DOSTOEVSKY AND ENGLISH MODERNISM, 1900–1930

When Constance Garnett's translations (1910–20) made Dostoevsky accessible in England for the first time they introduced a disruptive and liberating literary force, and English novelists had to confront a new model and rival. The writers who are the focus of this study – Lawrence, Woolf, Bennett, Conrad, Forster, Galsworthy, and James – either admired Dostoevsky or feared him as a monster who might dissolve all literary and cultural distinctions. Though their responses differed greatly, these writers were unanimous in their inability to recognize Dostoevsky as a literary artist. They viewed him instead as a pyschologist, a mystic, a prophet, and, in the cases of Lawrence and Conrad, a hated rival who compelled creative response. This study constructs a map of English modernist novelists' misreadings of Dostoevsky, and in so doing it illuminates their aesthetic and cultural values and the nature of the modern English novel.

PETER KAYE lectures at University College of Northwestern University, Evanston, Illinois, and is senior editor at educational publishers McDougal Littell. He has a particular interest in twentieth-century British literature and in strategies for teaching literature at school and college level.

DOSTOEVSKY AND ENGLISH MODERNISM, 1900–1930

PETER KAYE

CAMBRIDGE
UNIVERSITY PRESS

CAMBRIDGE UNIVERSITY PRESS
Cambridge, New York, Melbourne, Madrid, Cape Town, Singapore, São Paulo

Cambridge University Press
The Edinburgh Building, Cambridge CB2 2RU, UK

Published in the United States of America by Cambridge University Press, New York

www.cambridge.org
Information on this title: www.cambridge.org/9780521623582

First published 1999
This digitally printed first paperback version 2006

A catalogue record for this publication is available from the British Library

Library of Congress Cataloguing in Publication data
Kaye, Peter, 1952–
Dostoevsky and English modernism, 1900–1930 / Peter Kaye.
p. cm.
Includes bibliographical references and index.
ISBN 0 521 62358 8
1. English literature – 20th century – History and criticism.
2. Modernism (literature) – Great Britain. 3. Russian fiction –
Appreciation – Great Britain. 4. Dostoevsky, Fyodor, 1821–1881 –
Influence. 5. English literature – Russian influences. I. Title.
PR478.M6K34 1999
823'.91209–dc21 98–38085 CIP

ISBN-13 978-0-521-62358-2 hardback
ISBN-10 0-521-62358-8 hardback

ISBN-13 978-0-521-02419-8 paperback
ISBN-10 0-521-02419-6 paperback

Contents

Acknowledgments

This work began on a bright California morning many years ago, when I was asked by a Virginia Woolf enthusiast to name my favorite author. My answer of Dostoevsky prompted a fascinating response about Woolf's attraction to his work. One question suggested another, leading me eventually down the long and arduous road of this project, which began as a doctoral dissertation.

The members of my reading committee deserve my lasting gratitude. Bill Todd has nurtured this project from its tentative beginnings and served as its patient and clear-sighted guardian angel. Without his supportive direction, my work would have probably ended in futility. Lucio Ruotolo challenged me to rise to the most interesting questions, centered in the art of the novelists themselves; the texture of this study owes much to his stewardship. Will Stone gave me the benefit of his fine sense of our language, correcting my lapses and helping me realize that argument and elegance go hand in hand.

Others kindly assisted me at various stages. Helen Muchnic, whose 1939 publication *Dostoevsky's English Reputation (1881–1936)* inspired my own research, closely read my manuscript and sent delightful letters of encouragement. Joseph Frank lent support by his interest, his manuscript reading, and the example of his own scholarship. Thomas Moser assisted by sharing his articles on Conrad, which opened new paths of inquiry. Richard Garnett, the grandson of Constance and Edward, two distinguished literary people who figure prominently here, also deserves my gratitude for his interest and assistance. His letters, as well as his own biography of Constance, have given me a conduit to a rich past.

I am thankful to the English Department at Stanford University for its financial and moral support. Though the list of individuals is too long to itemize, I have learned that academic inquiry is truly a cooperative endeavor, and I hope one day to help others as I have been helped. I am also indebted to the Mellon Foundation and the Illinois Institute of

Technology for a one-year fellowship that enabled me to complete a significant portion of my work. A number of libraries deserve mention, including the Newberry Library and those at Stanford University, Northwestern University, and the University of Chicago.

Members of both sides of my family have assisted my project in word and in deed. I would especially like to thank my mother, Adeline, and my father for whom I am named, though he did not live to see this moment. I hope that my work, and my life, does justice to his memory. As a proud father, I believe that my children Jeremiah and Hannah have also contributed, sacrificing countless hours of my presence.

But I owe the greatest debt to my wife Nora. She has never wavered in her belief that all things are possible. Amid the Dostoevskian turmoil of my life, she has never lost her bearings or her spirit or her love. The next book – already completed in manuscript – is hers to publish.

CHAPTER I

Introduction

In 1912, Constance Garnett released her first major translation of Dostoevsky, *The Brothers Karamazov;* within the next nine years she would translate nearly the complete body of his fiction. During the year that marked Dostoevsky's triumphant entry, or more precisely, re-entry, into England's literary marketplace, the winds of modernism blew strong across Europe. The Russian composer Igor Stravinsky labored in Paris on *Rite of Spring,* a ballet celebration of pagan ritual that would provoke a near-riot when premiered in 1913. The unresolved dissonances and harsh, shifting rhythms of Stravinksy's music assaulted traditional expectations. Sergei Pavlovich Diaghilev's startling production of the ballet further discomforted the audience by its perpetual motion and asymmetry. During the first night's performance the lead dancer, the famed Nijinsky, had to clap the rhythm on stage because the orchestra could not be heard over the objections of the audience. In Berlin, the Austrian-born Arnold Schönberg challenged fundamental musical structures and dispensed with tonal organization entirely. His 1912 composition *Pierrot Lunaire,* vocal arrangements with chamber accompaniment, marked a further step in his revolutionary new direction.

In the visual arts, the Russian Wassily Kandinksy published a treatise in Munich, "Concerning the Spiritual in Art," that explained his need to move beyond representational art. According to W. H. Jansen, Kandinsky's aim "was to charge form and color with a purely spiritual meaning (as he put it) by eliminating all resemblance to the physical world."[1] Pablo Picasso experimented in Paris with collage Cubism. In his *Still Life* of 1911–12, letters and shapes are presented in layered planes, atop an actual piece of imitation chair caning, which had been pasted onto the canvas. An oval piece of rope encloses the painting. By merging three–dimensional objects with two–dimensional brushwork, Picasso seems to explode centuries-old traditions of perspective, for in his work illusion and reality, depth and surface are inextricably mingled. Also in

Paris, Matisse, the leading figure of the Fauves (the Wild Beasts), continued his radical simplification of form and space, perhaps best illustrated by his 1905–6 painting, *The Joy of Life*. The bold colors and non-representational distortions of his work alienated audiences in Paris and in London, where Roger Fry gave Matisse prominence in his 1912 second Post-Impressionist showing.

Revolutionary experiments in style and form also permeated the literary world. In Germany, Thomas Mann published *Death in Venice*, a masterful exploration of Dionysian decadence, the story of a rigidly self-possessed writer, Gustave Aschenbach, who, at the height of his power and popularity, vacations in a plague-ridden Venice. Aschenbach, a figure of Apollonian control and bourgeois respectability, becomes infatuated with a fourteen–year-old boy and gradually abandons himself to a corrupt and fatal sensuality. In its representation of unacknowledged desire, the heavy toll of repression, and mythic symbols of the psyche, the novella suggests the influence of Freud and Nietzsche, two writers whose works stirred the modernist literary imagination. In Trieste, James Joyce worked on drafts of *The Portrait of the Artist as a Young Man*, breaking new ground in its lyrical rendering of consciousness and its depiction of the alienated modern artist. In a failed effort to find a publisher for *The Dubliners*, Joyce made his last visit to Ireland in 1912; the interwoven short stories, which Joyce described as a series of chapters in the moral history of his community, would remain unpublished until 1914. In France, Marcel Proust was nearing the completion of *Swann's Way*, the first volume of *A Remembrance of Things Past* would be published in 1913. The French writer created a new type of novel, constructed around the narrator's recurring memories of emotional and aesthetic events central to his life, such as his experience of eating madeleine, and his sleepless nights at Combray. For the narrator Marcel – and for Proust – memory alone provides permanence and unity amid the chaos, flux, and disintegration of the modern world.

Dostoevsky's reception among English writers in the early part of the twentieth century needs to be understood within the context of modernism, which may be heuristically defined, to borrow from Malcolm Bradbury, as "that movement of artistic revolutionary self-consciousness that we associate with the work of painters like Matisse and Picasso, novelists like Joyce, Proust, Mann, and Gide, poets like Valéry, Apollinaire, Pound and Wallace Stevens, dramatists like Maeterlinck, Jarry and Pirandello."[2] While it is difficult to generalize about such a pluralistic international movement, a prototype of the modern artist might be delineated by the following attributes: skepticism about the creeds, ideals, and artistic traditions of the past; disdain for the middle class and its conventions; a preoccupation with change; an interest in the workings of perception, consciousness, and what Virginia Woolf called "the dark places of psychology"; a profound sense of alienation, often separating the artist from family, community, or the general audience; an obsession with technique and an attendant delight in formal experimentation; and a conviction that the present time differed radically from all previous eras. In the words of Carl Jung, "modern man is an entirely new phenomenon; a modern problem is one which has just arisen and whose answer still lies in the future."[3]

This study will focus on the writers, all touched by the modernist maelstrom that swept through England in the early decades of the twentieth century, who were most affected by their readings of Dostoevsky. In 1912, these seven writers – D. H. Lawrence, Virginia Woolf, Arnold Bennett, Joseph Conrad, E. M. Forster, John Galsworthy, and Henry James – were in different stages of their careers. The 27–year-old D. H. Lawrence published his second novel, *The Trespasser,* a work about illicit passion and the fear of physical intimacy, that pointed to the great novels to come. During that year, Lawrence was finishing *Sons and Lovers,* to be published in 1913. He became separated from the first important love of his life, Jessie Chambers, when she recognized herself as Miriam in the drafts of the work-in-progress and discovered the depths of Lawrence's resistance to her. Soon after, he met the married Frieda Weekley in Nottingham; before long, the two were scandalous lovers. Frieda left her husband and three children to accompany Lawrence to Europe, first to Rhineland, then to Bavaria, Austria, and Italy, following a migratory impulse that characterized much of their life together.

During the same year, Leonard Woolf, who had just returned from seven years in Ceylon, succeeded in wearing down Virginia's resistance to marrying him. On her honeymoon, she discovered her own aversion to physical intimacy with a man, though her biographer Quentin Bell reports that she was "still cheerfully expecting to have children."[4] At the age of thirty, Virginia Woolf had already experienced at least three serious mental breakdowns. For the last seven years, she had been writing reviews for the *Times Literary Supplement* and was hard at work on her first novel, *The Voyage Out,* which she completed in 1913 and published in 1915. This novel, a promising though fairly conventional work, follows Mr. and Mrs. Ambrose and their niece Rachel on a sea voyage from London to a resort on the South American coast. Essentially, it is the story of Rachel's coming of age.

The man who would eventually become Woolf's opponent in one of the famous literary quarrels of the time, Arnold Bennett, seemed at the height of his powers in 1912. Already an established writer and critic, Bennett worked on a sequel to his highly popular comic novel, *The Card* (1911). In *The Regeants*, which would be published in 1913, he again took up the story of Denry Machen, a joker, entrepreneur, and good-hearted adventurer, who left behind his life in the northern provinces – the Five Towns area based upon the pottery towns in Staffordshire where Bennett grew up – to settle in London, where he is engaged as a theatrical impresario and builds his own theater. In 1912, Bennett also enjoyed his first major theatrical success, *Milestones*, a play chronicling a family from 1860 to the current year. The drama, which ran for more than a year, added considerably to the author's wealth. Always a shrewd businessman, Bennett purchased his own yacht during this time; he also bought a country house in Essex.

Joseph Conrad, long acclaimed as a literary master but perennially denied commercial success, finally reached a larger audience at the age of fifty-five with his novel, *Chance*, first published serially in the *New York Herald* in 1912. This novel followed the 1911 publication of *Under Western Eyes*, a work that left Conrad in a state of mental collapse, in part because it proved the culmination of a bitter if unacknowledged rivalry with Dostoevsky, a battle in which the Polish writer refused to submit to the "destructive element." By contrast, *Chance* proved a fortunate affair; the novel won readers because it gave them both romance and a happy ending – two features not usually associated with the author. *Chance*, narrated by a pedestrian Marlow, is about a sea captain, Roderick Anthony, who falls in love with Flora De Barral, the daughter of a once wealthy man serving a prison sentence for fraud. Eventually, the father is freed and invited to join the newly married couple aboard ship. Of course, intrigue develops, based on misunderstandings, suspicion, and the isolation of seafaring, which lead to a thwarted murder attempt. In the end, all is well because that ever-menacing Conrad nemesis, Chance, proves unexpectedly beneficent.

By this time, the 43–year-old E. M. Forster had become firmly linked to the Bloomsbury circle, that iconoclastic collection of writers, painters, critics, and intellectuals who resided in a fashionable residential district of north-central London. This group of intimate friends included the Woolfs, the economist Maynard Keynes, the scholar Lytton Strachey, the critics Clive Bell and Desmond MacCarthy, the painters Vanessa Bell (Virginia's sister) and Duncan Grant, and Roger Fry, an art theorist and painter. Forster had already completed four major novels, the last of which, *Howards End,* had been published in 1910. His biographer, P. N. Furbank, reports that Forster wrote a "prophetic morality play" in 1912, but that the work was put in a drawer and never published.[5] Forster traveled to India in October of 1912 with his aunt and mother, a trip that led to his most significant work, *A Passage to India,* begun in draft on the return voyage and published in 1924.

John Galsworthy, a far more public figure than Forster, became involved in yet another social cause. A tireless humanitarian activist who had already campaigned for prison reform, women's rights, and divorce law liberalization, the 45–year-old Galsworthy turned his attention to animals and fought for the introduction of humane slaughtering laws in 1912 and 1913. As a matter of conscience, he had already given up hunting though, according to Margery Morgan, each September he sent his spaniel to a shooting party in Scotland so that the dog could still enjoy the sport.[6] In 1912, Galsworthy's play, *The Eldest Son,* was produced in London. The drama, about an affair between a wealthy aristocratic heir and a lady's maid, exposes the double standard and sympathetically portrays the working class. Ironically, in a declaration of equality the pregnant girl in the end refuses the young man's offer of marriage. Galsworthy also wrote *The Pigeon,* a play that looks critically at the practical effects of philanthropy while endorsing the need for philanthropic sensitivities.

Henry James, long settled into the retiring life of a distinguished man of letters at Lamb House in Rye, was nearing the end of his career. At the age of sixty-nine, James had already published his last novel, *The Outcry* (1911); he was working on the first volume of his memoirs, *A Small Boy and Others.* The man who did so much to establish the novel as a work of art became something of an inadvertently comical figure. Harry T. Moore tells the story of James, in full evening array, coming late to a Max Reinhold production of *Oedipus Rex* at Covent Garden, only to be caught up in an entrance procession of the actors playing the chorus, parading down the aisles with the perplexed master in tow.[7]

Each of these writers responded to Dostoevsky in a manner that mirrors the respective stages of their literary careers. James condemned with the peevishness of an old man, fearful of what might next corrupt the young. Lawrence denounced with the muscular, youthful vigor of one who knows his rivals and who is determined to make his own mark.

Woolf, more subtle and modulated, alternately praised or disapproved, a writer still in her formation tentatively weighing new possibilities of expression. Regardless of their critical judgment, the seven writers could not ignore the disruptive presence of Dostoevsky in the English house of fiction, any more than Rogozhin could be ignored after he burst into Nastasya's party in *The Idiot*. One critic compared the enthusiasm that greeted the Garnett installments to that of the Victorians waiting eagerly for the next release of Dickens or Thackeray.[8] The Russian author was acclaimed as mystic, prophet, psychologist, irrationalist, a chronicler of the perverse, and sometimes as a novelist. His reception in the second and third decades of the century can be compared to the earlier discovery of Van Gogh, whose paintings seemed to strip away all artifice to render an emotional power and spiritual depth unavailable to the classically trained. In Dostoevsky the English found a new primitive whose coarse strokes and jagged lines bespoke a tortured soul who expanded art's domain.

To understand how the modern novelists in England responded to Dostoevsky, it is helpful to keep monsters in mind. In *Violence and the Sacred*, René Girard offers an analysis of monsters as symptomatic of cultural crisis. He cites the monstrous images in Euripides' *The Bacchae* as an example of a culture threatened by disintegration and a blurring of differences. Monsters resist classification and hence pose a threat of dissolution, for they combine what is normally kept separate and distinct – head of man and torso of beast become one. In their "formless and grotesque mixture of things that are normally separate," they express the crisis of a "world caught up in the whirl."[9] In 1912, England was similarly caught up in a cultural and social whirl, the inescapable disruptions of modernity. A distant war in the Balkans ominously threatened European peace; Mrs. Pankhurst and her daughters broke laws and windows and bobbies' heads in a vociferous battle for women's rights; striking workers were engaged in pitched battles, countryman against countryman; even the King's army threatened insubordination in a cantankerous Ireland; and artists offended where once they sought to please. To anticipate Yeats, all had changed, changed utterly.

In such a cultural vortex, Dostoevsky was introduced as an exhilarating monster, a Sphinx on the English horizon, representing a suggestively barbaric combination of the literary and nonliterary, posing an enigma that each author felt compelled to address. That enigma was both cultural and literary, derived from a perceived defiance of literary conventions and the traditions that perpetuated order and continuity in an increasingly fragmented world. The writers who are the focus of this study all viewed Dostoevsky as a writer who could not be classified or assimilated within the traditions of the novel; his works were assumed to be unshaped by artistic intent and unloosed from social restraints. Our writers, along with most of the audience for Garnett's translations, read Dostoevsky as if he were a literary virgin, untainted by influence or knowledge of novelistic traditions. By disengaging him from his literary heritage, misunderstanding was assured.

Our study will begin with D. H. Lawrence, Dostoevsky's most outspoken and voluminous opponent. The writer from provincial Eastwood first encountered the Russian novelist at a crucial early stage of his own career; later, his best friend, Middleton Murry, "converted" to a strange hybrid Dostoevskianism, two factors which help explain the lifelong enmity. With admirable if misguided tenacity, Lawrence waged a ceaseless war against the author regarded as a false prophet of modernity's worst excesses: its perverse hyperconsciousness, blood-denying idealism, and sensual corruption. Though Lawrence shared Dostoevsky's belief in the novel as a sacred book that might give meaning and direction to an age of apocalyptic chaos, he insisted that his rival pursued the wrong grail, denouncing him as a diseased personality who mixed "God and Sadism."[10] Consequently, Lawrence never missed an opportunity to attack. In his letters, in his essays, in his reviews, and in his fiction, the curses of Dostoevsky resound with the intensity of a preacher trying to lure would-be believers away from a neighboring revival tent. At the same time, Lawrence learned from Dostoevsky's perception of evil and his use of the novel as a quest for wisdom. Indeed, his rival's subjects came perilously close to his own, and works such as *Kangaroo* and *The Escaped Cock* may be interpreted as a response to Dostoevskian themes.

Virginia Woolf also offered many public comments about Dostoevsky, though she felt no sense of rivalry and her most celebrated comments praised him as a means of modernist liberation. To a writer seeking to find her own voice, her Russian counterpart seemed a welcome salvo that might topple the stifling and materialist conventions of the Edwardian novel and defend her own literary experiments. In effect, he offered freedom from the shadow of Queen Victoria, the smug complacency of the Empire, the strictures of English class hierarchies, and the unquestioned assumptions of Arnold Bennett and his kind. Like most of her contemporaries, Woolf failed to see his indebtedness to the dethroned and neglected Dickens and other novelists representative of her father's world. She later turned away from Dostoevsky when he proved too far removed from the literary and cultural traditions that gave her comfort. Though she yearned for modernist disruption in the arts, she felt too much upheaval in his works, which produced "stranger monsters than have ever been brought to the light of day before," and rejected him for leaving his readers unguided by fictional and social signposts that might create harmonious order.[11]

Arnold Bennett, who had already read a great deal of Dostoevsky in French before Garnett's translations, played a key role in promoting the Russian novelist. In 1910 and 1911, Bennett, as a critic for the avant-garde *New Age*, lobbied for a complete translation of Dostoevsky. Alone among the writers of our study, he emphasized Dostoevsky's traditional values and realistic narrative methods, professing a safe distance from modern uncertainties and moral ambiguities. In his later years, he promoted him as an antidote to the heartless expressions of modern art and the dissonant negativity of England's literary vanguard, sentimentalizing Dostoevsky to advocate vaguely defined middle-class values. The Russian became a bulwark of simple, indisputable truths in Bennett's effort to slow the onslaught of modernity.

Conrad offers the most intriguing response. Aside from a handful of oblique allusions and a few comments in his letters to Edward Garnett, the Polish expatriate kept a virtual silence. For the purposes of this study, organized according to who said the most about Dostoevsky, a discussion of Conrad's response belongs after the three previously mentioned writers. Yet in Conrad's silence resides a wondrous antagonism. He spent years engaged in a sullen struggle against Dostoevsky in a rivalry that he refused to name, and his political fiction, especially *Under Western Eyes*, may be read as a direct if camouflaged response to his hated predecessor. To adapt the terminology of Harold Bloom, both Conrad and Lawrence wrestled with Dostoevsky as a strong novelist whose influence must be resisted and whose intimidating presence necessitated misreading to protect their own creative identities.[12] Conrad could not forgive Dostoevsky for stoking the fires of modernity's chaos while voicing support of outmoded values. He censured the unrestrained emotions of his characters, whom he regarded as monstrous, and dismissed his works for their failure to achieve ironic distance, a mark of their moral and literary turpitude. Ideological differences also motivated disdain for the writer believed to embody czarist autocracy and Orthodox servility. In the chaotic shouting of his novels,

Conrad heard the refusal to accept with stoic dignity the intractable dilemmas of modern life.

The last three writers included in this study have less to say than the others, once allowances are made for Conrad's indirection, which explains the grouping of the three in a single chapter. E. M. Forster vacillated in his views, perhaps because he never resolved his own attitude towards the modern. He shared Lawrence's interest in the prophetic and astutely recognized the common ground between the art of Lawrence and that of Dostoevsky. Echoing his Bloomsbury friend Woolf, he celebrated the Russian novelist for pointing to new fictional domains, at the same time failing to detect conscious artistry. Though his tone was more playful and less Olympian than Bennett's, he shared with him an appreciation of Dostoevsky's traditional values, limited by a simplistic account of his moral perspective. Forster was at times unsettled by the emotional and didactic nature of Dostoevsky's fiction, not because he regarded such content as impermissible, as Conrad did, but because of a class-bound discomfort with such explicitness. These diverse intersections reveal Forster to be the quintessential modern man who could not make up his mind.

John Galsworthy and Henry James, though less affected than the others, confronted Dostoevsky as an anarchic challenge to their own genteel values and cultural legacy. Galsworthy bitterly condemned his works as an expression of the violent and formless chaos of the modern world. Dostoevsky's raw power affronted the nostalgic beliefs of the writer who insisted that artists maintain a quiet decorum. Yet in a moment of surprising self-criticism, Galsworthy later recognized Russian literature as a legitimate criticism of English culture.

Henry James proved more recalcitrant, fighting vainly to resist Dostoevsky's English influence in the hope that young novelists would not be led away from the sanctuary of novelistic artistry. He resisted the use of the novel as a means of philosophical exploration, fearing the social and literary consequences of such inquiry. James dismissed Dostoevsky's works as monstrous excesses of a modern age, untouched by the graces of civility and intelligence, potentially lethal combinations of formless art and disrupted social hierarchies. Of course, James, like Conrad, was not English by birth. But the two writers were an important part of the English literary landscape, vocal participants in its public discourse, and their responses to Dostoevsky were greatly influenced by English friends and circumstances.

Besides our seven novelists, three others come to mind as major figures of the early modern era in English literature: H. G. Wells, Ford Madox Ford, and James Joyce. Where Dostoevsky is concerned, these men had little to say, and their stories and novels seem far removed from his influence. Ford Madox Ford offered intriguing comments relating his friend Conrad to the Russian author, which will be addressed in our discussion of the Polish writer. H. G. Wells apparently found in Dostoevsky a topic not worthy of comment – a Wellsian rarity – which suggests that he may not have read him. While James Joyce did read at least some novels, there is a scarcity of evidence about his response. Richard Ellman does report that Joyce purchased *The Idiot* while in Italy. Ellman also tells an amusing tale of the Irish writer subjected to the taunts of his adolescent son Giorgio, who chided his father with the claim that *Crime and Punishment* was the world's greatest novel and Dostoevsky the greatest novelist. Joyce enigmatically responded by saying that *Crime and Punishment* "was a queer title for a book which contained neither crime nor punishment."[13]

By studying Dostoevsky's intrusion into the English house of fiction, much will be revealed about its lively and disputatious inhabitants and the complexities of cross-cultural literary reception. Our analysis will give priority to direct comments about Dostoevsky; at the risk of violating the etiquette of current hermeneutic studies, we will take the authors at their word, unless evidence suggests otherwise. To make sense of those words, we will address the aesthetic agendas of the English writers, as delineated in their own nonfiction, and probe their relevant comments about other writers, especially the Russians. Where appropriate, we will draw comparisons between the English fiction of the moderns and Dostoevsky, an always fascinating juxtaposition. Our goal is to elucidate the response to Dostoevsky within the context of each writer's literary career and personal life. The Russian author may not have been appreciated as an artist, but ironically he did succeed in forcing these novelists to clarify their own literary values and their own distinctive vision of modern life. This study should help us to gain insight into the art of the English novelists as well as that of Dostoevsky.

First, however, we must set the stage by examining the historical evolution of Dostoevsky's English reception, from its earliest years in the 1880s to the time of the Garnett translations. Then we will turn our attention to the difficulties that his readers have historically experienced in discerning artistic intent and understanding the distinctive literary features of his work. Such background will help us to position our subject in a historical, cultural, and aesthetic framework.

THE ENGLISH HORIZON OF EXPECTATIONS

Though the judgments of the novelists were stamped with their distinctive personalities and artistic visions, each writer reflected the collective predispositions of the age, a condition that demands inquiry into England's horizon of expectations, defined by Wlad Godzick as "the sum total of reactions, prejudgments, verbal and other behavior that greets a work upon its appearance."[14] The novelists did not merely engage in Promethean struggles with Dostoevsky, bumping in the Freudian night, so admired by Bloom, in an anxious struggle to protect or to liberate their authenticity. Their opinions were shaped by collective codes representing the historical moment, reflecting "national patterns of literary perception" described in a different context by Jacques Leenhardt.[15] As readers, the English authors do not occupy privileged positions: their "I" always refracts a sociological "we" and its attendant stereotypes and reading schemes. While proving more articulate and provocative than their associates, they were not necessarily better readers of Dostoevsky.

Here, the pioneering research of Helen Muchnic, who first studied Dostoevsky's English reception in 1939, provides an invaluable descriptive tool.[16] Muchnic's thoroughly documented work explains the historical development of Dostoevsky's reception by identifying its three earliest stages: the first years (1881–88), the interval (1889–1911), and the period of the Constance Garnett translations (1912–21). While these stages do not exactly correspond to the readings of the English novelists, most of whom first became acquainted with Dostoevsky through French translations, Muchnic's chronological divisions enable us to trace the evolution of shared literary and cultural assumptions that shaped the writers' responses to his works.

Dostoevsky did not become well known in England until after his death in 1881. Both the *Athenaeum* and the *Academy* ran obituaries, which were probably the result of widespread European attention to the spectacle of Dostoevsky's funeral and the magnitude of public mourning in Russia.[17] A loose English translation of his fictionalized prison memoir, *House of the Dead*, was published the same year. Within the next eight years, translations of *Crime and Punishment*, *The Idiot*, *Injury and Insult*, and shorter works appeared. England's interest in Dostoevsky and other Russian authors was further stimulated by Melchior de Vogüé's *Le roman russe*, released in 1886, which catapulted Dostoevsky, Tolstoy, and Turgenev into the French literary spotlight.[18]

Vogüé exalted the author of *Crime and Punishment* for combining realism with compassion and religious sentiment, two qualities that he found absent in his contemporaries, Flaubert and Zola. He opened what was arguably the most influential essay ever written about Dostoevsky ("The religion of suffering" in *Le roman russe*) with the disarming words: "Here comes the Scythian, the true Scythian, who is going to revolutionize all our intellectual habits."[19] Vogüé called Dostoevsky "an incomparable psychologist" but complained that he had "traveled only by night" and that his studies were limited to "dismal and mangled souls." The French critic anticipated the responses of English novelists when he expressed the problem of classifying Dostoevsky, whom he regarded as a "phenomenon belonging to another world, a powerful but incomplete, intense and original monster": "He may with justice be called a philosopher, an apostle, a madman, a consoler of the afflicted or the murderer of peaceful minds, the Jeremiah of a convict prison, or the Shakespeare of an asylum."[20] Noticeably absent is the mention of literary artist.

Gilbert Phelps, who has studied the English response to Russian fiction, focusing mainly on Turgenev, cites Vogüé's work as an important stimulus for English translations: "in 1886 [the year of its publication] no less than 18 titles appeared in London and New York. By the end of the decade all the great Russian novelists were represented in English versions, and most of their major works had been translated."[21] The English audience of the 1880s shared Vogüé's interest in compassionate realism. Muchnic documents their attraction to Dostoevsky as a chronicler of Russian life and a realist in the Dickensian mold, the Dickens of *Hard Times*. Reviewers compared him favorably to Zola, whose *Nana* reportedly had sold more than 100,000 copies in England.[22] Following Vogüé's lead, the English praised Dostoevsky's dramatic power, insight into "moral disease," and sympathy for the suffering and oppressed.[23] Most reviewers saw in his works an accurate portrait of exotic and savage Russian life. When compared to Turgenev and Tolstoy, Dostoevsky was "absolutely Russian, the unWesternized Russian."[24] He was regarded as a novelistic Baedecker guiding the reader through the primitive terrain of Russia: "the country, society, feeling, and habits of thought are altogether different from anything to be met with amongst ourselves."[25]

Robert Louis Stevenson stands out among the readers of the 1880s, not only because of his enthusiasm but also because of his literary indebtedness. Stevenson probably read the French version of *Crime and*

Punishment, first published in 1884. That same year he published "Markheim," a short story about the brutal murder of a pawnbroker and the subsequent confession of his killer. Donald Davie has judged this story as "the best-authenticated example of an attempt to write a wholly Dostoevskian novel in English."[26] Davie, however, overstates his case. "Markheim" does employ certain unmistakable externals – the portrait of an obsessed criminal mind, the murder of a pawnbroker, a dialogue with a supernatural stranger, a confession marking an unexpected regeneration – yet the story bears little resemblance to the substance of its Russian predecessors. In the Stevenson work, the criminal exists primarily to advance the plot; we learn remarkably little about his motives. While the story owes much to the scenario of *Crime and Punishment*, all psychological depth, ideological conflicts, and spiritual turmoil have been banished from its domain. In a letter to A. R. Symonds written two years later, Stevenson praised Dostoevsky's novel as "easily the greatest book I have read in ten years," contrasting his reaction to that of Henry James, who could "not finish" the book. "It nearly finished me," Stevenson confided to his friend. "It was like having an illness."[27] Not coincidentally, Stevenson also published *The Strange Case of Dr. Jekyll and Mr. Hyde* in 1886, a work suggestive of Dostoevsky in its investigation of the mysterious sources of evil within the human psyche. In Stevenson's masterpiece, however, good and evil never appear simultaneously within the self; Jekyll and Hyde represent moral alternations that are far removed from the Manichean simultaneity that epitomizes the consciousness of Dostoevsky's most compelling characters.

Despite Stevenson's excitement, Muchnic reports that Dostoevsky entered a "long period of comparative neglect" after 1888.[28] Between the years 1889 and 1911 some studies became available, but only one new work of Dostoevsky's was translated – *Poor Folk*, with an introduction by George Moore and a frontispiece by Beardsley – while the previously translated novels went out of print. Maurice Baring, a diplomat and classical scholar who had traveled through Russia and knew the language, proposed a translation of Dostoevsky's novels in 1903 only to be told that "there would be no market for such books in England."[29] Lombroso's *Study of Genius*, translated in 1891, discussed the resemblance between Dostoevsky's epileptic seizures and the inspiration of genius.[30] *Impressions of Russia* by George Brandes, the Dane who helped to popularize Nietzsche throughout Western Europe, proclaimed Dostoevsky as a great though barbaric artist who embodied the Nietzschean concept of "slave morality."[31] The relative neglect during these years can be understood in terms of English insularity, which is explained by the critic Samuel Hynes: "In the last decade of Victoria's reign one could not buy a translation of Zola's *La Terre* or Dostoevsky's *The Idiot* or *The Possessed* or *The Brothers Karamazov* in London, or see a public performance of Ibsen's *Ghosts*, or look at any picture by a French Impressionist at any gallery, either public or private." "The new thought in Europe," Hynes reports, "had been kept out of England, as though by quarantine."[32]

It should be noted that few people in England knew Russian. The language was not recognized as a legitimate field of university study until the 1880s; even by the 1920s only a few programs were established.[33] As a result, the English depended almost entirely on translated works for their knowledge of Russian literature, and many of the translations were simply English versions of French and German editions. The first English history of Russian literature was not published until 1882. This work by Charles Turner, who served as Lector at the Imperial University of St. Petersburg, stopped short of Dostoevsky, an author mentioned only as a friend of Nekrasov.[34] Given the scarcity of information, it is not surprising that Russia's cultural emissaries, some of whom had migrated to England, played an important role in promoting and interpreting their country's literary heritage.[35]

Unfortunately, three of the most influential Russians distorted Dostoevsky and cast doubt on his artistic ability. Dmitri Merezhovsky, a novelist, symbolist poet, and critic, wrote an important essay that was translated into English in 1902. Merezhovsky, who lived intermittently as an exile in Paris throughout the early years of the twentieth century, called attention to Dostoevsky's "hasty, sometimes clearly neglected language" and his "wearisomely drawn out" plots.[36] Though the critic showed an appreciation of his dramatic power and unique use of dialogue as a means of defining character, the English paid far more attention to the celebration of Dostoevsky as a "poet of evangelical love" and "seer of the soul," as well as the oversimplified contrast between Dostoevsky and Tolstoy. Merezhovsky, despite his merits, contributed to the English tendency to read Dostoevsky as a zealot instead of an artist, and his influence can be detected in the responses of writers such as Bennett, Woolf, and Forster, all of whom regarded Dostoevsky as an inartistic sage.

Prince Peter Kropotkin, an anarchist who emigrated and joined the vocal ranks of those political exiles who had fled Russia for the safety of

England, went further and refused to admit any element of artistic intent in Dostoevsky. In a survey of Russian literature that was published in English in 1905, Kropotkin complained that Dostoevsky wrote too fast and cared little about literary form. He expressed discomfort with "the atmosphere of a lunatic asylum" that permeates the novels, insisting that the heroes were simply transparent reflections of the author himself: "whatever hero appears . . . you feel it is the author who speaks." While he recognized Dostoevsky as an important writer, his impatience with the novels' lack of "artistic finish" led him to confess that "one is never tempted to re-read them."[37] Kropotkin's influence extended beyond that of Merezhovsky, because he lived in England, he frequently gave lectures about Russian literature, and he was a friend of Constance and Edward Garnett, the couple who were largely responsible for leading the resurgence of interest in Dostoevsky.

Regrettably, the emigrant who knew the most about Russian literature, D. S. Mirsky, had only a limited appreciation of Dostoevsky. His authoritative *History of Russian Literature*, published in English in 1927, includes astute observations but also perpetuates a stereotype of Dostoevsky's disinterest in literary art. Mirsky objected to the "absence of all grace, and elegance . . . together with an absence of reserve, discipline, and dignity, and an excess of abnormal self-consciousness."[38] His intolerance of Dostoevsky was exasperated for Marxist reasons; he evaluated the author as a corrupt reflection of imperial Russia, "the first and greatest symptom of the spiritual decomposition of the Russian soul."[39] In a later work, Mirsky offered an interesting analysis of the English attraction to Dostoevsky: "Now that the hopes of the 1900s had come down to the catastrophe of the war [the First World War], the incomparably mystical, exaggeratedly irrational cult of faith in Dostoevsky was just what was needed to replace the rarefied naturalistically rationalistic faith of Shaw."[40]

Two other exiles, Sergei Stepniak and Felix Volkovsky – close friends of Kropotkin – introduced Constance Garnett to the Russian language and its literature and served as her first tutors. Their influence prompted her translations of Turgenev, Tolstoy, Dostoevsky, and other Russian writers. Garnett began her translations in the 1890s; she first translated Goncharov, then Tolstoy's *The Kingdom of God Is Within Us*. By 1899 she had translated the complete works of Turgenev, earning the praise of reviewers and novelists such as Conrad and Galsworthy. She went on to other translations of Tolstoy, including *War and Peace, Anna Karenina*, and numerous shorter works. Her husband's biographer, George Jefferson, reports that she translated "Dostoevsky from 1912 to 1920, Chekhov from 1915 to 1926, Gogol from 1922 to 1928, Herzen from 1924 to 1927."[41] The work of Constance Garnett put Russian literature on England's literary map.

English readers generally recognized Turgenev and Tolstoy as conscious literary artists. According to Gilbert Phelps, they immediately hailed Turgenev's formal perfection when his works were introduced in the later years of the nineteenth century. The author, who had once traveled to England and had met George Eliot, Robert Browning, Tennyson, Swinburne, Trollope, Henry James, and Ford Madox Ford, was appreciated as a writer working within discernible literary traditions and was often contrasted to Dostoevsky. For example, Conrad, James, and Galsworthy all sharply reproved Dostoevsky for his failure to adhere to Turgenev's lofty standards. Tolstoy, by comparison, was sometimes judged as Turgenev's artistic inferior, and interest in his moral philosophy and pilgrim quests overshadowed appreciation of his artistry. Yet he was usually recognized as a literary master. Virginia Woolf spoke for many of her contemporaries when she praised Tolstoy as a great artist, indeed the greatest of all novelists, while she judged Dostoevsky a psychologist but no artist.[42]

Perhaps the assumption that Dostoevsky was the least accomplished artist of the Russian trinity contributed to the tardiness of his translations. Three pivotal works did, however, pave the way for his reintroduction to the English reading public. Edward Garnett took an important step towards creating a market for Dostoevsky when he wrote a short essay for the *Academy* in 1906. The essay masterfully presented the author to an audience that had lost touch with his works. "The present generation," Garnett complained, "knows not Dostoevsky. So much the worse for the present generation." He lambasted the English for their neglect, which he traced to cultural differences: "no doubt the reason for our neglect lies in the Englishman's fear of morbidity." Garnett went on to praise Dostoevsky for his spiritual depth, a depth far removed from the wholesome chatter of England's vicars, and his exploration of consciousness that "yields us insight into deep, dark ranges of spiritual truths." Where the generation of the 1880s had praised Dostoevsky as a realist who depicted Russian life and society, Garnett now acclaimed him as a psychologist of the abnormal, the "one who has most fully explored the labyrinthine workings of the mind unhinged." Novels once read as a peculiarly Russian vision were now regarded as a psychological road map of humanity's darker vistas. Significantly, Garnett disagreed with Vogüé and identified *The Brothers Karamazov*, a novel brutally dismissed by the French critic, as Dostoevsky's greatest work. Throughout his essay, Garnett voiced his regret about the absence of English translations of Dostoevsky.[43]

That regret was likewise expressed by Maurice Baring whose *Landmarks in Russian Literature* sparked a great deal of interest. Baring's work, published in 1910, served as a popular introduction to nineteenth-century Russian literature, with an emphasis on Gogol, Tolstoy, Dostoevsky, Turgenev, and Chekhov. Nearly half of the book was devoted to Dostoevsky's life and literature. Baring praised him as a Shakespeare whose genius "soared higher and dove deeper than that of any other novelist, Russian or European."[44] With missionary fervor, Baring called upon his countrymen to seek spiritual and Christian truth from Dostoevsky that they might learn his lessons of love and pity. After the publication of *Landmarks in Russian Literature*, the author became an apostle for Russian literature and culture, writing numerous articles and books over subsequent years, endorsing the stereotypical view of Dostoevsky's artlessness. He found his works "shapeless," comparing them to quarries where "granite and dross, gold and ore are mingled." Dostoevsky's greatness, according to his popularizer, could only be attributed to his "divine message" that "emanates, like a precious balm, from the characters he creates."[45]

The interest generated by Baring's work made the prospect of publishing Dostoevsky in England more attractive. The campaign for a complete edition of his fiction was aided by Arnold Bennett, who promoted the cause of translation through his *New Age* column. Bennett used his review of *Landmarks in Russian Literature* to generate interest in Dostoevsky. He concluded his article by naming the desired publisher and calling for action: "And now, Mr. Heinemann, when are we going to have a complete Dostoevsky in English."[46] When an immediate response was not forthcoming, Bennett again used his column as a bully pulpit in an apparently successful attempt to shame Heinemann into action. His work in securing publication for Dostoevsky cannot be underestimated. Yet the popular novelist and influential critic contributed to the English misunderstanding of Dostoevsky's merit. While he praised Baring for providing a much-needed work, he criticized him for not discussing the "grave faults" of Dostoevsky's novels. Repeating a notion that had become a critical commonplace in France, Bennett announced: "The fact is that the difficulties under which he [Dostoevsky] worked were too much for the artist in him."[47]

By 1912, when Constance Garnett published *The Brothers Karamazov*, the English were predisposed to ignore its artistic qualities. Indeed, many even refused to judge it as a novel, mistakenly assuming that it reached beyond all typologies of genre. Garnett's starting point is significant because it reveals the symbolic and psychological interests that characterized the early twentieth-century fascination with Dostoevsky. Unlike the generation of the 1880s, which heralded *Crime and Punishment* and *House of the Dead* as the author's finest achievements, Garnett's audience paid more attention to his later novels, which seemed furthest removed from English traditions. Readers now found in Dostoevsky an intensity, depth, and complexity that they could not find in their own literary heritage. The modern English audience, unlike their predecessors of the 1880s, admired "his ideal of extreme individualism which made heroes of unconventional and anti-social beings. No longer were Dostoevsky's people queer Russians. They were everybody seen by a genius."[48]

Garnett's readers approached his characters through the filter of his life and everywhere found evidence of psychological imbalances and diseases presumed to be Dostoevsky's own. Ivan, Alyosha, Raskolnikov, and Stavrogin – indeed, virtually all the dominant characters – were thought to be transparent reflections of their author; some readers, such as Middleton Murry, even insisted that Dostoevsky endorsed the views of his most criminal and perverse creations. The psychological orientation reflected the recent influences of Nietzsche and Freud, two writers who mined irrational depths and who posed a radical challenge to England's intellectual and psychological definitions of the self.

Nietzsche became well known in England after his death in 1900, and a complete translation of his works was published between 1909 and 1913. The iconoclastic writer, who once claimed that "Dostoevsky was the only psychologist from whom I had anything to learn," was heralded as a prophet of the irrational, a powerful voice from the underground.[49] W. B. Yeats, exemplifying the response of the moderns, found Nietzsche to be a "strong enchanter." In a study of Nietzsche's influence among modern writers, John Burt Foster, Jr., reports that Yeats "was so fascinated that he injured his eyes in reading him."[50] During the same period, Sigmund Freud slowly made inroads into England. In 1911, he was named an honorary member of the prestigious Society for Psychical Research. Two years later the London Psycho-Analytical Society was founded, though the ranks were admittedly slim – a total of nine members.[51] In a sense, Freud's studies of sexuality, dreams, and the unconscious toppled the last vestiges of Victorian optimism. Because of Freud and Nietzsche – and, we might add, Dostoevsky – the recesses of the self took on a darker, more menacing hue.

Apparently, intellectual England loved such dark places. Muchnic entitles the chapter that deals with the initial response to the Garnett translations, "The Dostoevsky cult." She provides ample evidence that there was indeed a cult-like response marked by excessive devotion. Parties were given in his honor; diaries were punctuated with references to him; writers of distinction engaged in "great Dostoevsky nights" of philosophical dispute; and Middleton Murry became an "amanuensis" for the spirit of the author which dwelt within him.[52] The response resembled a Dionysian frenzy, as readers sought religious, psychological, philosophical, and, at times, literary truth from his pages. Katherine Mansfield playfully compared England's frenetic enthusiasms to the heated atmosphere of a Dostoevsky novel, observing that the author himself could not have exaggerated "the discussions he has provoked, the expenditure of enthusiasms and vituperation, the mental running to and fro . . . the added confusion of young gentleman-writers declaring (in strict confidence) that they were the real Dostoevsky."[53] Edmund Gosse later complained that every member of England's literary elite had "been subjected to the magic of this epileptic monster," the writer whose "genius led us astray" and whose works represented "the cocaine and morphia of modern literature."[54]

The impassioned reactions to the Garnett translations can be seen as an expression of a larger cultural phenomenon: the fascination with all things Russian that characterized the end of the Edwardian era. When the Russian ballet visited London in 1910, the English discovered a new world, as described by Frank Swinnerton: "Diaghilev and Nijinsky created a new state of mind . . . [the ballet's] rich decor, so bold and at times so bizarre, the triumphs of its strangeness and its beauty, the unfamiliar rhythms of its musical contributions – all had the glory of a new world."[55] Interest in Russian ballet, music, and literature was at various times compared to a fever, a virus, a drug, and an epidemic. The English borrowed a new word, "intelligentsia," from the Russians, enabling fashionable highbrows to describe themselves. According to a Somerset Maugham novel, "Everyone was reading the Russian novelists . . . the Russian composers set shivering the sensibility of persons who were beginning to want a change from Wagner . . . New phrases became the fashion, new colours, new emotions."[56] Samuel Hynes has aptly summarized the Russian "vogues" that occurred between 1910 and 1914: "Admiration for Russian art had reached such a pitch that Russianness alone sometimes seemed a measure of value."[57]

Perhaps the most amusing preoccupation of the age was the earnest interest in that strange nebula called the Russian soul. Dorothy Brewster discusses sundry views about this soul in *East–West Passage: A Study in Literary Relationships*, a broad overview of English responses to Russia from the Renaissance to the modern times. Brewster cites a 1916 anthology entitled *The Soul of Russia* as representative of England's interest. The anthology included articles on drama, folklore, folk song, music, painting, poetry, language, and even peasant industries. Jane Harrison's 1915 study, *Russia and the Russian Verb*, tried to establish a link between the grammatical state of the Russian verb and the spiritual state of the Russian people. Her work, according to a less-than-sympathetic reviewer, "caused a boom in the imperfective aspect of the Russian verb" and led to "much amateur psychical research into the manners and customs" of the Russian people.[58] Predictably, *The Brothers Karamazov* was read as a symbolic presentation of the Russian soul: "Russia inarticulate, dreaming her great Byzantine dreams, half choked, half strangled by barbarism, and yet retaining always a vision that sweeps upward into vistas beyond the morass of her passions."[59]

Despite the absurd excesses of many readers, Dostoevsky represented a serious challenge to the culture and traditions of England.[60] The resurgence of interest in his work can be compared in its importance to the first Post-Impressionist exhibition sponsored by Roger Fry. That exhibit, which opened in London on 8 November 1910 and ran until 15 January 1911, included the first English showings of Cezanne, Van Gogh, Gauguin, Matisse, Picasso, and Seurat. It provoked an extraordinary response because it challenged artistic sensibilities and pointed towards radically new directions, prompting Virginia Woolf's famous remark that "on or about December 1910 human character changed."[61] Samuel Hynes interprets her comment as indicating that she "chose that occasion as an appropriate symbol of the way European ideas forced themselves upon the insular English consciousness during the Edwardian years and so joined England to the Continent."[62] Dostoevsky presented a similar challenge to the sensibilities of the time, though he never had the equivalent of a Roger Fry or Clive Bell who could explain his formal significance to an otherwise uncomprehending audience. Owing to the absence of people who understood his distinctive artistic forms, Dostoevsky was either reduced to the status of a psychological, moral, and literary dissolvent or heralded as a regenerative visionary working beyond the borders of art.

The English writers who might have helped their countrymen understand his fictional art proved incapable of detecting artistic intent. The seven novelists of this study, like their contemporaries, did not have access to the diaries, articles, and rough drafts that reveal his commitment to his art. Nor did they have the benefit of discerning critics, with the minor exception of Lytton Strachey, who could intelligently and accurately address his work in terms of European literary traditions. As products of their age, they were influenced by Russian critics who themselves did not understand Dostoevsky and English critics who shared their assumption that he paid no attention to art.

Interestingly, Dostoevsky's reputation soared amid the ebbing of interest in Balzac, Hugo, Dickens, and other giants of nineteenth-century realism whose works were creatively filtered through his artistic consciousness, a neglect which aggravated English tendencies to judge his products as virgin novelistic births. Biographical knowledge only augmented the problem: the available information distorted Dostoevsky's artistic dedication by drawing upon the sensationalist aspects of his life, his epilepsy, his gambling, and his political imprisonment. History, in effect, conspired to render the English incapable of understanding Dostoevsky's art.

Literary reception theory helps to explain the inability to recognize artistic form. According to Hans Robert Jauss, misunderstanding occurs when the aesthetic distance between a given work and the prevailing horizon of expectations is too great. Jauss defines "aesthetic distance" as the "disparity between the given horizon of expectations and the appearance of a new work." He argues that works embodying innovative aesthetic principles always challenge the expectations of their audience and will be met with resistance, illustrated by the first responses to Flaubert and Baudelaire. If the aesthetic distances are not too formidable, such works can change the horizon of expectations "through negation of familiar experiences or through raising newly articulated experiences to the level of consciousness." In the case of Dostoevsky, however, the distance between expectations and the author's intentions could not be bridged, a phenomenon explained by the application of Jauss's theory: "The distance between the actual first perception of a work and . . . the resistance that the new work poses to the expectations of its first audience can be so great that it requires a long process of reception to gather in that which was unexpected and unusable within the first horizon."[63] Of course, Dostoevsky's works were not historically new at the time of Garnett's translations, but her audience approached them as virtually new creations, demonstrating the descriptive power of Jauss's model.

Unlike other modernist works built upon new aesthetic principles and delineating new genre boundary lines, such as *Ulysses* and *To the Lighthouse*, which were at least identified as art by a minority, Dostoevsky's works could not significantly alter the artistic expectations of his English readers, largely because the author was not acknowledged as someone self-consciously engaged in the task of redefining the novel. While it is true that the works of Joyce and Woolf met with great aesthetic resistance because both sought to redefine the prevailing horizon of expectations, the two writers helped their cause through their own statements about their efforts. Dostoevsky's English readers, by contrast, had no such help. To an audience that often equated literary art with stylistic beauty, upholding the conviction of James and Conrad that each sentence must bear the Olympian imprint of an artist in control, that fiction must resonate with a melodic, unifying authorial voice, Dostoevsky proved aesthetically deficient. The stylistic, structural, linguistic, social, and thematic heterogeneity of his literature, attributes heralded by Bakhtin as essential to the novel, merely confirmed the audience's expectations of artlessness.

Other theoretical models representing diverse hermeneutic stances underscore the importance of expectation in individual acts of reading. E. D. Hirsch contends that expectations shape our understanding of what we find in a text: "an interpreter's preliminary generic conception of a text is constitutive of everything that he subsequently understands."[64] Hirsch uses Piaget's notion of corrigible schemata to discuss the process of understanding: "A schema sets up a range of predictions or expectations, which if fulfilled confirms the schema, but if not fulfilled causes us to revise it." Understanding, then, may be "conceived as a validating, self-correcting process – an active positing of corrigible schemata which we test and modify in the very process of coming to understand an utterance."[65] In terms of Hirsch's conceptual model, the readers of the Garnett translations can be viewed as having a faulty "preliminary generic conception" of Dostoevsky's texts. Because these readers typically approached the Russian writer with an inappropriate set of expectations, their responses were miscued.

A reader's expectations, Hirsch argues, must be aligned with the author's because understanding "can occur only if the interpreter proceeds under the same system of expectations" as the author.[66] Hirsch adopts a conservative hermeneutics for he argues that the author's intention is the "determiner of meaning," and he insists that literary interpretation can achieve validity only if it approximates the author's intended meaning.[67] Meaning, as Hirsch defines it, is "that which is represented by a text: it is that which an author meant by a particular sign sequence."[68] Such assertions render Hirsch vulnerable to the charge that he gives too much power to the author; the reader seems required to practice Buddhist-like self-abnegation to enter the temple of authorial meaning. Yet his work provides a cautionary counterweight to those post-modernists who blithely jettison authorial intent as a vestige of our authoritarian predecessors.

Unlike Hirsch, Wolfgang Iser pays scant attention to the author behind the text in his conceptualizing about the dynamics of reading. Though he offers a more protean and fluid concept of the act, one more amenable to modernist literature, he, like Hirsch, gives expectation a paramount role in the construction of meaning. Iser does allow the reader greater freedom than Hirsch and stresses the creative interplay between text and reader, but he recognizes that a reader's expectations must be circumscribed by the text. If a "work is to come together in a polyphonic whole, there must be limits to the tolerable level of indeterminacy, and if these limits are exceeded, the polyphonic harmony will be shattered or, to be more precise, will never come into being."[69] Unfortunately, Dostoevsky's twentieth-century English audience, possessing a scarcity of reliable guides for understanding authorial intention and textual construction, seldom recognized polyphonic harmony in his works. The failure to comprehend his artistry – and the meaning of his literary creations – can be traced to the uninformed and unguided expectations that led readers to assume that his fiction was not shaped or structured. Denied credence as an artist by both admirers and detractors, Dostoevsky remained a literary outcast in England.

DOSTOEVSKY AND THE PROBLEM OF ARTISTIC INTENTION

The particular responses of the English novelists exemplify the historic difficulties that numerous readers have experienced with Dostoevsky. According to D. S. Mirsky, even the author's contemporaries "deplored his lack of taste, his misrepresentation of real life, his weakness for crudely sensational effects." Though Dostoevsky's "great natural gifts" were recognized, the Russians regretted his "insufficient artistic discipline."[70] Dostoevsky's audiences, from the France of Sartre and Camus to the Germany of Hesse and Mann to the England of Lawrence and Woolf, have often been unable to discern an underlying artistic intent, in large part because of the author's relative silence. Dostoevsky did not follow the usual agenda of modern artists who seek to create new artistic forms. In contrast to the voluminous legacy of novelists such as Woolf, James, Lawrence, Joyce, Flaubert and Zola, Dostoevsky offered his readers relatively little that would explain the characteristics of his art. He never fully developed an aesthetic theory to defend, explain, and legitimize his narrative methods, nor did he write manifestos to enlighten or attack his audience. Perhaps because his role as an artist was so closely aligned with his other roles as moralist, social critic, religious visionary, philosopher, and patriot, Dostoevsky seldom treated artistic issues in isolation. He may have realized that his new agenda for the novel could only be accomplished through the exploratory act of fiction writing. A manifesto, after all, typically requires the suppression of dissent, and Dostoevsky required a minimum of two conflicting voices, two world views, to express himself artfully.

He did operate with carefully thought-out aesthetic assumptions, but most of these were implied rather than stated directly. Evidence has been compiled from numerous sources that elucidates his extraordinarily ambitious attempts to meld his unique content with innovative artistic forms. Scholars such as Leonid Grossman, Mikhail Bakhtin, Edward Wasiolek, Robert Belknap, Robert Louis Jackson, and Joseph Frank have thoroughly traced the development of Dostoevsky's artistic mission. They have done so by exploring his omnivorous readings, his correspondence, journal articles, the indirect evidence of his own literature and its drafts, his relationships to other authors and theories of art, and the intellectual culture of Russia.[71] In discussing the problems of understanding Dostoevsky's art, one must not lose sight of the obvious: much of this information was unavailable to earlier audiences.

Perhaps the most common cause of the failure to recognize his artistry resides in his means of characterization. He created such powerful and philosophically profound characters, allowing them to voice their views with great freedom and without interruption, that readers often felt compelled to argue and debate with them, without discerning a directive authorial presence. As Bakhtin points out, readers either reduced Dostoevsky to a series of "disparate, contradictory philosophical stances" represented by "author–thinkers – Raskolnikov, Myshkin, Stavrogin, Ivan Karamazov, the Grand Inquisitor, and others" – or they regarded him as "a peculiar synthesis of all these ideological voices."[72] In both cases, they assumed that artistry had been sacrificed to the heated passions of ideological disputes, and Dostoevsky's intricate polyphonic structures were misunderstood as a disparate assortment of philosophical monologues. Bakhtin has persuasively argued that readers became "enslaved by the ideology of Dostoevsky's heroes," delaying the recognition of the author's profoundly original "artistic intention."[73]

Bakhtin's analysis will be frequently used throughout this study because it provides a means of explicating the persistent nonliterary assessments of Dostoevsky with their collapsed distinctions between author and characters. D. H. Lawrence, for example, could not separate the writer from his creations, and he interpreted Myshkin, Ivan, Rogozhin, and others as biographical evidence of Dostoevsky's sensual and intellectual corruption. Though Virginia Woolf regarded the author as a healthy sage rather than a diseased prophet, she too could not move beyond his characters to find a controlling artistic will. She heard only individual voices, shrill, monstrous, and chaotic. The other novelists, in varying degrees, were similarly overwhelmed by myriad voices preventing the recognition of art.

The intense immediacy and chaotic effects of Dostoevsky's narratives further contributed to the impression that he artlessly reported the volcanic fury within his mind. Unaware of his conscious effort to break down the distance between text and reader, audiences believed that he lacked the discipline to achieve aesthetic distance and control. His fictional methods – Gothic plots of surprise and coincidence, riotous group scenes, frenzied pacing, interior monologues, confessional outbursts, philosophic debates, dreams, hallucinations – often disoriented readers. Historically, audiences have interpreted the whirlwind narration as evidence of failed artistry rather than the intentional reflection of a society in the midst of dissolution. They have not recognized his narratives as the result of what Joseph Frank describes as Dostoevsky's "attempt to grapple with the chaos of his society." Frank reminds us that the author defined himself as the "chronicler of the moral consequences of flux and change, and of the breakup of the traditional forms of Russian life."[74] Frank's monumental five–volume study, when completed, may one day serve as the final corrective to the excesses and misunderstandings of Dostoevsky's early twentieth–century readers. In contrast to those readers, Frank locates Dostoevsky's genius in "his ability to fuse private dilemmas with those raging in the society of which he was a part," and he patiently discerns the social and cultural roots of his fiction .[75]

As might be expected, Dostoevsky's narrative techniques proved a stumbling block to English novelists, especially those most dedicated to the art of the novel. Virginia Woolf described his works as "seething whirlpools, gyrating sandstorms, waterspouts which hiss and boil and suck us in."[76] Though she found manic excitement therein, she feared the delirium was further evidence of abdicated control. Joseph Conrad, who dismissed *The Brothers Karamazov* as "fierce mouthings from prehistoric ages," could not admire fiction so far removed from the restraint, stylistic beauty, and narrative indirection of his own work.[77] Henry James shared his repulsion, deploring Dostoevsky along with Tolstoy as a creator of "fluid puddings."[78] John Galsworthy similarly found a lack of restraint, condemning Dostoevsky's popularity among the English as a "mark of these cubistic, blood-bespattered-poster times."[79] Even Arnold Bennett and E. M. Forster could find little evidence of shaping amid the passionate tumult.

The heterogeneous nature of Dostoevsky's subject matter and style further supported the perception of artlessness. His fiction juxtaposed religious believers and debased idolaters, philosophic quests and violent sensuality, the sacred and the scandalous, using not one style but a mixture of many, from grotesque farces to religious parables. Perhaps the best explanation of the connection between subject and style is supplied by Leonid Grossman:

> Dostoevsky merges opposites. He issues a decisive challenge to the fundamental canon of the theory of art. His task: to overcome the greatest difficulty that an artist can face, to create out of heterogeneous and profoundly disparate materials of varying worth a unified and integral artistic creation. Thus the Book of Job, the Revelation of St. John, the Gospel texts . . . [are] combined here in a most original way with the newspaper, the anecdote, the parody, the street scene, with the grotesque, even with the pamphlet. He boldly casts into his crucibles ever newer elements, knowing and believing that in the blaze of his creative work these raw chunks of everyday life, the sensations of boulevard novels and the divinely inspired pages of Holy Writ, will melt down and fuse in a new compound. [80]

Bakhtin goes even further than Grossman, for what the latter regards as Dostoevsky's compositional principle, the former identifies as characteristic of an entirely new genre, the polyphonic novel. According to Bakhtin's controversial thesis, Dostoevsky merged elements of carnival literature and menippean satire to create a new genre that would at last do justice to the complexity of the modern world.

Bakhtin credits Dostoevsky with the creation of a new form of artistic discourse uniquely suited to capture modernity's unstable dialogical oppositions, its relativized, indeterminate plurality of languages, ideologies, and social experiences. The blurring of aesthetic and linguistic boundaries, the commingling of oddly incongruous elements, for which many ostracized Dostoevsky from the ranks of artists, became for Bakhtin the definition of a new poetics of the novel. According to Bakhtin, the polyphonic novel is marked by its contending, autonomous voices: "A plurality of independent and unmerged voices and consciousnesses, a genuine polyphony of fully valid voices is in fact the chief characteristic of Dostoevsky's novels."[81] These voices speak simultaneously and contentiously, the living embodiments of the "multi-leveledness and contradictoriness" that Dostoevsky found in "the objective social world," which refused to submit to a single, controlling authorial voice.[82] In this view, Dostoevsky's major characters are "not voiceless slaves . . . but *free* people, capable of standing *alongside* their creator, capable of not agreeing with him and even of rebelling against him."[83]

Always an intriguing and provocative thinker, Bakhtin offers an explanation of Dostoevsky's power that accommodates form as well as content. In effect, he presents the Russian novelist as the ultimate democrat: in Dostoevsky's dialogues all voices are equal, so equal in fact that the author's own voice cannot be distinguished. No wonder Bakhtin has been so popular in recent decades: he killed off the author as a philosophical construct long before Foucault. Bakhtin's critics, however, take him to task for disengaging Dostoevsky from his European literary heritage and for granting full sovereignty to his heroes. Victor Terras, for example, makes the convincing point that Dostoevsky's fiction owes its success to "a controlling narrative voice." Contrary to Bakhtin's interpretation, Terras finds a "clear hierarchy of voices" in the novels. To those who have done their homework, the imprint of Dostoevsky's own judgment and values is everywhere evident. Ivan Karamazov's voice, however compelling, cannot be given the same status as Zossima's; likewise Svidrigailov's voice, for all its poignant decadence, cannot be ranked as equal to Sonya's. The author tilts the dialogic scale, regardless of Bakhtin's claims.[84]

For our purposes, Bakhtin's theory must be recognized as fundamentally flawed because it claims too much. Still, Bakhtin wields a power not easily dismissed. If his foundational claims are inflated, his insights into our habits of misreading Dostoevsky retain their utility. The Russian novelist might not be the Promethean innovator who cast aside all previous artistic modes, but Bakhtin remains an invaluable ally in our struggle to resist the legion of those who have discerned little or no artistry in Dostoevsky. Bakhtin's critical study gives us a vocabulary for naming key attributes of Dostoevsky's art.

Robert Louis Jackson, another critic who has keenly penetrated Dostoevsky's artistry, offers a religious dimension to our appreciation of the author's aesthetic values and his reliance on contradictory raw materials. Jackson notes that Dostoevsky believed that art shared in the power of the Holy Spirit because it was capable of transfiguring humanity. Jackson argues that Dostoevsky's distinctive aesthetic vision derives from the contrast between *obraz* and *bezobrazie*. *Obraz*, Jackson contends, "is the axis of beauty in the Russian language, it is 'form,' 'shape,' 'image;' it is also the iconographic image, or icon – the visible symbol of the beauty of God."[85] *Bezobrazie*, in contrast, names "that which is 'without image,' shapeless, disfigured, ugly" – in other words, that which is monstrous. The opposition between the two terms is moral as well as aesthetic, for *obraz* points to moral perfection, while *bezobrazie* leads in the direction of "cruelty, violence, and . . . sensuality."[86] Dostoevsky, according to Jackson, found the subject matter of his art in the intersection of *obraz* and *bezobrazie*. He re-created in his fiction a monstrous world, disfigured in violence, despair, and depravity, yet a world yearning for ideal beauty and the presence of God. In this contrast between historical reality and spiritual ideals can be found the explanation for Dostoevsky's reliance on subject matter and stylistic polarities.

Those who castigated Dostoevsky as a monster in the house of fiction did not realize the new aesthetic possibilities that flowered from his disfigured subjects. Profound art can indeed grow from the intersection of *obraz* and *bezobrazie*, an insight denied to the seven novelists of this study. Still, when novelist meets novelist, interesting things occur. As we shall see, the lively and cantankerous misreadings of our seven novelists illuminate the vortex of modernity.

CHAPTER 2

Prophetic rage and rivalry: D. H. Lawrence

Like Birkin in his wrestling match with Gerald, Lawrence struggled with fierce intensity against Dostoevsky, a hated and loved rival whose strength flowed from the decadence of modernity. Lawrence grappled with him as a false prophet, a false artist, whose works endorsed the modern sickness and its symptoms of self-division, egoism, cankered sensualism, and devouring consciousness. Repeatedly, Lawrence stalked his rival in letters, essays, reviews, and fiction. His assaults blur, but cannot mask, his affinity with the passionate visionary who evoked a "subterranean love" and a reluctant "great admiration."[1]

Lawrence felt the cloying presence of his rival because the height of Dostoevsky's English influence coincided with his own most creative and troubled years. Lawrence's closest friends, including Jessie Chambers, Edward and Constance Garnett, S. S. Koteliansky, and Middleton Murry, admired Dostoevsky with an irritating ardency. Murry's zeal proved especially galling; in a move tantamount to John the Baptist abandoning the camp of the Nazarene, he exchanged devotion to Lawrence for the worship of his rival. Lawrence's correspondence with Murry and others shows how his views were antithetically shaped, or misshaped, by his friends and the prevailing literary climate.

Lawrence's essays and fiction help to explain his judgment and the mutable complexity of his values. The theoretical essays illuminate the bitter depths of his response, especially his charge that Dostoevsky embodied a diseased mental consciousness. The essays about other Russian, American, and Italian authors are equally useful, for Dostoevsky became an inverse and self-reflective measure of value. Perhaps the best explanation of Lawrence's anger can be found in his fictional mining of the Dostoevskian terrains of ambivalent passion, social dissolution, hyperconsciousness, and pilgrim quests. For an author who proclaimed his romantic singularity, the thought of shared domains in the modern underground could not have been pleasing.

The rivalry with Dostoevsky culminated with an end-of-life essay on *The Grand Inquisitor*. Lawrence's deconstructive and self-liberating reading provides a case study of his persistent misunderstanding of Dostoevsky while highlighting the vacillations and contradictions in his own thinking and creative art. To borrow from Harold Bloom, Dostoevsky played the paternally chafing role of a "predecessor" whose influence spurs creation and compels a destructive misreading. In seeking to unmask Dostoevsky, Lawrence reveals far more about himself than about his antagonist.

FIRST CONNECTIONS

The first stage of Lawrence's response occurs between 1909 and 1916, the span from his earliest recorded comment to the Dostoevsky-induced demise of his friendship with Middleton Murry. During this time, Lawrence published his first four novels, including *Sons and Lovers* and *The Rainbow*, and he drafted *Women in Love*. He also broke away from Jessie Chambers, eloped with Frieda, faced the suppression of *The Rainbow*, planned a utopian community to be called Rananim, suffered prosecution for suspicion of German sympathies, lived penuriously, and struggled against the early effects of tuberculosis. He managed to write his best fiction amid such difficulties, all the while fighting tirelessly against Dostoevsky.

The first reference to Dostoevsky appears in a letter of 8 May 1909 to Blanche Jennings. Lawrence denounced *Crime and Punishment* as "a tract, a treatise, a pamphlet compared to Tolstoy's *Anna Karenina* or *War and Peace*."[2] Lawrence had first read Tolstoy while at college in Nottingham, and he acclaimed *Anna Karenina* as the greatest novel in the world because of its frank sexuality.[3] Later, as a young man of twenty-three in his first year of teaching at Croydon, he had written to Jessie Chambers's older sister recommending Tolstoy's works as a remedy to the provincial isolation and narrowness of Eastwood.[4] Though he later turned against Tolstoy for allowing his moralism to suppress libertine energies, Lawrence always found a sexual vitality in Anna and Vronsky that he could never find in Dostoevsky. Lawrence came to view Anna's suicide as evidence that Tolstoy denied the natural, sensual part of himself, the "God-flame" of free individualism, and submitted to the false dictates of social morality.[5] Only a coward, and a false artist, could thwart the passionate vitality of Anna and Vronsky.

Jessie Chambers, Lawrence's first love and the model for Miriam in

Sons and Lovers, also reports about his first encounter with *Crime and Punishment*. She notes that Lawrence read a French translation soon after the death of his mother which occurred on 9 December 1910. Though her date is contradicted by the letter to Blanche Jennings, the spirit of her account seems plausible when judged against her other descriptions of Lawrence's early readings. Chambers recounts, "I remember how he frowned in a puzzled way and said: 'It's very great, but I don't understand it. I must read it again.'"[6] Perhaps Lawrence had felt compelled to reread *Crime and Punishment* after the death of his mother, and Chambers remembered his response to a second reading.

Her book about Lawrence, regardless of the accuracy of its dates, provides an intellectual barometer of a rebellious generation. The young lovers read Ibsen, Schopenhauer, William James, Euripides, Baudelaire, Verlaine, Turgenev, Whitman, and Dostoevsky, searching far beyond the shores of the British Isles, as far as possible from the shadow of Queen Victoria. At first, Dostoevsky was only available in French translations. Within a couple of years, the translations of Constance Garnett would be ensconced on the shelves of the community library so that all of Eastwood would become acquainted with him. Chambers herself would read *The Brothers Karamazov* for solace after discovering that Lawrence had finally abandoned her for Frieda. When she returned it to the library, she "left it refreshed in spirit . . . able to face [her] own inner chaos."[7]

Edward Garnett, a crucial figure in Lawrence's early years, provided a link to Dostoevsky. A powerful figure in London's literary world, Garnett had close ties to publishers and novelists such as Conrad, Bennett, Galsworthy, and Wells. As a reader for Duckworth, he helped secure publication for Lawrence's second novel *The Trespasser*. Lawrence sent him everything he wrote in his early years, seeking his critical appraisal. Garnett substantially edited *Sons and Lovers* and prepared the manuscript for publication. He also influenced Lawrence's decision to give up teaching for full-time writing. Garnett's home, the Cearne, served as the location for energetic, late-night literary and intellectual discussions which often focused on Lawrence's own writing. When the young novelist met Frieda in 1912, Garnett became a confidant as well. The scandalous couple even stayed at the Cearne shortly before their elopement to Germany.

Garnett and his wife Constance were pivotal figures in promoting Dostoevsky. Edward wrote a stirringly eloquent essay in 1906, urgently recommending that England pay attention to the neglected, out-of-print novelist.[8] Edward also persistently drew attention to Dostoevsky and other Russian writers in his critical essays and reviews; his friend Joseph Conrad even labeled him the "Russian Embassador to the Republic of Letters."[9] Lawrence read at least some of his mentor's comments about Dostoevsky and was probably influenced by his judgment.[10] During the time that Edward and Lawrence were becoming close friends – 1911 to 1914 – Constance was translating Dostoevsky. Lawrence marveled when he saw her busily at work in her garden, piling page upon page of her finished copy.[11] She too became a friend of Lawrence and Frieda, later corresponding with them and visiting them in Europe.[12] Given the Russian interests of the Garnetts, the nights that Lawrence spent at the Cearne would certainly have included discussions of Dostoevsky.

S. S. Koteliansky, a Ukrainian emigrant and translator, considerably broadened Lawrence's interest in Russian writers. Koteliansky gained the friendship of Leonard and Virginia Woolf, Katherine Mansfield, Middleton Murry, T. S. Eliot, W. B. Yeats, E. M. Forster, G. B. Shaw, and even Jessie Chambers, but he is best remembered as a friend of Lawrence.[13] The young novelist met "Kot," as he was known to his friends, in 1914 on the eve of the outbreak of the First World War. He was an industrious translator who ranks second only to Constance Garnett in the number of Russian works that he introduced to the English public. Though Lawrence apparently had a rudimentary knowledge of Russian, he depended on English translations for his readings in Russian literature and philosophy, though he also read some works in French. The translations of Koteliansky and Garnett enabled him to become familiar with Tolstoy, Turgenev, Chekhov, Gorky, I. A. Bunin, Andreyev, Gogol, V. V. Rozanov, Alexander Kuprin, Dmitri Merezhkovsky, Vladimir Solovyov, and Leo Shestov.[14] Koteliansky also translated a selection of Dostoevsky's letters, excerpts from his *Diary of a Writer*, and *Stavrogin's Confession and the Plan of the Life of a Great Sinner* (previously unpublished material from *The Possessed* and Dostoevsky's notebooks). In 1930 he translated *The Grand Inquisitor* as an independent work and enlisted Lawrence to write the preface. According to George Zytaruk, Lawrence read everything that Kot translated.[15]

Kot sought Lawrence's collaborative help in his translating activities. Though the emigrant's knowledge of Russian language and literature was great, he never became completely fluent in English, so he used collaborators, including Lawrence, the Woolfs, Katherine Mansfield, and Middleton Murry, to help smooth the rough edges. Leonard Woolf has described Kot's method as follows:

His method was to write the translation in his own strange English and leave a large space between the lines in which I then turned his English into my English . . . After I turned his draft into English English, we then went through it sentence by sentence . . . He would pass no sentence until he was so absolutely convinced that it gave the exact shade of meaning and feeling of the original and we would sometimes be a quarter of an hour arguing over a single word.[16]

The extent of Lawrence's translating role is difficult to assess because he wanted no public acknowledgment of his contributions. According to Bertram Rota, Koteliansky said that "Lawrence felt it would be damaging to his reputation with publishers as a creative writer if he should appear as a translator."[17] Evidence points to Lawrence's collaboration in the translation of Shestov's philosophic work, *All Things Are Possible*.[18] Lawrence also helped Kot with I. A. Bunin's *The Gentleman from San Francisco*, and he played a role in Maxim Gorky's *Reminiscences of Leonid Andreyev*. Kot reported that his friend assisted in the translation of *The Grand Inquisitor*, though his claim has been disputed on the grounds of Lawrence's failing health and his physical distance from Kot.[19]

Lawrence's correspondence with Koteliansky provides valuable information about his response to Dostoevsky. In a letter of ?8 April 1915 he admitted ambivalent feelings after reading a collection of letters.

What an amazing person he was – a pure introvert, a purely disintegrating will – there was not a grain of the passion of love in him – all the passion of hate, of evil. Yet a great man. It has become, I think, now, a supreme wickedness to set up a Christ-worship as Dostoevsky did: it is the outcome of an evil will, disguising itself in terms of love.

But he is a great man and I have the greatest admiration for him. *I even feel a sort of subterranean love for him.* But he never, never wanted anybody to love him. He exerted a repelling influence on everybody [emphasis mine].[20]

The proximity of admiration and hatred expressed here is essential for understanding the depths of his antagonism.[21] In a manner reminiscent of the narrator's response to the Russian officer in *Notes from the Underground*, Lawrence found himself seeking again and again to confront Dostoevsky to demonstrate his superiority and contempt. Beneath his need for confrontation there resided a masked identification, a "subterranean love."

One year later, Lawrence wrote again to Koteliansky about Dostoevsky, this time condemning him with no trace of identification. Apparently, Lawrence read the novels in the same way that he read the letters, mining the texts for biographical revelations and evidence of the author's personal credo.

I could do with Dostoevsky if he did not make all men fallen angels. We are not angels. It is a tiresome conceit. Men want to be Sadists, or they don't. If they do, well and good. There's no need to drag in the fallen angel to save ourselves in our own sight. I am most sick of this divinity-of-man business. People are not important – I insist on it. It doesn't matter what Stavrogin does, nor whether he lives or dies. I am quite unmoved when he commits suicide. It is his affair. It bores me.

Lawrence's letter concludes with a statement that blurs the distinction between Dostoevsky's fiction and the blackness of his own life during the war years: "People are so self-important. Let them die, silly blighters, fools, and twopenny knaves."[22]

Ironically, Lawrence found his own work compared to Dostoevsky's; friends and enemies alike found many similarities. In 1912, his second novel *The Trespasser*, was jointly reviewed in the *Athenaeum* with Garnett's first major translation of Dostoevsky, *The Brothers Karamazov*. The reviewer praised Lawrence in terms of Dostoevsky, noting "psychological intensity" and "poetic realism of a Dostoevskian order." *The Trespasser*, according to the review, "recalled the best Russian school."[23] The joint review has a larger significance, for it points to a convergence that was to trouble Lawrence for years to come. Both writers had a powerful, scripture-like effect upon their English audience, though devotion was not always accompanied by intelligence or perceptiveness. Their readers during the 1910s and 1920s can usually be identified as either believers or unbelievers, converts or infidels. If Dostoevsky enthusiasts evoked comparisons to a cult, the same fervor extended to Lawrence's admirers. For example, Ivy Low reported that she "read *Sons and Lovers* in one all-night sitting." The next morning she sent postcards to her friends, including one to Viola Maynell: "Be sure to read *Sons and Lovers!* This is a book about the Oedipus complex! The most marvelous novel I have ever read." Later, she wrote that "Viola and I adopted D. H. Lawrence as our creed." In person, Lawrence could have the same effect. Cynthia Asquith, the prime minister's daughter-in-law, described her meeting with him in religious terms: "He is a Pentecost to one, and has the gift of intimacy and such perceptiveness that he introduces one to oneself."[24] While Lawrence sometimes enjoyed playing a messianic role, he certainly did not welcome competition. Yet wherever he turned, he could not escape Dostoevsky.

LAWRENCE, MURRY, AND DOSTOEVSKY: A TRIANGLE
OF DISPUTE

The convergence of the two novelists has its clearest focal point in Middleton Murry. Murry and Katherine Mansfield, whom he later married, became close friends with Lawrence and Frieda in 1913, the publication year of *Sons and Lovers*. Both women were still legally bound in marriages to men who no longer participated in their lives. The intimacy of the Lawrences and Murrys, as they were known, derived from common literary interests and a shared scorn of social proprieties. The Murrys witnessed the wedding of Lawrence and Frieda and faithfully supported them, even living with them for a while, during the dark, early years of the First World War when *The Rainbow* was suppressed by censors and Lawrence was severely strained by the hostilities and hysterias of wartime England.[25]

Murry found in Lawrence literary genius, visionary strength, and personal charisma. One senses an almost sacramental bond between them, with each man seeking a communion that went beyond ordinary friendship. Lawrence in these years had a Birkin-like reverence for Murry; he characterized him as "one of the men of the future . . . the only man who is quite simply with me. One day he'll be ahead of me. Because he'll build up the temple." In 1915 the two friends worked together to produce a short-lived fortnightly paper, the *Signature*. Their plan called for Lawrence to be the main contributor. He identified his purpose in religious terms: "I am going to do the preaching – sort of philosophy – beliefs by which one can reconstruct the world." Murry, in turn, was to make contributions that shared "his ideas on freedom for the individual soul."[26] Together, they would give voice to a new vision, a new world. Only three issues were published, however, and the reconstruction of the world was postponed due to a lack of subscribers.

According to the accounts of Murry and others, the two friends often included Dostoevsky in their discussions.[27] With a monkish fervor, Murry exulted in his love of Dostoevsky. John Carswell records the remarks of a Murry acquaintance:

We had wonderful conversations, especially on Dostoevsky and the "higher" consciousness. They would last for hours, and during them he would mount, as it were, from one transcendental height to another, the ascent culminating with some such remark as "the inhuman is the highest form of the human," and in the ensuing silence he would gaze vaguely at the corner of the ceiling with a faint, wondering smile.[28]

Between 1913 and 1916 Lawrence and Murry read the translations of Dostoevsky as they were released by Heinemann. They came to terms with his novels while coming to terms with one another. Though their opinions of Dostoevsky diverged, Lawrence was almost persuaded to collaborate with Murry on a book about him. Murry went on to write the book himself.

Murry's *Dostoevsky: A Critical Study*, published in 1916, marked an irreparable fissure in their friendship. According to his *Reminiscences of Lawrence*, Murry had been disturbed by Lawrence's attacks as early as 1914: "It started with Dostoevsky. Lawrence was all against him for his humility and love." Murry was further disturbed by the salvos fired in "The Crown," a Lawrence essay which was partially published in the *Signature*. The book itself, however, proved the final break: "For the first time an issue had emerged between us on which I really knew my mind. I felt I must stick to my guns; and I did. I wrote my book on Dostoevsky."[29]

Murry later described the act of writing his book in terms that undermine the title's claim to be a critical study. Dostoevsky proved the occasion for "an unprecedented flood of illumination," a means of "inward revelation." For the "first time in his life," Murry "had the experience of certitude." He was "hardly more than an amanuensis of a book that wrote itself": "all that happened . . . was that the objective pattern of Dostoevsky declared itself, through me as an instrument."[30] The experience of the novels even produced visionary terror: "There are times when thinking about the spirits which he [Dostoevsky] has conjured up – I use the word deliberately – I am seized by a suprasensual terror. For one awful moment I seem to have a vision of suns grown cold, and hear the echo of voices calling out without sound across the waste and frozen universe."[31] In Dostoevsky, Murry discovered a spiritualized vision that invoked a new life far removed from Lawrence's concern for the blood and the body.

Dostoevsky's vision, according to Murry's idiosyncratic account, requires the denial of physical life to attain a higher and more privileged consciousness. Murry even claims that Dostoevsky "existed more truly as an idea than as a man." "He was consciousness incarnate and in him the preponderance of the spirit over the body reached the extreme beyond which lay the death of physical man and the dissolution of the spiritual being."[32] Murry's study reveals him as a Lawrencean apostate who had abandoned his friend's creed of sensual vitality for "consciousness incarnate." The man who had agreed to work with Lawrence to reconstruct the world now sought to baptize in the name of Dostoevsky.

Murry approaches the novels as sacred writ with a decidedly Nietzschean cast.[33] Dostoevsky "was not a novelist, and he cannot be judged as a novelist." Too singular a being to be approached in such mundane terms, "his living spirit was incommensurable with the forms of life, his art with the forms of art. He cannot be approached by the same road as other men."[34] Equating Dostoevsky with his most tormented characters, Murry praises the "superhuman," those "mighty champions" who "battle life for its secret," "men who in their combat dared to will evil."[35] He identifies the author with a quest for limitless knowledge, the quest of an Ivan or Raskolnikov or Stavrogin, and he wholeheartedly approves: "The man who is most truly man can acquiesce to no limitations to his knowledge, for to know is to be a man, and to know utterly is to be most wholly man."[36] In his midrashic excess, Murry wrongly assumes that Dostoevsky endorsed the views of his strongest characters, siding always with the willful romantic egos, the thought-tormented, and the transgressors. Murry's preoccupation with consciousness and knowledge evokes the intellectualized posings of Hermione in *Women in Love,* so brutally satirized by Lawrence.

By ignoring literary context, Murry arrives at ludicrous interpretations. For instance, he exonerates Raskolnikov because of his status as a superior being: "Raskolnikov had done no crime. He had done no more than to transgress the Laws which are human institutions . . . No wonder he does not repent, when he has done no sin . . . Right is on his side."[37] Raskolnikov's only failure can be attributed to a weakness of character and resolution. When he accepted punishment, he mistakenly allowed society's conventional standards to usurp his own privileged position. The "real hero" of *Crime and Punishment* for Murry is Svidrigailov. He has "dared to face life alone, to measure his individual will against all things."[38] He has "passed beyond good and evil . . . and willed that his will should be omnipotent."[39] In Murry's perspective, Svidrigailov symbolizes Dostoevsky's "passionate denial of God," a denial that is necessary "to assert one own's divinity."[40] In order to make such claims for Svidrigailov, however, Murry has to ignore the novel itself. Dostoevsky's Svidrigailov, with his lust for children, his near-rape and intended blackmail of Raskolnikov's sister, his treachery towards Sonya, and his pathetic suicide, emerges as a less-than-ideal romantic hero. Yet in Murry's work he walks as proudly as a Zarathustra.

Murry ignores any hint of complexity and praises all main characters as a scriptural model for heroic life. He celebrates Stavrogin of *The Possessed* as a demi-god for his proud will, his rebellion against life, and his cynical denunciation of ideals.[41] Alyosha of *The Brothers Karamazov* is praised as a Christ-like champion of humanity, a fulfillment of all those heroes who have gone before him. According to Murry, he has even "passed beyond Christian revelation," for a character so superior has no such need: he has a "knowledge in the Great Oneness which needs no belief in God for its support."[42] All the Dostoevsky characters stand on the same jerrybuilt stage as heroes without meaningful distinction. One might as well put together Pickwick, Uriah Heep, Little Nell, and Fagin and declare their sameness.

Murry's comments fueled Lawrence's rage and provoked letters of opposition aimed at both the Russian and his acolyte.[43] What might otherwise seem to be unsolicited anger can be understood more readily when placed within the context of Murry's devotional excess. Lawrence's railing against Dostoevsky's destructive mental consciousness and self-absorption is elucidated by Murry's penchant for hyperconscious characters who define the world in egoistic terms. Lawrence reacted with similar vehemence against Murry's belief that all of Dostoevsky's major characters participated in a single movement towards new heights of consciousness and wholeness. Lawrence, instead, found evidence of division everywhere, a division produced by the author's split psyche. In key respects, Murry's warped version of Dostoevsky is inseparable from the Dostoevsky that Lawrence rejects.

While Murry's work was still in progress, Lawrence wrote to him and Katherine Mansfield to express his contempt. This letter of 17 February 1916 provides some of the most important evidence about Lawrence's response to his rival. After reading *The Possessed*, he found that he had "gone off Dostoevsky and could write about him in very cold blood." Though Lawrence found the novel boring – "nobody was possessed enough really to interest me" – his reading led him to a summary statement about the author's deficiencies as a writer and man.

1. He has a fixed will, a mania to be infinite, to be God.
2. Within this will, his activity is twofold:
   a. To be self-less, a pure Christian, to live in the outer whole, the self-less whole, the universal consciousness.
   b. To be pure, absolute self, all-devouring, and all consuming.

Lawrence's "main statement" about Dostoevsky echoes Murry's generalizations about the selfless Alyosha and the absolute egoism of Svidrigailov, but Lawrence condemns what his friend praises.

The letter proceeds to identify three kinds of corrupt desire in the novels, the sensual, the spiritual, and the "unemotional will." Lawrence's condemnation of sensual desire in Dostoevsky should not be confused with what is celebrated in his own writing. In his view, Dostoevskian sensuality is always diseased, for it results from the mind and egoism, not the body and the transcendent self. Lawrence astutely describes the nihilistic, despairing causes of such corruption in Dostoevsky's fiction, but he wrongly insists that all disorder stems from the diseased personality of the author himself. Dmitri, Rogozhin, and Stavrogin are raised as unambiguous evidence of Dostoevsky's destructive "desire to achieve the sensual, all devouring consummation." Dmitri, for example, is symptomatic of the author's need to experience a "dark sensual ecstasy" that makes it seem as if "universal night" has "swallowed everything." When Zossima bows to Dmitri in his monastic cell, he is simply acknowledging Dostoevsky's own hidden allegiance to sensual rather than Christian ecstasy. The logical conclusion of sensual corruption is exemplified by Rogozhin's murder of Nastasya: "for mind, the acme of sensual ecstasy lies in devouring the other, even in the pleasures of love it is a devouring, like a tiger drinking blood." Dostoevsky, according to Lawrence, shares that murderous desire.

Lawrence explains the genesis of spiritual desire in novels such as *The Idiot* and *The Brothers Karamazov* in a manner that recalls Freud's reluctance to accept any notion of healthy spirituality. Dostoevsky's "desire for the spiritual, turn-the-other-cheek consummation, comes out in the Idiot himself, in Alyosha, partly in Stavrogin." In contrast to sensual ecstasy, "Christian ecstasy" seeks oblivion by being passively "devoured in the body, like the Christian lamb," rather than by devouring others. It seeks to lose the self, lose the body, and achieve oneness with the universe by becoming "transcendently super-conscious." With venomous glee, Lawrence confesses that he likes *The Idiot* "best" because it reveals the self-devouring consequences of Christian striving. The novel shows the "last stage of Christianity, of becoming purely self-less, of becoming disseminated out into pure, absolved consciousness." Such selflessness represents a false transcendence that leads only to death and, in the case of Myshkin, "imbecility." Even Zossima, according to Lawrence, suffers from this spiritual disease. Though he is a "pure Christian, selfless, universal in the social whole," his life ends in meaningless dissolution – "dead, he stinks." The spiritual Zossima shares with the sensual Rogozhin a disintegration that proves the futility of his desires.

By presuming a conflation of spiritual and sensual desire, which traces the shared genesis of their corruption to the twin pillars of

Western civilization, the mind and the self, Lawrence strives to undermine not only Dostoevsky but 2,000 years of Christianity's moralistic ideals. His insistence that Rogozhin and Zossima are equivalently diseased manifestations of desire is part of a larger attempt to destroy the philosophic and psychological paradigms of Western thought. If the ideals represented by Zossima and Myshkin can be shown to lead to disintegration, then a path may be opened to a new order, which exchanges a transcendent, noncorporeal god for a god of fleshly immanence, self-abnegating altruism for a spontaneous primitivism. Zossima, the humanely compelling icon of the old order, must be destroyed, his ideals trampled, before Lawrence can be free to utter his new word.

The third type of desire diagnosed by Lawrence is the "pure unemotional will." His discussion avoids mention of the author's personality, perhaps because he sensed a distance between Dostoevsky and the characters that illustrate this desire. Ivan Karamazov, Ganya Ivolgin (the greedy, scheming suitor in *The Idiot*), and Pyotr Stepanovitch (the coldly vicious conspirator in *The Possessed*) embody "the Will, the pure mental, social, rational, absolved will." These characters portray the latest, most corrupt phase of social evolution, "the last stage of our social relation." Their rationalism precludes all true and false possibilities of transcendence. Lawrence points out that "when Stepan [i.e., Ivan] Karamazov talks with the devil, the devil is a decayed *social* gentleman – only that. The mechanical social forms and aspirations and ideals, I suppose, are the devil." The social, rational will does not share in the great though misguided passions of the sensual or spiritual ecstasy. Ivan's vision, from Lawrence's perspective, is too contagioned with consciousness and social convention to move beyond the dull, sublunary world. Modern rationalists, like Lawrence's own Gerald Crich and Clifford Chatterley, presumably share in such a disease of the will.

Lawrence seems unwilling to admit that the male characters, with the exception of Stavrogin, can embody more than one type of desire. However, he explains Dostoevsky's women in terms of mixed desires and finds them less interesting as a result: "All the 'great' women" in the novels contain elements of the three kinds of desire. Lawrence declares that "they *desire* the sensual ecstasy" but that they also possess "the opposite wild love for purity, selflessness, extreme Christianity." The women, however, are "bound to social convention," the standard by which they define themselves, and convention lies in the province of the third desire, rational will. In Lawrence's final view, "the women are not important. They are mere echoes and objectives of the men."

Lawrence's pathology of Dostoevskian desire proves provocatively reductive, impaired by assumptions that the characters are simple and static. For example, Dmitri, even in the "highest pitch" of sensuality, maintains an ambivalence towards his desires; his "ecstasy," as a result, is never complete, even in the midst of drunken orgies. Lawrence ignores Dmitri's changes within the novel and his subsequent acceptance of suffering as a means of purification. He also disregards the complexity of Alyosha by refusing to acknowledge the sensual and social elements of his desire; though dressed in a monk's cassock, Alyosha does allow the seductive Grushenka to sit on his lap, which at least suggests a male body beneath the religious vestment. Alyosha may be defined by his spiritual longings, but true spirituality in Dostoevsky can never be totally isolated from other desires, as evidenced by the character of Zossima himself, who is criticized by fellow monks for his joyous acceptance of earthly pleasures. More importantly, Zossima never shrinks from any manifestation of human desire, be it Fyodor Karamazov's licentious buffoonery or Dmitri's patricidal impulses. The three types of desire that Lawrence identifies as predominantly unmixed and isolated can be found in varying proportions in virtually all of Dostoevsky's major characters. Indeed, one may infer from the novels that personal and social harmony can only be achieved if all desires are recognized, balanced, and integrated. Lawrence blithely assumed Dostoevsky to be incapable of such an insight. A holy war fought in the modern wasteland and in the solitary depths of the imagination does not encourage a warrior to recognize the subtle complexities of his enemy, especially when the enemy's camp is growing.

Lawrence concludes his letter to Murry with his most serious charge: Dostoevsky's novels "are great parables . . . but false art"; "All the people are *fallen angels* – even the dirtiest scrubs. This I cannot stomach. People are not fallen angels, they are merely people. But Dostoevsky uses them as theological or religious units, they are all terms of divinity, like Christ's 'Sower went forth to sow,' and Bunyan's *Pilgrim's Progress*. They are bad art, false truth."[44] Dostoevsky, according to Lawrence, subordinates humanity to his own religious quest for univocal meaning. As a result, he fails to render justice to human complexity. This charge will be discussed later within the context of Lawrence's own views of art.

Murry's reminiscences of conversations with Lawrence help to clarify the attacks voiced in the letter. Lawrence believed, in Murry's words, that Dostoevsky "strove to identify himself with the urge toward the selfless ecstasy of Christianity." He made the inevitable corollary "mistake" and believed that "his sensual seekings were wrong; therefore he was cruel, he tortured himself and others, yet found pleasure in the tortures." As a result, Dostoevsky became emblematic of modern, divided consciousness, with "the complete selflessness" opposed to "the complete self-assertion of sensuality." His novels document the fateful consequences of the split between spirit and body, self and other. Murry reports that in the life of Myshkin, "Lawrence found what he desired to find proved, namely, that the movement towards spirituality must end in death." By the same standard, Lawrence dismissed Alyosha as a "retrograde fantasy," another destructive embodiment of "the will towards selfless Christian ecstasy."[45]

After Murry's Dostoevsky study was published, he received another letter from his now erstwhile friend, dated 28 August 1916. Here, Lawrence condemns both Murry and Dostoevsky for perversely enslaving "being" to the "mind."

You've got the cart before the horse. It isn't the being that must follow the mind, but the mind that must follow the being. And if only the cursed cowardly world had the courage to follow its own being with its mind, if it only had the courage to know what its unknown *is*, its own desires and its own activities, it might get beyond to the new secret.

The will to knowledge, according to Lawrence, obstructs revelation, for truth resides beyond the realm of knowledge and includes the dark, knowledge-defying forces of the blood. Murry and Dostoevsky are chastized for damming the primal instincts that are the source of life.

Lawrence condemns "the cursed cowardly world" for its failure to break through false visions to a "new secret" of living, and he uses an amusing simile to make his point: "But the trick is when you draw somewhere near the 'brink of revelation' to dig your head in the sand like the disgusting ostrich; and see the revelation there." Presumably, all modern visionaries, such as Murry and Dostoevsky, "with their heads in the sand of pleasing visions and secrets and revelations," "kick and squirm with their behinds most disgustingly." The ostrich is Lawrence's symbol of modern consciousness. Its self-protecting actions represent modern man's refusal to enter into a complex, active relationship with all that is beyond the self. The letter to Murry concludes with an ostrich image of Dostoevsky sticking "his head between the feet of Christ" and waggling "his behind in the air." Even Christ, that other rival of Lawrence's, functions as an obstruction to truth, a "bluff for the cowards to hide their eyes against."[46]

A letter to S. S. Koteliansky, dated 15 December 1916, reinforces Lawrence's sense of the complete identification between Murry and Dostoevsky. After reading Murry's introduction to Koteliansky's translation of excerpts from Dostoevsky's *Diary of a Writer*, Lawrence bitterly complained:

Both [Dostoevsky and Murry] stink in my nostrils. Dostoevsky is big and putrid, here. Murry is a smaller stinker, emitting the same kind of stink. How is it that these foul-smelling people ooze with such loving words. "Love thy neighbor as thyself" – well and good, if you'll hate thy neighbor as thyself. I can't do with this creed based on self-love, even when the self-love is extended to the whole of humanity.

Lawrence denounces the two of them for preaching a false creed, one that negates the passions to promote an impossible universal love. Dostoevsky in his "preaching" denied "the lusting in hate and torture" that he confessed "in his art." Lawrence admits that his art had elements of truth, but he dismisses his "credo" as "filth."[47]

It should be noted that Lawrence never accuses Murry of misreading. He never comments on his persistent habit of wrenching characters from their novelistic context, nor does he complain about Murry's simplistic identification of author and characters. That is because Lawrence approached Dostoevsky in the same way.

Lawrence and Murry assume an absence of artistic design and novelistic intention. Characters as diverse as Rogozhin, Ivan, Alyosha, and Stavrogin are interpreted as a kind of primal ooze from the depths of the author's consciousness, whether prophetic or diseased, and the novels are read as transparent biographical documents. Lawrence and Murry blithely ignore issues of literary *form* in their attempts to explain the meaning of *content*. Each pays virtually no attention to how a story is told, ignoring issues of plot, irony, style, point of view, and setting. They recognize no literary antecedents for Dostoevsky and pay no attention to literary structure. Dostoevsky's unique artistic elements are viewed simply as eruptions of his personality; the scandalous scenes, ideological confrontations, and unremitting crises are strictly interpreted in personal terms. Using Bakhtin's study as a framework, Lawrence and Murry can be categorized as critics who approach Dostoevsky as a writer of romantic novels, the type of novel which "knew consciousness and ideology solely as the pathos of an author or as the deduction of the author – and which knew the hero solely as an implementer of authorial pathos or as an object of authorial deduction."[48] By ignoring issues of literary form and denying an author's freedom to create characters who do not resemble himself, Lawrence and Murry ensure their misunderstanding of Dostoevsky's content.

Lawrence viewed Dostoevsky as a victim and carrier of the modern disease of "mental consciousness." His letters to Murry can be read as a failed attempt to warn a friend away from a contagious influence. To understand the dread and hatred of Dostoevsky, their relationship needs to be placed in the context of Lawrence's philosophical and psychological theories.

Mental consciousness, according to Lawrence's essay, "Psychoanalysis and the unconscious," is not a disease by itself. It only becomes so when it is allowed to dominate the "passional soul."[49] Then, it becomes life-denying, for it separates man from the "deepest form of consciousness," "pure blood consciousness," which is "non-ideal and non-mental."[50] While Lawrence does not provide a completely worked-out model, and his terminology often shifts, blood consciousness is associated with passion, sensuality, interrelationship, spontaneity, the living moment, and wholeness. Blood consciousness maintains a vital connection with the unconscious and its "spontaneous life-motives," though Lawrence sometimes blurs the distinction between the two.[51] By contrast, the abstractions and ideals of mental consciousness raise dams to thwart the life-promptings of the unconscious.

Mental consciousness in its diseased state denies the blood because blood cannot be assimilated within the mind. Evidence of this disease can be found in Hermione and Gerald in *Women in Love*, Miriam in *Sons and Lovers*, Clifford Chatterley, Middleton Murry – and Dostoevsky. Such individuals are characterized by a lack of vital relatedness to the world around them; their illness prevents a true experience of life and a full achievement of being. Miriam, for example, cannot abandon herself to a sexual relationship with Paul Morel; though she offers herself to him, her sexual gesture is a product of her idealizing mind, which reduces experience to a romantic abstraction. Gerald Crich, though hardly a romantic knight, shares in Miriam's habits of abstraction; he rationalizes all operations of his father's coal mine in an effort to impose his will upon a recalcitrant world. Those who are plagued by this disease can never gain true knowledge of the world or of themselves, because "knowledge is always a matter of whole experience," and whole experience can never be achieved by those enthralled by mental consciousness.[52]

By using the novels as diagnostic instruments, Lawrence concludes that every part of Dostoevsky's literature and life was infected with this characteristic disease of the modern age. All of Dostoevsky's major characters, according to his analysis, were mind-obsessed: the rationalists (such as Ivan and Raskolnikov), the sensualists (such as Dmitri and Rogozhin), and the spiritualists (such as Alyosha and Myshkin). All Dostoevskian desires, for Lawrence, flow from the corruption of mental consciousness, not from the vitality of the blood. The author himself is therefore assumed to share in the diseased desires of his characters. Dostoevsky's novels, in Lawrence's perspective, function as biographical battlegrounds for the author's contagioned desires. He approaches the Russian writer as a psychoanalyst would approach a disturbed patient: he believes that all linguistic evidence betrays deep-rooted psychic turmoil. Of course, Dostoevsky is no mere patient; he represents the entire hospital of modernity, with its wards of Christian enthusiasts and murderers, ostrich-philosophers and fallen sensualists: all diseases gather in his name.

Ironically, Dostoevsky would have agreed with Lawrence's diagnosis of the harmful effects of mental consciousness. Robert Louis Jackson has drawn attention to Dostoevsky's notebook statement that "consciousness kills life . . . consciousness is a disease." "The greater the accumulation of consciousness," Dostoevsky warned, "the greater the loss of the capacity to live." Elsewhere, he announced his intent to unmask the hidden tragedy of the hyperconscious underground: "I am proud that I was the first to bring forward the real man of the Russian majority and the first to expose his disfigured and tragic side . . . Only I brought out the tragedy of the underground, consisting in suffering, in self-punishment, in the consciousness of something better and in the impossibility of achieving it."[53] Of course, Dostoevsky knew that his most tormented characters were victims of their own thinking, but he did not celebrate such self-division as a triumph of the romantic self. Ivan Karamazov, the narrator of *Notes from the Underground*, Raskolnikov, and others need to be understood as the ideological products of their epochs; their egoism, disbelief, and hyperconsciousness owe their genesis to the ideological battles that dominated Russian culture in the 1860s and 1870s, as Joseph Frank so carefully substantiates in his biography. Dostoevsky's thought-tormented characters live out "the tragedy of the underground" because their faithless rationality leads to a blind alley; in the end, the modern intellect, for all its visions of a brave new world and its Rousseau-like proclamations of a new self, cripples the will and pollutes the soul. Dostoevsky would not have agreed with Lawrence's answers to the problems of modern civilization – especially his celebration of "John Thomas" and "Lady Jane" – but he would have found truth in his diagnosis of the modern sickness.

Lawrence voiced his alternative to Dostoevskian sickness in "The Crown," his evocative parable about the lion and the unicorn, which illuminates the oppositions necessary to maintain balance and health. The mutually dependent unicorn and lion are Blake-inspired emblems of life's contradictions: light and darkness, love and power, creation and destruction, spirit and flesh. These oppositions are embodied within the human self: "And we, fully equipped in flesh and spirit, fully built up of darkness, perfectly composed out of light, what are we but light and shadow lying together in opposition, or lion and unicorn fighting, in these two eternities which nullify each other." The self can only achieve wholeness "when the opposition is complete on either side," "the perfect opposition of dark and light that brindles the tiger with gold flame and dark flame."[54] Though Lawrence does not cite examples from his own literature, perhaps this balance is best embodied in his creation of Birkin, that ever-mutable hero who lithely straddles elemental oppositions, achieving a Heraclitean balance amid the flux of the sentient self.

Lawrence cites three Dostoevsky characters to illlustrate the disintegration that occurs when balance between the lion and unicorn is not maintained. Dmitri and Rogozhin, agents of sensuality-induced disintegration, "will each of them plunge the flesh within the reducing agent, the woman, obtain sensation and the reduction within the flesh, add to the sensual experience, and progress towards utter disintegration to nullity." Myshkin, an agent of spirituality-induced disintegration, "will react upon the achieved consciousness or personality or ego of everyone he meets, disintegrate this consciousness, this ego, and his own as well . . . reduced further and further back, till he himself is a babbling idiot, a vessel full of disintegrated parts, and the woman is reduced to nullity." For Lawrence, Dostoevsky's novels are emblematic of all that has gone wrong with civilization: "Dostoevsky has shown us perfectly the utter subjection of all human life to the flux of corruption."[55] His characters sought the absolute instead of Lawrence's approved "pure relationship." By attempting to deny or enslave their sensual or spiritual opposites, they failed to achieve balance and to acknowledge the dark, liberating passions of the blood.

OTHER WRITERS AND THEIR DOSTOEVSKY VEXATIONS

Lawrence's essays on other writers, published between the war and 1928, reveal his continued preoccupation with Dostoevsky as a symptom of mental consciousness. Lawrence's comments during this period are somewhat less vitriolic than before, perhaps because he spent most of this time living abroad, far removed from the daily annoyances of the English "Dostoevsky cult."

Lawrence found great similarities between Dostoevsky and Hawthorne, whom he diagnosed in 1919 as a victim of the Dostoevskian disease, a man "divided against himself." Though Hawthorne stands "openly for the upper, spiritual, reasoned being," "secretly, he lusts in the sensual imagination, in bruising the heel of this spiritual self and laming it forever." Lawrence concludes that "All his reasoned exposition is a pious fraud, kept up to satisfy his own upper and outward self."[56] In Lawrence's judgment, Arthur Dimmesdale reflects the author's self-torture and self-division. The Puritan preacher "hates his body with morbid hate" and "lusts to destroy it," a self-loathing that provides "the whole clue to Dostoevsky." When the preacher walks to his Election Day Sermon, he has urges to give a pure young girl a lecherous look and whisper arguments against the immortality of the soul to a pious old widow; his desire, according to Lawrence, "is the fatal, imbecile or epileptic state of the soul, such as Dostoevsky's, which makes one half of the psyche malevolently act against the other half, in leering malignant progress of futility."[57] Lawrence later accused Dostoevsky in *Studies in Classic American Literature* (1923) of "posing," in Dimmesdale fashion, "as a sort of Jesus, but most truthfully revealing himself all the while as a little horror."[58]

In 1927 Lawrence found evidence of Dostoevskian sickness in *Max Havelaar*, an obscure Dutch novel about the inhumane colonial treatment of the Javanese. The novel, which Lawrence compares to *Uncle Tom's Cabin*, was written by Multatuli (the pseudonym for E. D. Decker) and was originally published in the 1860s. Though Multatuli speaks as a "preacher," Lawrence finds in his work "a mad-dog aversion from humanity." Multatuli has not traveled as far along the path of human revulsion disguised as preacherly moralism as has his Russian counterpart: he "never quite falls down the fathomless will of his own revulsion, as Dostoevsky did, to become a lily-mouthed missionary rumbling with ventral howls of derision and dementia." According to Lawrence, Dostoevsky "though a great nervous genius," was so overcome with human revulsion that he "never felt a moment of real physical sympathy in his life."[59]

In the same year Lawrence reviewed and condemned a translation of *Solitaria*, an introspective, fragmentary philosophic work by V. V. Rozanov, the self-styled follower of Dostoevsky who knew him personally and even married his former mistress, Apollinaria Suslova. Rozanov's work reveals him as "another of these morbidly introspective Russians, morbidly wallowing in adoration of Jesus, then getting up and spitting in His beard." He is "a pup out of the Dostoevsky kennel," one of those characters "such as Dostoevsky has familiarized us with, and of whom we are tired."

They have a spurting, *gamin* hatred of civilization, of Europe, of Christianity, of governments, and of everything else in their moments of energy; and in their inevitable relapses into weakness they make the inevitable recantation; they whine, they humiliate themselves . . . and call it Christ-like, and then with the left hand commit some dirty little crime of meanness, and call it the mysterious complexity of the human soul. It's all masturbation, half-baked, and one gets tired of it.

Lawrence's attack on *Solitaria* resembles his attack on Murry's *Critical Study* of Dostoevsky; in both cases, the larger, more important target is Dostoevsky.

However, the excerpts from Rozanov's *The Apocalypse of Our Times*, included in the edition of *Solitaria*, earn the reviewer's praise. Lawrence judges this work as the product of a "real man" who was "integral, and grave, and a seer, a true one." Here, he finds that the author, after all, "is not really Dostoevskian," for Rozanov "has more or less recovered the genuine pagan vision, the phallic vision, and with these eyes he looks, in amazement and consternation, on the mess of Christianity." Lawrence claims that Rozanov "is the first Russian who has ever said anything to me." In contrast to Tolstoy and Dostoevsky, the writer offers "a real positive view of life." "His vision is full of passion, vivid, valid. He is the first to see that immortality is in the vividness of life, not in the loss of life." Unfortunately, Rozanov's vision of "the living and resurrected pagan" sometimes lapses; then he "again starts to Russianize, and he comes in two." At such moments, "he becomes aware of himself, and personal . . . and almost always dual!" Lawrence bitterly complains that "these Dostoevskian Russians" delight in being "dual and divided against themselves." But he concludes that the "voice of the new man" in Rozanov, "not the Dostoevsky whelp," "means a great deal."[60]

Lawrence's unpublished preface (written in 1928) to *Mastro-don Gesualdo*, a novel by Giovanni Verga and translated by Lawrence himself, celebrates another work that endorses Lawrencean values and refutes Dostoevskian ones. The novel represents a welcome relief from "this subjectively-intense every man his own hero business in which the Russians have carried us to the greatest lengths." It does not attempt to convey "the phenomenal coruscations of the souls of quite commonplace persons"; its hero lacks the self-consciousness, self-flattery, and self-obsession that Lawrence finds characteristic of "Dostoevsky or Chekhov," where "every character" believes "himself a nonesuch, absolutely unique." Lawrence praises the novel for its depiction of physical life and the passions: "How utterly different it is from Russia, where the people are always – in the books – expanding to one another, and pouring out tea and their souls to one another all night long." He admires the main character Gesualdo for the pure physical nature of his being, "so potent, so full of nature." Gesualdo "never says anything." His silence "is the very reverse of the Russian who talks and talks, out of impotence."[61]

The shorter version of this essay, which was published with the novel, contrasts the hero of *Mastro-don Gesualdo* with Dostoevsky's Myshkin. Lawrence notes that the Italian hero "still has a lovable flow in his body, the very reverse of the cold marsh-gleam of Myshkin." Gesualdo's life may have ended in "a tumour of bitterness," but Lawrence says that "I would rather have lived it than the life of Tolstoy's Pierre, or the life of any Dostoevsky hero."[62] For Lawrence, the passionate, unreflective life would always be preferable to a life governed by mental consciousness, spiritual idealism, and sensual denial. An earthy Mellors will always count for more than an idealistic Myshkin.

TWINS OF PROPHECY: SUPPRESSED NARRATIVE AFFINITIES

Lawrence may not have liked what he read in Dostoevsky, but his own characters bear unacknowledged similarities to those of his rival, betraying a common literary territory. Ivan Karamazov, with his "mechanical" will and his frustrated desire for rational harmony, is not far removed from Gerald, who ruthlessly imposes his will for the sake of a perfectly run mining operation. Though Ivan protests the suffering of innocents and yearns for a utopian society, he is the cruelest of the legitimate Karamazov sons, in part because he cannot stand to see his abstract yearnings thwarted by a muddy reality. Neither Gerald nor

Ivan can tolerate an imperfect universe that resists rationalist agendas. The "sensual ecstasy" of Rogozhin that ends in murder resembles Gerald's death-lust for Gudrun; both characters would kill what they cannot possess, becoming victims of their own failed mastery. Svidrigailov, who in his genteel corruption yearns pornographically for young female flesh, bears a striking affinity to Loerke, whose desires are equally corrupt and who shares his artful decadence and chilled disengagement. Even apparent opposites such as the narrator of *Notes from the Underground* and Hermione share a common fate: both are imprisoned in the culture of consciousness. Lawrence's vision of human evil – most notably, its strong-willed male expressions – owes much to his reading of Dostoevsky. To support such an interpretation, one merely has to imagine how readily Lawrence's life-denying villains, at least those created from *Women in Love* to *Lady Chatterley's Lover,* could blend into a Dostoevskian landscape.

George Panichas argues that Lawrence and Dostoevsky have a shared "vision of evil" that "reaches a most terrifying effectiveness in their depiction of Svidrigailov and Loerke, who, as the embodiment of unbridled depravity and immorality, indicate that ultimate point of no return in the breakdown of human life and the triumph of the forces of anti-life."[63] According to Panichas, Svidrigailov embodies carnal corruption while Loerke's degradation results from "the excesses of intellect." Both are "cynical and indifferent men, who have chosen to cut themselves from the body of humanity."[64] In their leering eyes, beauty exists merely for the sake of exploitation; for that reason, Svidrigailov becomes engaged to a sixteen-year-old, whose blushing virginity spurs his voluptuousness, and Loerke can only sculpt naked teenage girls, innocent maidens to be sacrificed to a heartless art. Both men wear a public mask, Svidrigailov's that of the aristocratic dandy, Loerke's that of the dedicated modern artist; their charming personas simultaneously attract and repel. Yet the self beneath the image thrives in a vermin-ridden underworld. Gudrun's judgment of Loerke can be applied with equal justice to Svidrigailov: "He seemed to be the stuff of the underworld of life. There was no going beyond him."[65] Panichas interprets Lawrence's portrayal of Loerke "as an admission of his debt to Dostoevsky and an acknowledgment and vindication of the Russian novelist's prophetic and visionary powers."[66]

Interestingly, one of Birkin's comments about the sculptor echoes a statement that Lawrence himself had made about Dostoevsky. Birkin tells Gerald that Loerke "lives like a rat in the river of corruption, just where it falls over into the bottomless pit. He's further than we are. He hates the ideal more acutely. He *hates* the ideal utterly, yet it still dominates him."[67] After reading *The Idiot*, Lawrence wrote to Lady Ottoline Morrell and compared Dostoevsky to a rat "slithering along in hate." Unlike Loerke, Dostoevsky outwardly professed "love, all love," but Lawrence found a rodent's nose beneath love's artifice, a nose "sharp with hate."[68] Lawrence, like Nietzsche, reduced all talk of Christian ideals to suppressed hatred, the evidence of *ressentiment* cleverly disguised. Accordingly, the moral ideals raised by *The Idiot* must owe their genesis to the same river of corruption that bathes Loerke. Dostoevsky, a self-deceived priest of the ascetic ideal, swims in the same waters.

Though Lawrence demonizes his enemy, the two novelists share an apocalyptic vision of death-ridden civilizations, from the brutality of the coal mines to the inhumanity of Baden-Baden roulette tables. Lawrence's parables of love in the modern world, *Women in Love* and *Lady Chatterley's Lover*, elicit a correspondence with *The Idiot*, which depicts a world where decaying social structures threaten to defile the aspirations of love and reduce human beings to frenetic poseurs obsessed with money, power, and egoistic achievement. In such societies, human worth is devalued by the imposition of false standards and relationships become a stuggle between dominance and humiliation, an endless repetition of a capitalist nightmare that transmutes individuals to commodities. The works of Lawrence and Dostoevsky, both profoundly indebted to the Book of Revelation, are imbued with a sense of millennial crisis, of civilization reaching a dead and fruitless end. Clifford Chatterley, Gerald, Rogozhin, and Ivan Karamazov are not merely defeated characters; they are the death rattles of entire epochs. Yet each novelist also pointed to the possibility of a regeneration capable of transforming death. Each clung to utopian hopes for a new world, for the re-birth of society as well as the self.

Their protagonists are often seekers of wisdom in the Old Testament sense of the word. Characters as diverse as Birkin, Somers, Mellors, Alyosha, Ivan, and Myshkin seek to establish harmony between themselves and their surroundings, a harmony that incorporates their deepest longings. Faced with the psychic disintegration of their societies, they envision paradisiacal wholeness, unity, and integration. Acting as modern prophets, they debate their opponents in confrontations which test their own beliefs and lead to either clarification or confusion. Such characters are typically restless wanderers in the modern desert, pilgrims who search for ultimate meaning and the life-giving word.

Given the labyrinthian difficulties of proving literary influence, it would be foolish to assert that Lawrence's prophetic role can only be attributed to his reading of Dostoevsky. Clearly, he drank from a Pierian Spring, and other prophetic voices, from Nietzsche to Freud, Blake to the Methodist hymnal, resonate throughout his works. Yet as a novelist Lawrence traveled a distinctively Dostoevskian path after the publication of *Sons and Lovers*, which moved him away from the English tradition of the novel as biography, the story of individual lives largely immune from metaphysical debate and cultural crisis. In a manner worthy of Dostoevsky, he sought to combine the particular with the universal, the concrete with the abstract, to explore the foundations of modern dilemmas and create a fiction that weighed possible solutions. As a result, individuals became less important than their hidden philosophical, erotic, and cultural origins, and biography gave way to "thought adventures." Thus, Lawrence became the philosopher-novelist seeking to unravel basic questions of existence, sometimes at the expense of his art, especially when he mistook shrill earnestness for redemptive insight.

That is not to say that Lawrence recognized all resemblances between his works and Dostoevsky's, but he did recognize a novelist who confronted problems central to his own art. He recoiled with indignation verging on repugnance mainly because, in his opinion, Dostoevsky went wrong when he chose non-Lawrencean solutions to the problems of modern civilization. His spiritualized answers to the dilemma of modern life were ineffective, in Lawrence's view, for the suggested cure would be as destructive as the original illness. Lawrence believed that mental consciousness and the divided psyche could not be overcome by a moralistic recognition of guilt or an acceptance of suffering, such as that shown by Dmitri or Raskolnikov. True, vivid life could not be achieved by an emptying of the self in the service of others, as exhibited by Zossima and Myshkin. Lawrence refused to take such courses of action seriously, associating them with platitudinous orthodoxy, the dying gasps of a Christianity that could no longer meet humanity's most profound needs. Dostoevsky's "cure" for the modern illness, according to Lawrence, would lead only to further divisions and imbalances. His prescriptions for living failed to acknowledge the passions of the blood.

Lawrence's simplistic reductions of Dostoevsky's profound spiritual, moral, and psychological insights can be partially explained by his assumption that the Russian novelist used heroes in the same way that he did. Because his own novelistic heroes often embody his most cherished values and represent various aspects of his own life, Lawrence assumed that Dostoevsky's characters provided similar biographical revelations, that the distance between narrator and hero was close and relatively free from irony or criticism. If Ivan proposes to turn the state into a church – a view cherished by Dostoevsky himself – then Ivan himself must be approved by the author, in all his intellectual posing and psychic disintegration. If the Inquisitor speaks compassionately about such Dostoevskian concerns as human weakness and suffering, then he must be seen as a speaker for the author's deepest longings. Lawrence, like so many other readers in his generation, denies Dostoevsky the freedom of artistic creation and mistakenly approaches the novels as confessional tracts, missing their polyphonic depth while hearing only the droning voice of Dostoevsky.

Lawrence's misunderstanding of Dostoevsky may in part be attributed to their radically opposed conceptions of desire. As René Girard has persuasively argued in *Deceit, Desire, and the Novel*, Dostoevskian desire is essentially mimetic.[69] For better or worse, desire is typically mediated by the presence of the other. The self does not sire its own desires, which means that characters must choose between contending models. Alyosha, for example, may follow the path of Zossima or be detoured by the cynicism of Rakitin and Ivan. Raskolnikov must choose between his Napoleonic posings – the creation of a nihilistic intellectual culture – and Sonya's submissive faith. Lawrence, however, creates heroes of autonomous desire. Birkin, the post-Nietzschean romantic individualist, seeks the deepest reservoirs of the self, where being and nonbeing, self and nonself merge. He must both create and destroy to find that self, becoming his own Apollo and Dionysus. In an important sense, Birkin, Mellors, and even Paul Morel are seeking a paradise within, the human form divine that offers the only heaven worth the having. Clearly, Dostoevsky offers no comparable paradise of the self; indeed such longings consistently end in tragedy, best exemplified by Kirillov's suicide in *The Possessed*.

Lawrence's persistent misreading can be further explained by his discomfort with the mixture of heterogenous materials in Dostoevsky's novels. In contrast to Lawrence's pilgrim quests, which are marked by the purity and decorum that characterize heroes such as Birkin and Mellors, Dostoevsky's quests are marked by a mixture of radically disparate elements. His works combine spiritual altruism with sensual depravity, high tragedy and low comedy, idealism and farcical ridicule, within the same scene and even in the same character, a combination brilliantly achieved in the events that take place in Zossima's cell near the beginning of *Brothers Karamazov*. That is why Lawrence complained bitterly to Lady Ottoline Morrell that Dostoevsky mixed God and sadism, a comment prompted by the scandalous juxtapositions in *The Possessed:* "It seems as though the pure mind, the true reason, which surely is noble were made trampled and filthy under the hoofs of secret, perverse, indirect sensuality."[70] Lawrence insisted that the contradictory materials within the novels were evidence of the author's own psychological corruption, not the product of intentional artistic choices. He could not recognize Dostoevsky's innovative compositional principles, what Leonid Grossman has described as his monumental effort "to subordinate polarly incompatible narrative elements to the unity of the philosophical plan and to the whirlwind movements of the event . . . to create a unified and integral work of art from heterogeneous, profoundly foreign materials of unequal value."[71] Lawrence could not tolerate the sacrileges and travesties that pervade Dostoevsky's novels, because, in his view, the sanctuary of the novel was too sacred a place to allow for such constant mockery and scandal. Dostoevsky may have written about Lawrencean subjects, but his rival ultimately judged him as a heretic in the temple of art.

THE GRAND INQUISITOR: TRUTH OF THE TALE, PERVERSITY OF THE TELLER

Lawrence's introduction to *The Grand Inquisitor*, which was translated by S. S. Koteliansky and published as a self-standing work in 1930, represents the last stage of his response. Written after the cresting of England's interest in Dostoevsky, the essay admits a newfound affinity: after four readings, Lawrence found hidden in the legend a view of humanity with which he could agree. Despite its sympathetic interest, the essay typifies Lawrence's rivalry and the pattern of his misreading.

Lawrence defends the arguments presented by the Grand Inquisitor as "the final and unanswerable criticism of Christ," reflecting a correct assessment of human limitation.[72] The Inquisitor, who shares Lawrence's distrust of democratic impulses, recognizes that the masses lack the strength to live "free and limitless." He has identified their essential and inalterable needs for mystery, miracle, and authority, needs antithetical to freedom, best served by bread and a heroic authority to worship. According to Lawrence, the vision of the universal state led by a select, heroic few is born of compassionate realism. The Inquisitor seeks to serve "the great wholeness of humanity."[73] In contrast, Christ "overestimates human abilities"; his "inadequacy . . . lies in the fact that Christianity is too difficult for man, the vast mass of men." Christianity offers an impossible ideal "because it makes demands greater than the nature of man can bear." The man who would be savior offered a freedom nearly impossible to achieve, unlike his interlocutor who loved humanity "more tolerantly and more contemptuously than Jesus loved it . . . for itself, for what it is and not what it ought to be."[74] Christ's idealism places too heavy a burden on the masses, thus ensuring destructive consequences: "Most men cannot choose between good and evil, because it is so extremely difficult to know which is which." Lawrence argues that Christ undermines visionary leadership that alone can give meaning to the life of the masses. His insistence on free choice does not "let the specially gifted few make the decision between good and evil, and establish the life values against the money values." "The many," in Lawrence's view, would "accept the decision with gratitude and bow down to the few, in the hierarchy."

Lawrence acknowledges only two central mistakes in the Inquisitor's philosophy. First, the Inquisitor incorrectly identifies the need for authority as a sign of human weakness and failure. While the rare heroic and superior man has no need to submit to an authority beyond himself, most people are not so gifted. Lawrence affirms, "It is not man's weakness that he needs someone to bow down to. It is his nature, and his strength, and it puts him in touch with far, far greater life than if he stood alone." Echoing Plato's belief in an enlightened rulership, Lawrence maintains that "The sight of a true lord, a noble, a nature-hero puts the sun into the heart of the ordinary man, who is no hero, and therefore cannot know the sun direct."[75] The Inquisitor has falsely applied the standards of the heroic few to the masses, mistaking genetic limitation for moral degeneration.

The other crucial mistake can be found in his admission that his views reflect an alliance with the devil. Contrary to the Inquisitor's own interpretation, Lawrence insists that there can be no link between a love of humanity "with all its limitations" and the "spirit of annihilation and not-being" that Satan represents.[76] He refuses to see the Inquisitor's denial of freedom as the result of a satanic alliance, because unlike the Inquisitor himself Lawrence does not associate freedom with the God-like. Conclusions about the impossibility of freedom follow inexorably from human nature, which means that the Inquisitor has merely sacrificed an impossible ideal for the greater good of humanity.

An uneasy ambivalence permeates Lawrence's reading. On one

hand, he celebrates the Inquisitor as a champion of humanity, a brave
advocate of previously unacknowledged truths. On the other hand,
Lawrence has to deal with an Inquisitor who kills anyone judged as a
heretic. If such a man were in a position of authority in the First World
War, he certainly would have supported Lawrence's own harassment
and exile from Cornwall, for he would always deny individual freedom
for the sake of communal stability. To resolve this dilemma and preserve
his own integrity as a sexually charged and oligarchical Galahad, the
one pure voice of truth in the modern world, Lawrence finds the
Russian author guilty of "epileptic and slightly criminal perversity," a
phrase that suggests Lawrence attributed Dostoevsky's epilepsy to his
divided psyche.[77]

> Where Dostoevsky is perverse is in his making the old, old wise governor of man
> a Grand Inquisitor. The recognition of the weakness of man has been a
> common trait in all great, wise rulers of people . . . And the man who put those
> sad questions to Jesus could not possibly have been a Spanish Inquisitor. He
> could not possibly have burnt a hundred people in an *auto-da-fé*. He would have
> been too wise and far-seeing.[78]

Because Dostoevsky could not admit the validity of the arguments
against Christ, he placed them within the corrupt context of the Spanish
Inquisition.

Lawrence happily concludes that Dostoevsky "is always perverse,
always impure, always an evil thinker and a marvelous seer." The
tensions of contradiction, the "wild love of Jesus" mixed with "perverse
and poisonous hatred of Jesus," the moral hostility to the devil "mixed
with secret worship," reside entirely in Dostoevsky, not Lawrence.[79]
Literature born of a psyche divided between love and hate, truth and
falsehood, can never be free from contamination. Dostoevsky's impuri-
ties dictate that he house the pearls of his visionary wisdom within
swinish bodies, and for this Lawrence is outraged. Presumably, truth
belongs in a Birkin-like body, far removed from the corruption of the
Inquisition.

Lawrence's sense of the disjunction between diseased personality and
artistic truth is best explained in his introduction to *Classic Studies in
American Literature*, where he separates art from the artist, truth from the
teller: "Art speech is the only truth. An artist is a damned liar, but his art,
if it be art, will tell you the truth of his day. And that is all that matters."
The artist, not knowing the liberating depth of his own vision, assumes a
public role in relation to his creations, which requires a moralistic
defense of social conventions within the boundaries of the literary work.

Yet the eruptive force of artistic truth undermines all such convention, regardless of disclaimers. Beneath the moralistic proclamations that congeal on literary surfaces lies a truth capable of exploding society's Promethean shackles. Dostoevsky as public apologist may have sided with the democratic Jesus, but truth belongs to the Inquisitor. Though Hawthorne judged Hester Prynne a sinner and Tolstoy punished the illicit love of Anna and Vronsky, truth glimmers only in their libidinal passions and social defiance. Conventional morality always denies artistic truth, hence the maxim: "Never trust the artist. Trust the tale."[80]

True art, for Lawrence, can be equated with true life, which owes its vitality to the promptings of the unconscious and the free, creative impulses of the blood. The artist's personality, however, usually overrides impulse; the conscious will and social self suppress imaginative insight. Such prohibitions prevent the artist from experiencing "true relatedness"; as a result, the teller cannot accept the truth of the tale. That is why Dostoevsky's truth is distorted and masked. The artist can glimpse the promised land but cannot find the courage to live there.

Lawrence acts as a precursor to Derrida, unflinchingly confident of his ability to perceive and explain ruptures unknown to the author. His deconstructive effort, however, reduces rather than amplifies meaning. Lawrence remains oblivious to the irony that undercuts the Inquisitor's compassionate pose. His arguments are interpreted as monological statements that can be disengaged from all particular settings, thus dispensing with the story's richly layered complexities. Satisfied that the Inquisitor shares his own benevolent disdain for the masses, Lawrence is blind to the obvious link between stated compassion and unstated ambition, nor can he see that confirmations of human weakness provide an easy excuse for turning a spiritual agenda into a strategy for empire-building. All details that would diminish the stature of the Inquisitor's views are either ignored or assumed to be the result of Dostoevsky's perversity.

Lawrence's weaknesses as a reader of *The Grand Inquisitor* become more evident when the work is placed within its literary framework. Christ and the Inquisitor, after all, are creations of their narrator, Ivan, who even supplies a preface naming relevant literary antecedents. Malcolm Jones makes the compelling point that *The Grand Inquisitor* cannot be understood as a simple expression of Dostoevsky's own views.

It is presented as the product of the literary imagination of a cultured and well-read young man who has no faith in a loving God; to whom the world appears essentially hostile; who has in his heart a burning ideal of a world at peace and harmony; but who sees no possibility for realising it and who revolts against whatever principle it is that has ordained things.[81]

The debate between Christ and the Inquisitor may be read therefore as an internal debate between two sides of Ivan: a cynical, life-denying, Inquisitor side and a sentimental, romantic, idealistic Christ side. Both characters can be interpreted as images of his sceptical despair and inability to reconcile internal oppositions.

Despite its appearance of self-containment, *The Grand Inquisitor* needs to be addressed within the context of the entire novel. As Ivan stands between the views of Christ and those of the Inquisitor, so he stands between Alyosha and Smerdyakov: his divided thoughts and desires pull him in mutually exclusive directions, an ambivalence made apparent in his literary creation. Robert Belknap persuasively argues that the behavior and beliefs of Rakitin, the self-serving and unbelieving seminarian, and Kolya, the Voltaire-spouting thirteen-year-old radical, serve as comic prickings of Ivan and his legend. The viciousness of Rakitin and the boyish absurdity of Kolya contribute to the confutation of Ivan's despairing arguments, for the former highlights Ivan's debased motives and the latter "trivializes the ideas of the Grand Inquisitor and the Devil, as well as those Ivan expresses himself."[82] Later in the novel, Ivan's hallucinatory conversation with the devil provides a burlesque unmasking of his divided consciousness and romantic pretense. The devil uses Ivan's own tender and defiant pronouncements to deflate his Schillerian self-delusions; the comic low style of their dialogue mocks the somber formality of Ivan's earlier narration. The conversation shows the advanced state of Ivan's tragic disintegration: his heroic vision and idealized rebellion have been reduced to the level of schizophrenic buffoonery. *The Grand Inquisitor* needs to be understand in terms of that tragedy.

Contrary to Lawrence's assumptions, the political and religious debates of the legend provide more than just an obfuscation of Dostoevsky's secret malaise. The Inquisitor represents the culmination of the author's disputes with Roman Catholicism and atheistic socialism, parties found equally guilty of abandoning the kingdom of heaven for earthly power. Dostoevsky judged attempts to turn the church into a state (Catholicism) and the state into a godless church (socialism), two ambitions manifested by the Inquisitor, as obverse sides of the same destructive coin. Both philosophies embody a materialistic corruption of spiritual ideals, a suppression of human freedom, and, in the end, a ruthless authoritarianism. The Inquisitor's philosophic views are not in opposition to the historical Inquisition: they are its perfect flowering, for they are founded on a denial of freedom and a refutation of human nobility. The Inquisitor is more than Ivan's self-reflective creation; he is Dostoevsky's nightmare of evil.

Such interpretations of *The Grand Inquisitor*'s meaning and novelistic function, of course, are by no means complete or immune from disagreement. But they do serve to measure the distance between Dostoevsky and Lawrence, highlighting the radical differences in their conceptions of freedom. Dostoevsky defined freedom in moral and religious terms, insisting on the autonomy of every human being, a theologically sanctioned birthright that could be ignored only at grievous cost. Each individual, whether whore or saint, bears iconic witness to the presence of God, an image which can be defiled but never eradicated. Obviously, Lawrence had no patience for this universal idealism. He chose to define freedom as a release from moral constriction, a dethroning of false transcendence for the sake of immanent and sensual vitality. To dance with the lithe spontaneity of Birkin, one could not conform to the crowd or compromise the One by binding it to the Many. In Lawrence's world, freedom comes only to the proud and defiant few.

RESPONSES FROM A MUTABLE MESSIAH: *KANGAROO* AND *THE ESCAPED COCK*

Lawrence's comments about *The Grand Inquisitor* have a ring of irrevocable Olympian authority typical of his criticism. His fiction, more tentative and exploratory, is needed to understand the intriguing depths of his ambivalence towards Dostoevsky and the eddying inconstancy of his own thought. Two works in particular are engaged in a creative dialogue with *The Grand Inquisitor*. *Kangaroo*, though preceding the preface by seven years, addresses the same issues of leadership and the masses. *The Escaped Cock*, a sexually charged parable about heroic divinity and its responsibility to the crowd, answers the Inquisitor's call for enlightened despotism.

Kangaroo, published in 1923, is Lawrence's most overtly political novel. Its protagonist, a Lawrence-like writer named Richard Lovat Somers, lives in self-imposed exile with his wife in Australia. He encounters a people who are crassly materialistic, boisterously democratic, and contemptuous of authority and singular talents. Even their housing reflects the monotonous sameness of the Australian democracy. At the novel's beginning, Somers maintains a proud distance; gradually, he is drawn in with a fascist underground movement, led by a charismatic man known as Kangaroo, that plans to seize control of the government. Intrigued by Kangaroo and his organization's fiercely male camaraderie, Somers considers joining, enchanted by the prospect of overthrowing the past to build a new future, one dependent on male bonds and a reverence for the authority of those who are innately superior. But Somers cannot commit himself to being either a "mate" or a leader in the movement. Despite his yearning for solidarity, he cannot relinquish himself in the service of others.

Somers's attraction to "the mystery of lordship" helps to explain Lawrence's defence of the Inquisitor: "The mystery of innate, natural, sacred priority. The other mystic relationship between men which democracy and equality try to deny and obliterate. Not arbitrary caste of birth aristocracy. But the mystic recognition of difference and the sacred responsibility of authority."[83] Kangaroo's anti-democratic beliefs and his yearning for a life of true spirituality appeal to Somers. The writer feels a strong affinity with the leader who seeks to remake the world in the likeness of his own values. Kangaroo knows the power of lordship's mystery; he plans to use it as the basis of a new political order.

The leader reveals his debt to Dostoevsky for his political philosophy. When Somers tells him, "you don't believe in education," Kangaroo replies, "not much." Though he believes that education is useless for "ninety percent of the people," he wants those people "nonetheless to have full substantial lives: as even slaves have had under certain masters." Kangaroo advocates government based upon a kind of constitutional tyranny, where the leader would serve the function of "a patriarch, or a pope: representing as near as possible the wise, subtle spirit of life." "I should try to establish my state of Australia as a kind of Church," Kangaroo continues, "with the profound reverence for life, for life's deepest urges, as the motive power. Dostoevsky suggests this and I believe it can be done."[84]

His philosophy seems to have two antecedents in *The Brothers Karamazov*. The willingness to consign the vast majority of people to slave-like conditions due to their inferior abilities can be traced to the Inquisitor's view of the masses. Like the Inquisitor, Kangaroo plans to organize society according to his sense of human limitation, creating a state based upon a shared respect for authority. His proposal to turn the state into a "kind of Church" is a restatement of what Ivan proposes in his article on church–state relations: "every earthly state should be, in the end, completely transformed into the Church and should become nothing else but a church."[85]

Kangaroo's political vision reflects the values endorsed in Lawrence's preface to *The Grand Inquisitor*, which advocates an oligarchy. The Guardians of Lawrence's state would bestow earthly bread, but it would be bread with a "heavenly taste." These lord–leaders would be able to put "the sun into the heart of the ordinary man, who is no hero, and therefore cannot know the sun direct."[86] The leaders would bestow life values upon all common men, those weak minions who are "as babes or children or geese."[87] Such statements show that Lawrence was no enemy to a closed, tyrannical society as long as those in power were capable of a true and vivid life. Throughout his life, he willingly denied humanity to a large portion of the human race; only a select few could even be said to have souls. Theoretically, Lawrence had no difficulty admitting that the soulful few have privileged rights of leadership, that the Few should be encouraged to take control of the Many.

Given Lawrence's comments on *The Grand Inquisitor*, one might expect that Somers would accept Kangaroo, as Lawrence accepted the Inquisitor's views. Somers flatly rejects Kangaroo, however, even at the hour of the leader's death. He rejects him in a manner that resembles the Inquisitor's rejection of Christ: Somers judges Kangaroo's vision as inadequate for it does not include the whole of human nature. Where the Inquisitor rejects Christ for not recognizing the human incapacity for freedom, Somers rejects Kangaroo for not recognizing the dark gods of the sensual, physical self.

I know your love, Kangaroo. Working everything from the spirit, from the head. You work the lower self as an instrument for the spirit. Now it is time for the Son of Man to depart, and leave us dark, in front of the unspoken God: who is just beyond the dark threshold of the lower self, my lower self. There is a great God on the threshold of my lower self, whom I fear while he is my glory. And the spirit goes out like a spent candle.[88]

Somers rejects Kangaroo so that he can follow the "dark god at the lower threshold."[89]

The death-bed rejection of Kangaroo represents Lawrence's own political negations. Though he often sounded a fascist trumpet, or at least a Platonic one of similar tones, he could not carry a fascist gun. He never committed his allegiance to any leader or cause, for he never encountered a soul superior to his own. Though he continued to explore political questions until the end of his life, he could never resolve the demands of politics with the demands of the dark gods. In an important sense, he abandoned politics because he could not live with any political answers. *Kangaroo* marks his adventure through politics of both the fascist and Marxist variety (the latter represented by the labor leader Willie Struthers), two sides attractive because of their destructive potential and their derision of the middle class. Both, if given power, could overturn the corrupt existing order, an order governed by money, materialism, and mental consciousness, that needs apocalyptic cleansing. At the novel's end, however, the dark gods prove more compelling than any political movement or leader. Somers has learned that political ideals, themselves a creation of mental consciousness, always seek to rationalize and control and thus prove antithetical to the dark gods. To work for a political cause would require abandoning the dark, "passional" self so precious to Somers and Lawrence. *Kangaroo*, then, can be read as a sceptical response to the Grand Inquisitor's vision. Like Kangaroo, the Inquisitor has neglected the dark gods.

The Escaped Cock, a novella published serially in 1928, sermonizes about the unhealthy motives of messiahs, explicitly refuting the aristocratic values of the preface to *The Grand Inquisitor*. The preface suggests that political leaders serve an essentially religious function. The enlightened few must act as a priestly elite; they must "take charge of the bread – the property, the money – and then give it back to the masses as if it were really the gift of life."[90] The lords will give life a ritualistic rhythm, establishing a harvest that will again become the occasion for "ever renewed consciousness of miracle, wonder and mystery."[91] This vision of a priestly class, capable of answering the religious needs of the masses, is undermined by *The Escaped Cock*.

Like Dostoevsky's Ivan, Lawrence tells a return-of-Christ story, but this story, far removed from concerns of politics and the state-as-church, takes place immediately after Christ's death. "The Man who had died" returns to life but no longer believes in his salvific mission. No longer does he seek to control the destinies of others, nor does he try to sway others or himself by the motives of heaven. When he encounters a peasant, he has a vision of a new truth. Though he still views the peasant "with compassion," he "no longer wished to interfere in the soul of man who had not died": "let him return to earth in his own good hour, and let no one try to interfere with when the earth claims her own."

When he meets Mary Magdalene, Christ preaches his new message of non-involvement.

"My triumph," he said, "is that I am not dead. I have outlived my mission and know no more of it. It is my triumph. I have survived the day and the death of my interference, and am still man . . . The teacher and the savior are dead in me, now I can go about my business, into my single life . . . For I have died, and I know my own limits. Now I can live without striving to sway others anymore. For my reach ends in my finger-tips, and my stride is no longer than the ends of my toes."[92]

Christ embraces the way of the solitary self and the life of the flesh: "Now he knew that he had risen for the woman, or women, who knew the greater life of the body."[93] A woman would show him the life of the flesh, but he would be bound to no one. "Now I can be alone," Christ says with relief, "and leave all things to themselves . . . My way is my own alone."[94] The one who once proclaimed himself the truth and the way for all now seeks a solitary path.

Christ eventually succeeds in his quest to experience sexual passion. The Christian pilgrim learns the pagan lessons of the body with a priestess of Isis, in a passage that strives for a scriptural effect, the scripture of the Lawrencean word.

He crouched to her, and he felt the blaze of his manhood, and his power rise up in his loins, magnificent.
"I am risen."
Magnificent, blazing indomitable in the depths of his loins, his own sun dawned, and sent its fire running along his limbs, so that his face shone unconsciously . . . he saw the white flow of her white-gold breasts. And he touched them, and he let his life go molten. "Father!" he said, "why did you hide this from me?"[95]

Shortly after Christ's ecstasy of the flesh, he sets off in a boat by himself. The story closes with his tired words: "So let the boat carry me. Tomorrow is another day."[96]

The new gospel presented by *The Escaped Cock* subverts what Lawrence endorses in his *Grand Inquisitor* essay. According to the Inquisitor's view, one would be correct to interfere in the lives of others, as long as the one who interferes is superior. Such a view allows no respect for those who would lead single, isolated lives, for it insists that all lives be coordinated within a hierarchical whole. The Guardians do not have the luxury of leaving the cave to pursue the singleness of their souls. Presumably, the Christ of *The Escaped Cock* would have harsh words for anyone who sought to dictate so thoroughly how life is to be lived. Lawrence's solitary figure would not be likely to kiss an Inquisitor who held him in captivity. He would not remain silent before someone who preached interference and ignored the truths of the flesh. A basic incongruence exists, then, between the novella and the essay. One cannot lead a solitary, fleshly life and seek lordship over the lives of others. One cannot gain the pleasures of Isis and the praises of the multitudes at the same time.

Taken together, the essay, *The Escaped Cock*, and *Kangaroo* point to a central problem in Lawrence's life and literary career: the prophet's vision of the promised land wavered with uncertainty. Lawrence sought to create a messianic role for himself, complete with a scripture and a colony, Rananim, that would lead the way to a new world. He borrowed symbols from both the Christian and pagan traditions – the rainbow, the phallus, the phoenix, Christ, and Isis – to clothe his gospel in legitimacy. His gospel sought to liberate the self by purging the legacy of Puritanism with paganism, by freeing blood consciousness from the death grip of mental consciousness. At his most audacious moments, he saw himself as one who pointed to a new millennium of human possibility. Lawrence, the prophet, urged man "to behold God, and to become God"; he shared his dream of "the one glorious activity of man: the getting himself into a new relationship with a new heaven and a new earth."[97] Yet Lawrence never completely believed his own prophecies. His recurring self-mockery reflected his persistent doubts about his messianic role. Perhaps that was because he knew his followers too well; Mabel Dodge Luhan, Middleton Murry, Dorothy Brett Singer, and the rest had apostolic fervor but not much else. More importantly, Lawrence often became confused about the specific direction he should take. His desires were many and complex, and they often led in opposing directions. Too many gods spoke within Lawrence at the same time. His fiction and nonfiction alike reflect the contradictions and Byron-like mutability of those voices.

Such contentious voices help to explain the inconsistencies among *Kangaroo*, *The Escaped Cock*, and the *Grand Inquisitor* preface. Lawrence restlessly experimented with different solutions to the problems of modern life, solutions that often negated one another: the boot of Mussolini, the breast of Isis, the earnestness of Christ, the blood of Marxism, and the scepter of the Inquisitor all prove alluring but unsatisfactory. With a modernist bravado, he celebrated his own manic mutability, advising that truth could only be found in Heraclitean flux, which accounts for the contradictory multiplicity of his scriptural messages. He praised the novel – *his* novels – as "the one bright book of life," a "tremulation" to "make the whole man alive tremble," precisely because of its capacity to register change.[98] "The novel can help us to live, as nothing else can" only because it reveals "the changing rainbow of our living relationships."[99] Lawrence spent his life trying to capture that evanescent rainbow. His visions of truth changed not simply because of personal doubts or philosophic uncertainties but also because truth itself was always revisable.

Lawrence's life, however, did maintain one constancy: he could not escape the presence of Dostoevsky on his pilgrim road. He wrestled continuously with the author whom he regarded as a fellow writer of gospels. Dostoevsky may have written monstrously false gospels, but Lawrence saw him as a fellow explorer of the human soul, flesh, and spirit, one who addressed the most important issues of life in his novels. His lifelong antagonism, in a sense, was the highest compliment that one artist–prophet could pay to another: he paid serious attention to what was said and never let his rage subside. Unfortunately, Lawrence's stubborn insistence that Dostoevsky was incapable of irony, unconcerned with literary craft, and a victim of diseased desires led him to separate the prophetic message from its artistic context, ensuring misreading rather than understanding.

In the end, Lawrence's combative encounter teaches us virtually nothing about his rival. As might have been expected, we read what Lawrence says about Dostoevsky to learn about Lawrence alone, an always interesting and exasperating topic.

CHAPTER 3

A modernist ambivalence: Virginia Woolf

Like Lawrence, Woolf first encountered Dostoevsky through a French translation of *Crime and Punishment*. She read the novel in 1912 while on her sexually disappointing honeymoon with Leonard.[1] Lawrence, by contrast, had read it in the midst of the impassioned ambivalence of his romance with Jessie Chambers. The differing passional contexts of their first readings set the tone of all future readings. Unlike Lawrence, who could never escape the abrasive, discordant presence of his rival, Woolf always kept a safely ironic distance from Dostoevsky, never viewing him as a competitor. Her comments about his works, typically more balanced and penetrating than Lawrence's, reflect a patrician uncertainty about how the barbarian in the foyer of modern fiction should be treated.

Her response to Dostoevsky can be divided into three stages. The first, 1912 to 1920, covers the period in which the Constance Garnett translations were released. Woolf's letters and reviews during this time reveal her attraction to Dostoevsky's psychological portraits, especially his graphic renderings of tumultuous consciousness, and her discomfort with his alleged absence of form. Perhaps because she too readily subscribed to Dostoevskian stereotypes of her era and too easily dismissed Dickens, Balzac, Hugo, and other romantic realists, Woolf could not place Dostoevsky within the traditions of the novel and found no evidence of artistic control or literary shaping.

The second stage of her response, 1921 to 1925, represents the high point of her interest and marks a number of important crossroads in her own career. During these years, Woolf attempted to learn Russian, assisted S. S. Koteliansky in translations, and through Hogarth Press helped to publish a number of important Russian works. As a creative writer she struggled to define her artistic vision and established herself with the publication of *Jacob's Room* (1921) and *Mrs. Dalloway* (1925) as an important and innovative modernist. The evidence about her attitude towards Dostoevsky, primarily conveyed in three pivotal essays, shows that her perspective had expanded considerably. He now provided her with valuable ammunition to topple the outworn edifice of the Edwardian novel, to define the merits of literature produced by "the moderns" and to justify her own experimental approach. Dostoevsky pointed the way to a "new panorama of the human mind" in support of Woolf's quest for a fiction that would at last do justice to the depth and complexity of Mrs. Brown, Woolf's emblem for common humanity.[2]

Woolf's enthusiasm cooled considerably in the last stage of her response, evidenced by comments made between 1929 and 1940 (the year of her last recorded remark). Increasingly uncomfortable with what she perceived as the sacrifice of art for the spontaneous expression of life, she admitted in a 1933 diary entry that "one can't read D. again."[3] A few days later, when Koteliansky asked her to write an introduction to their translation of *Stavrogin's Confession*, she politely refused. Unlike Lawrence who had accepted a similar request from Kot, which led to his famous preface to *The Grand Inquisitor*, Woolf felt no need to return to Dostoevsky. Her aloofness suggests that his works never fully touched the artist in her.

The fictional differences between them, illustrated by their party scenes, further explain Woolf's detachment. While both writers shared a fascination with social festivities and gave them prominent roles in their fiction, the radical differences in content, style, tone, and setting reveal an artistic and social distance that cannot be spanned. Woolf's parties are dominated by the restraint and social homogeneity of upper-middle-class England, where unspoken rules govern speech and action and the inhibitions, deceptions, and masks of civility reign. Her absorbing interest in the subjective self reflects a romantic suspicion of public discourse as a threat to private autonomy and assumes a radical disjunction between the private and public selves, positing an interior self that may in its freest expression be uncontaminated by other people. Her characters, as a result, typically retreat to the protected domain of private consciousness, where less-than-respectable desires and contradictory thoughts are allowed to surface and mingle freely. Dostoevsky's parties allow for no such leisured retreats because the antagonisms are too great, the personalities too heated, the public confrontations too scandalous. As will be seen, his parties reflect a conception of personality that challenges Woolf's epistemology of the self. Though admitting her attraction to the power and passion of such scenes, Woolf could not move beyond her uneasiness with their embarrassing travesties and

frankly stated passions to discover an underlying artistic intent. In her
view, Dostoevsky was too passionate, too intense to be an artist.

ENCOUNTER WITH AN ARTLESS SAGE (1912–1920)

Woolf's first recorded comments about Dostoevsky appeared in a 1912
letter to Lytton Strachey.

> I have now run full tilt into *Crime et Châtiment*, fifty pages before tea, and I see
> there are only 800; so I shall be through in no time. It is directly obvious that he
> is the greatest writer ever born: and if he chooses to become horrible what will
> happen to us? Honeymoon completely dashed. If he says it – human hope –
> had better end, what will be left but suicide in the Grand Canal.[4]

Four months later, she wrote again to Strachey: "I'm reading *An
Adolescent* . . . Dostoevsky more frantic than any, I think, twelve new
characters on every page and the mind quite dazed by conversations."[5]
The experience of reading his novels would often leave Woolf bewildered: the frantic pacing, emotionally charged confrontations, and
confessional outbursts provided excitement yet also impeded her ability
to recognize design.

Strachey, it should be noted, had already read most of the major
novels of Dostoevsky in French translations, as well as a number of his
shorter works. His enthusiasm for Dostoevsky may even have spurred
Woolf's interest though no evidence has yet been found to document his
influence. Strachey published an intelligent and lucid essay, presumably
a response to the publication of Constance Garnett's translation of *The
Brothers Karamazov*, that appeared in the same month that Woolf reported her first reading, raising themes that Woolf herself would later
take up. After contrasting Dostoevsky's "agitated, feverish, intense"
style with the "ordinary English novels," Strachey praises "the wonderful intensity and subtlety" of his "psychological interest" and finds that
his works lead "to a new understanding of the mysterious soul of man,"
which earns him standing "among the great creative artists of the
world." Strachey also reports his first impression of the "disconcerting"
and "extremely disorganized" characteristics of the novel. In his view,
its "construction seems often to collapse entirely," apparently due to "a
singular incoherence" of "outward form" characteristic of Dostoevsky's
novels. However, Strachey moves beyond his first impression, in a
manner that Woolf was never able to imitate, to discover "a vital
unexpected unity to the whole," a unity that dominates the "most

heterogeneous" parts of the novels. To illustrate his sense of the fusion between form and content, he compares the construction of Dostoevsky's novels to "some gigantic Gothic cathedral, where, amid all the bewildering diversity of style and structure, a great mass of imaginative power and beauty makes itself mysteriously felt," the unique artistic form adding power to the psychological insight.[6] Unfortunately, few, if any, readers of the Garnett translations shared Strachey's intuitive sense of form.

Three years later, Woolf again wrote to Strachey about Dostoevsky. Her letter of 22 October 1915 informs him of her progress, as one might inform a tutor: "I am beginning the *Insulted and Injured*, which sweeps me away."[7] During the same year, she also read *The Idiot*, noting in her diary the first evidence of her frustration: "I can't bear the style of it very often." Yet Woolf finds "same kind of vitality in him that Scott had; only Scott merely made superb ordinary people. And D. creates wonders, with very subtle brains, and fearful sufferings." The entry concludes by noting that "the likeness to Scott" may be partly attributable to "the loose, free and easy style of the translation."[8]

Woolf often complained about the dangers of Russian translations; her gifted facility with language made her all too aware of what might be lost in the translating process. Yet the barrier of translated texts never stopped her from recognizing Tolstoy, Turgenev, and Chekhov as great stylists in command of their material. As a reader of Chekhov, she reported feeling "that we hold the parts together, and that Chekhov was not merely rambling disconnectedly, but struck now this note, now that with intention, in order to complete his meaning." She recognized Tolstoy as "the greatest of all novelists": "Even in a translation we feel that we have been set on a mountain-top and had a telescope put into our hands. Everything is astonishingly clear and absolutely sharp."[9] In Turgenev, she found "the rare gift of symmetry, of balance." Like other Russian writers, "his scope is wide . . . but we are conscious of some further control and order."[10]

Such an assumption of an artist in control never extended to Dostoevsky though she made efforts to excuse his otherwise inexcusable lapses of style as deficiencies of translation. Woolf, sharing the insistence of James and Conrad that art must make itself felt in every sentence of a work, viewed well-wrought sentences of grace and beauty as the best evidence of an artist's shaping hand. Perhaps because Dostoevsky often wrote plebeian sentences, which reflected the common language of uncivil speakers and unrefined narrators, Woolf failed to recognize the innovative and intentional elements of his craft. The contemporary translator Richard Pevear notes that Dostoevsky "delighted in the richness of spoken language, its playfulness, its happy mistakes, its revealing quirks and peculiarities."[11] The spoken word, in an eclectic variety of quotidian manifestations, dominates Dostoevsky's fiction; Woolf was not alone in her inability to detect artistic intent behind the use of such common, low-brow language.

In 1917 Woolf made her first public comments about Dostoevsky in a review of Garnett's translation of *The Eternal Husband and Other Stories*. By this time she recognized him as having thoroughly infiltrated the English literary climate: "His books are now to be found on the shelves of the humblest English libraries; they have become an indestructible part of the furniture of our rooms, as they belong for good to the furniture of our minds." With some trepidation, Woolf concludes that the stories in the collection "leave the reader with the feeling that something strange and important had happened."

Her review focuses on "The eternal husband" as a problem of literary evaluation, claiming that the story is obviously flawed but that its "extraordinary power" constrains the reader's aesthetic judgment: "nor while we are reading it can we liberate ourselves sufficiently to feel certain in this or that respect that there is a failure of power, or insight, or craftsmanship." The usual signposts of literary merit are of little use here because a Dostoevsky story makes the reader forget about evaluative standards; while reading, it does not "occur to us to compare it with other works either by the same writer or by other writers." As a result, "it is very difficult to analyze the impression it has made even when we've finished it."

The difficulty of assessing Dostoevsky's literary stature, Woolf asserts, derives from the strangeness of his content and the singularity of his vision, illustrated by the plot of "The eternal husband," which depicts the complex relationship between Pavel Pavlovitch, "the eternal husband," and his rival Velchaninov, "the eternal lover," who had seduced his wife and fathered a child by her. The story describes what happens after the wife dies and the husband pursues his rival, torn between his desires to emulate him and to kill him. Pavel Pavlovitch engages his rival in a macabre cat-and-mouse game: he befriends Velchaninov in order to taunt him with elusive hints that make the lover suspect that the husband knows his secret. In typical Dostoevsky fashion, the husband vacillates between abject timidity and brazen insolence in his hatred and admiration for the lover. After summariz-

ing the plot, Woolf acknowledges her descriptive difficulties in the face
of "monstrous" creations: "These, at least, are the little bits of cork
which mark a circle upon the top of the waves while the net drags the
floor of the sea and encloses stranger monsters than have ever been
brought to the light of day before."[12] Because of such dark, unsettling
subject-matter, Woolf regards Dostoevsky as a literary alien, disengaging him from a legion of nineteenth-century writers, such as Poe,
Hoffman, Hugo, and Dickens, who shared his preoccupation with the
grotesque, perhaps a mark of Woolf's own limitations as a student of
the novel.

Her stress on Dostoevsky's literary discontinuities does not diminish
her appreciation of his ability to reconstruct states of consciousness. Her
encounter with the powerfully bizarre scene of Velchaninov awaking to
find the husband standing over him, poised to kill the man who is both
his role model and his rival, leads her to the realization that Dostoevsky
is duplicating the flow of consciousness that we all experience: "Velchaninov, as he broods over the blood-stained razor [the would-be
murder weapon], passed over his involved and crowded train of thought
without a single hitch, just, in fact, as we ourselves are conscious of
thinking when some startling fact has dropped into the pool of our
consciousness." According to Woolf, Dostoevsky stands "alone among
writers" in his "power of reconstructing these most swift and complicated states of mind, of rethinking the whole trains of thought in all its
speed." She especially values his ability to suggest desires that lie beyond
expressed thought, his explorations of "the dim and populous underworld of the mind's consciousness where desires and impulses are
moving blindly beneath the sod."

Dostoevsky's presentation of character, "the **exact** opposite" of the
method adopted by "most of our novelists," offers an illuminating
alternative to the English tradition with its empiricist habits of mind and
its reliance on external details. In Woolf's judgment, the English novelists "reproduce all the external appearances – tricks of manner, landscape, dress, and the effect of the hero upon his friends – but very rarely,
and only for an instant, penetrate to the tumult of thought which rages
within his own mind." The Russian novelist never evades the "tumult of
thought": "the whole fabric of a book by Dostoevsky is made out of such
material." Interestingly, Woolf ignores the genesis of such tumult,
glossing over the dialogical nature of Dostoevskian consciousness and its
replication of social, ideological disputes that always bear the mark of
the other, even in the most private musings. To twist Husserl, one might

note that consciousness in Dostoevsky is always consciousness of someone else.

Woolf admires his works for challenging readers to redefine their
vision of humanity and of themselves.

> To him a child or a beggar is as full of violent and subtle emotions as a poet or a
> sophisticated woman of the world; and it is from the intricate maze of their
> emotions that Dostoevsky constructs his version of life. In reading him, there-
> fore, we are often bewildered because we find ourselves observing men and
> women from a different point of view from that to which we are accustomed.
> We have to get rid of the old tune which runs so persistently in our ears, and to
> realize how little of our humanity is expressed in that old tune.

Dostoevsky forces readers to cast aside their habitual stances, an accom-
plishment that she herself will later emulate in novels such as *To the
Lighthouse* and *Mrs. Dalloway,* and *The Waves,* in which perspectives are
constantly shifted, disrupting conventional modes of reading and cate-
gories of thought. In her fictional world, the emotional complexities of a
Septimus Smith or Mrs. Dalloway can only be discerned if traditional
standards of judgment are disrupted; our usual frames of perspective
must be exploded in the service of truth. As Lily Briscoe reflects about
Mrs. Ramsey, "One wanted fifty pairs of eyes to see with. Fifty pairs of
eyes were not enough to get round that one woman with."[13] Woolf
shares with Conrad a commitment to an art that will make us see, an art
that can liberate the self from false vision. For that reason, she appreci-
ates Dostoevsky's manner of unsettling his readers: "we constantly find
ourselves wondering whether we recognize the feeling that he shows us,
and we realize it in ourselves, or in some moment of intuition we have
suspected it in others."

The act of reading Dostoevsky serves a psychoanalytic function,
taking the reader on a self-reflective journey to discover unacknowledged truths, to discard past distortions, and to develop a more accurate view of the self. In contrast to Lawrence, Woolf regarded Dostoevsky's psychology as a cleansing instrument of health. Psychological
depth, however, cannot be equated with craft; in her verdict Dostoevsky
is a genius lacking literary discipline and aesthetic sensibility: "Intuition
is the term which we should apply to Dostoevsky's genius at its best.
When he is fully possessed by it he is able to read the most inscrutable
writing at the depths of the darkest souls; but when it deserts him the
whole of his amazing machinery seems to spin fruitless in the air."[14]

Her next public comments about Dostoevsky surface in an essay
published on 25 July 1918 that sought to revive the reputation of the late

Victorian novelist George Meredith. Dostoevsky, along with Tolstoy and Turgenev, is blamed for seducing the English reading public and blinding them to the merits of Meredith, who was rendered "an insular hero bred and cherished for the delight of connoisseurs in some sheltered corner of a Victorian hothouse." The Russian novel, "larger, saner and much more profound than ours," seemed to offer the English "an entirely new conception of the novel," "one that allowed human life in all its width and depth, with every shade of feeling and subtlety of thought, to flow in their pages." While recognizing the Russians' "undeviating reverence for truth," Woolf judges them to be unconcerned with art: "Life was too serious to be juggled with. It was too important to be manipulated. Could any English novel survive in the furnace of that overpowering sincerity?"[15] Her essay cautions the English to temper their new-found Russian enthusiasms so that they will not undervalue their own literary heritage.

In her 1919 review of Garnett's translation of *An Honest Thief and Other Stories*, Woolf again voices her concern about the author who writes "in his big rough way" beyond the pale of literary tradition. Where she previously praised Dostoevsky's liberation of the novel from stifling conventions, Woolf now laments his lack of restraint. His stories "read as if they were improvisations of a gigantic talent reeling off its wild imaginations at breathless speed"; "they have the diffuseness of a mind too tired to concentrate, and too fully charged to stop short. Slack and ungirt as it is, it tumbles out rubbish and splendour pell-mell." Woolf regards Dostoevsky as one who wrote merely to transcribe the pain and depth of his experience, who refused to pay attention to formal restraints and remained insulated from the cross-winds of literary influences. Readily admitting his genius – "we are perpetually conscious that, if Dostoevsky fails to keep within the proper limits, it is because the fervour of his genius goads him across the boundary" – she is increasingly reluctant to grant him the title of artist.[16]

Still, his works are to be preferred over those that contain beautiful prose about unimportant matters. In a 1920 review of an anthology entitled *A Treasury of English Prose*, Woolf makes an apparent about-face, excusing Dostoevsky's *absence* of style as the price of greatness.

The greatest of novelists – Dostoevsky – always, so Russian scholars say, writes badly. Turgenev, the least great of the Russian trinity, always, they say, writes exquisitely. That Dostoevsky would have been a greater novelist had he written beautifully into the bargain no one will deny. But the novelist's task lays such a load upon every nerve, muscle, and fibre that to demand beautiful prose in addition is, in view of human limitations, to demand what can only be given at the cost of sacrifice.

Her comments, however, must be appraised in context; Dostoevsky's novels serve not to justify his absence of "exquisite" writing but to warn readers against judging novels according to an anthologizing standard that would mistakenly identify quotable prose as the sole determinant of greatness. The primary goal of a novelist is to capture human complexity, giving the reader "the priceless privilege of living with human beings," not the creation of beautiful prose.[17]

DOSTOEVSKY AND THE STRUGGLE OF THE MODERNS (1921–1925)

The second stage of Woolf's response, while not representing a change of mind, conveys a new conviction that Dostoevsky and Russian literature could advance the cause of modernism. During these years Woolf strained to find new artistic forms that would do justice to her ambitions. Her publications included *Jacob's Room* (1922), two versions of "Mr. Bennett and Mrs. Brown" (1923 and 1924), *The Common Reader* (1925), and *Mrs. Dalloway* (1925). Russian writers proved invaluable in the effort to define and defend her own modernist values; she now believed that their works could impel the English novel to new directions. Her interests prompted her to begin learning Russian in 1921, though she stopped her lessons within the year and never mastered the language. She even assisted her friend S. S. Koteliansky in three translations that were published by her own Hogarth Press in 1922 and 1923.[18] Though not forgetting her previous concerns, Dostoevsky became an important ally in her modernist campaign, and she used his fiction to exemplify the multiplicity and expansiveness of literary possibilities.

In the original abbreviated version of her "Mr. Bennett and Mrs. Brown" essay, published in 1923, Dostoevsky helped Woolf to sound the death knell of the Victorian tradition of characterization and to highlight the limitations of Galsworthy, Wells, and Bennett.

After reading *Crime and Punishment* and *The Idiot* how could any young novelist believe in "characters" as the Victorians had painted them? For the undeniable vividness of so many of them is the result of their crudity. The [Victorian] character is rubbed into us indelibly because its features are so few and so prominent. We are given the key word (Mr. Dick has King Charles' head; Mr. Brooke, "I went into that a great deal at one time"; Mrs. Micawber, "I will never desert Mr. Micawber"), and then, since the choice of the keyword is astonishingly apt, our imagination swiftly supplied the rest.

The reader encounters a troubling depth in Dostoevsky's characters that allows no return to Victorian simplicities: "what keyword could be applied to Raskolnikov, Myshkin, Stavrogin, or Alyosha? These are characters without any features at all." In Woolf's view, we "descend" into his characters "as we descend into some enormous cavern. Lights swing about; we hear the boom of the sea; it is all dark, terrible, and uncharted."

Woolf argues that Dostoevsky's influence blocked the Edwardian novelists from following in the steps of their Victorian predecessors. Unhappily, the Edwardians allowed their social activism to dictate their new novelistic choices: "A sensitive man like Mr. Galsworthy could scarcely step out of doors without barking his shins upon some social iniquity . . . so the young novelist became a reformer." The Edwardian turned his attention away from individual character to the panorama of society. As a result, "Every sort of town is represented, and innumerable institutions; we see factories, prisons, workhouses, law courts, Houses of Parliament." Woolf implies a historical inevitability about the novel's decline into sociological generalities: "We need not be surprised if the Edwardian novelist scarcely attempted to deal with character except in its more generalized aspects. The Victorian version was discredited; it was his duty to destroy all those institutions in the shelter of which character thrives and thickens; and the Russians had shown him – everything or nothing, it was impossible as yet to say which."

Yet Woolf condemns the Edwardian choice of subject-matter, which threatens to dissolve the novel into an artless tract. These writers, she argues, "gave us a vast sense of things in general; but a very vague sense of things in particular." Deflecting a charge that Arnold Bennett had made about her own *Jacob's Room*, she finds a grievous weakness in their work: "Their books are already a little chill, and must steadily grow distant, for 'the foundation of good fiction is character-creating and nothing else,' as Mr. Bennett says; and in none of them are we given a man or woman whom we know." To escape this fictional dead end, Woolf summons the Georgian writers to rescue Mrs. Brown, the prototype of common humanity, from the damage done by the Edwardians. The new generation of English writers must "bring back character from the shapelessness into which it had lapsed, to sharpen its edges, deepen its compass, and so make possible those conflicts between human beings which alone arouse our strongest emotions." From "the ruins and splinters" of the Edwardian house of fiction, the "Georgian writer must somehow reconstruct a habitable dwelling place" for Mrs. Brown.[19]

Despite the elegance of her argument, Woolf's claim that Dostoevsky influenced Edwardian choices is dubious for there is little evidence to suggest that Galsworthy, Bennett, and Wells were so constrained. While Galsworthy and Bennett read his novels in French translation, most of their comments about Dostoevsky were made in response to the Constance Garnett translations, which did not appear until they were both well established. In the case of Wells, there is not even any evidence that he read Dostoevsky. Perhaps because Woolf realized the anachronism of her argument, she omitted all reference to Dostoevsky in the more famous 1924 version of her essay. That expanded version, presented to Cambridge University on 18 May 1924, avoided any hint of historical determinism that might excuse Edwardian choices. Instead, Woolf held her counterparts wholly accountable for the limitations of their fiction, a move that considerably strengthened her attack against the three novelists.

It seems clear, however, that the Russian author did affect *her* choices. In a crucial diary entry made in the same year of the essay (1923), Woolf uses Dostoevsky as a test of her novelistic worth.

> But now what do I feel about *my* writing? – this book, that is, *The Hours* [later to be retitled *Mrs. Dalloway*], if that's its name? One must write from deep feeling, said Dostoevsky. And do I? Or do I fabricate with words, loving them as I do? No, I think not. In this book I have almost too many ideas. I want to give life and death, sanity and insanity; I want to criticize the social system, and to show it at work, at its most intense. But here I may be posing . . . Am I writing *The Hours* from deep emotion?

She continues, employing Dostoevsky as a defense against Arnold Bennett's charge that she could not create convincing characters: "People, like Arnold Bennett, say I can't create, or didn't in *Jacob's Room*, characters that survive. My answer is – but I leave that to the *Nation*: it's only the old argument that character is dissipated into shreds now: the old post-Dostoevsky argument." In effect, Dostoevsky gives license to those who depart from Bennett's formulaic realism, supporting Woolf's new directions for the novel. Though confident of her aesthetic goal, she voices trepidation about her own abilities: "Have I the power of conveying the true reality. Or do I write essays about myself."[20]

Woolf's 1925 "Modern fiction" essay provides a more substantial account of that "true reality." Once again relying on polarities, she names Bennett and the Edwardians as the antithesis of Joyce, Woolf, and other "moderns," as well as the "Russians" (presumably, Dostoevsky, Tolstoy, Turgenev, and Chekhov). The Edwardians are faulted not for a failure to pay attention to character – the argument of the first "Mr. Bennett and Mrs. Brown" essay – but because their characters are not sufficiently vital, interesting, or important. Woolf's polemic is given philosophical underpinnings as she now denounces her Edwardian antagonists as "materialists." "Because they are concerned not with the spirit but with the body," she contends "that they have disappointed us, and left us with the feeling that the sooner English fiction turns its back upon them, as politely as may be, and marches, if only for the desert, the better for its soul."[21] Again, Woolf singles out Bennett, ostensibly because he "is by far the best workman" and therefore poses the gravest fictional threat. She admits that his characters have life but laments their lack of depth: "His characters live abundantly, even unexpectedly, but it remains to ask how do they live, and what do they live for?"

At first, Woolf seems to base her attack on the fictional lives of his characters, immersed as they are in middle-class domesticity, complacency, and security. Bennett and his counterparts "write of unimportant things . . . [and] spend immense skill and immense industry making the trivial and transitory appear the true and the enduring." The greatest problem, however, flows from their choice of method. These novelists plod "perseveringly" as they create arbitrary constructions of "two and thirty chapters," as if held in thrall by some "unscrupulous tyrant . . . to provide a plot, to provide comedy, tragedy, love interest, and an air of probability embalming the whole." In their fiction, "the essential thing," which can be called "life or spirit, truth or reality," "has moved off, or on, and refuses to be contained any longer." With amused understatement, Woolf describes her "momentary doubt" and "a spasm of rebellion" about pages that "fill themselves in the customary way": "Is life like this? Must novels be like this?"[22] Her criticism extends by implication to the genealogy of the realistic novel, exemplified by writers such as Defoe, Trollope, and Thackeray. To capture the life that Woolf values – the swift, mysterious, and evanescent flow of consciousness – the conventions of realism must be radically expanded.

"Modern fiction" calls for a new way of rendering reality. A new, liberated novel must pierce through old ways of seeing, obscured as they are by conventions which mask what they purport to reveal, and move towards the unfettered activity of the mind itself: "Let us record the atoms as they fall upon the mind in the order in which they fall, let us trace the pattern, however disconnected and incoherent in appearance, which each sight or incident scores upon the consciousness." Woolf

identifies James Joyce as one who discards conventions for the sake of
moving the novel "closer to life."

Mr. Joyce is spiritual; he is concerned at all costs to reveal the flickerings of that
innermost flame which flashes its messages through the brain, and in order to
preserve it he disregards with complete courage whatever seems to him adven-
titious, whether it be probability, or coherence or any of those other signposts
which for previous generations have served to support the imagination of a
reader when called upon to imagine what he can neither touch nor see.[23]

Woolf's insistence on Joyce's "spiritual" qualities seems to negate a
large part of his writing, especially the delightful physicality of Leopold
and Molly Bloom and the concrete, heterogeneous vitality of Dublin.
Her dichotomy between the spiritual and material represents an unfortunate choice of words and argumentative base, misleading because of
the suggestion that writers must neglect the material world in favor of
the spiritual, or more precisely, the mental. The force of Woolf's
argument, however, does not depend on a gnostic separation between
matter and spirit.[24] Rather, her essay can be best understood as an
argument against fiction that does not do justice to the open-ended,
fluid, and profound complexity of life.

Woolf uses Joyce's new fictional paths to support her call for artistic
emancipation, a freedom that is the ultimate basis of her dispute with
Bennett and the Edwardians. The modern novelist must be "set free to
set down what he chooses. He has to have the courage to say that what
interests him is no longer 'this' but 'that': out of 'that' alone must he
construct his work." Such freedom promises new depths and new forms
for those bold enough to unloose their imaginative vision: "For the
moderns 'that,' the point of interest, lies very likely in the dark places of
psychology. At once, therefore, the accent falls a little differently; . . . at
once a different outline of form becomes necessary, difficult for us to
grasp, incomprehensible to our predecessors." Dostoevsky, it should be
remembered, also pointed to the "dark places of psychology." His
unfettered narrative approach, though not named explicitly here, serves
as a model for the emancipated novelist.

To support the cause of the moderns further, Woolf addresses the
"Russian influence." Russia's fiction, in its absorbing, relentless focus on
the tragic dimensions of human existence, "turns so many . . . famous
novels" in the English tradition to "tinsel and trickery." With an
admiration that is perhaps tongue-in-cheek, Woolf acknowledges that
"If the Russians are mentioned one runs the risk of feeling that to write

any fiction save theirs is a waste of time. If we want understanding of the soul and heart where else shall we find it of comparable profundity?" While recognizing that cultural differences militate against an assimilation of Russian modes of thought or writing, she draws upon their fiction to illustrate the infinite elasticity of the literary imagination: "they flood us with a view of the infinite possibilities of art and remind us that there is no limit to the horizon, and that nothing – no 'method,' no experiment, even of the wildest – is forbidden, but only falsity and pretense."[25]

Another 1925 essay of Woolf's, "The Russian point of view," should be read as a companion piece to "Modern fiction" (both were first published in *The Common Reader*). After opening with a warning about the liabilities of reading translated texts, Woolf confidently identifies "the chief character" of all Russian fiction – "the soul."[26] She contrasts the soul that is "delicate and subtle" in Chekhov with the one "of greater depth and volume in Dostoevsky, liable to violent diseases and raging fever." Woolf extols Dostoevsky's exploration of new, alien underworlds far removed from the English literary landscape. Yet there are hints of discomfort in her praise of the writer regarded as the strangest and most foreign of all Russians.

Perhaps that is why it needs so great an effort on the part of the English reader to read *The Brothers Karamazov* or *The Possessed* a second time. The "soul" is alien to him. It is even antipathetic. It has little sense of humour and no sense of comedy. It is formless. It has slight connection with the intellect. It is confused, diffuse, tumultuous, incapable, it seems, of submitting to the control of logic or the discipline of poetry.

Like Joyce, Dostoevsky is heralded as an emancipator unbound by the conventions of realism; his novels "are composed purely and wholly of the stuff of the soul." Unfortunately, Woolf's insistence on Dostoevsky's grim, formless illogic masks his sardonic wit, intellectual complexity, aesthetic ambitiousness, and boisterous sense of the absurd.

Woolf discusses the bracing immediacy of his novels, finding an excitement matched only by Shakespeare. In the absence of the usual signposts of authorial control, the reader plunges into a new world: "We open the door and find ourselves in a room full of Russian generals, the tutors of Russian generals, their stepdaughters and cousins, and crowds of miscellaneous people who are all talking at the tops of their voices about their most private affairs." Though Woolf seems nettled that the writer does not locate the scene for us – "Where are we? Surely it is the part of a novelist to inform us whether we are in an hotel, a flat, or hired lodging" – she is fascinated by the lack of barriers between text and reader. Indeed, the reader becomes a participant: "We are souls, tortured, unhappy souls, whose only business it is to talk, to reveal, to confess, to draw up at whatever rending of flesh and nerve those crabbed sins which crawl on the sand at the bottom of us."

Woolf continues her playfully imaginative description by noting how the reader's "confusion slowly settles." Her choice of metaphor is most revealing; the novelist provides a rope to a reader drowning in a sea of chaos: "holding on by the skin of our teeth, we are rushed through the water; feverishly, wildly, we rush on and on, now submerged, now in a moment of vision understanding more than we have ever understood before, and receiving such revelations as we are wont to get only from the press of life at its fullest." Woolf then abruptly changes to a flying metaphor, which calls to mind the superhuman speed of the trip that Marlowe's Dr. Faustus made with Mephistopheles.

As we fly, we pick it all up – the names of the people, their relationships, that they are staying in an hotel at Roulettenburg, that Polina is involved in an intrigue with the Marquis de Grieux – but what unimportant matters these are compared with the soul! It is the soul that matters, its passion, its tumult, its astonishing medley of beauty and vileness. And if our voices suddenly rise into shrieks of laughter, or if we are shaken by the most violent sobbing, what more natural? – it hardly calls for remark. The pace at which we are living is so tremendous that sparks must rush off our heels as we fly.

The comments disclose that Woolf's subject is *The Gambler*, a novella written in the form of a first-person diary. The narrator, Alexsey Ivanovich, serves as a tutor for a Russian general, temporarily residing abroad. The intricate plot, which includes Alexsey's pursuit of the general's stepdaughter Polina, his obsession for roulette, his romantic rivalry with the Marquis who secretly controls the general's finances, and a debauched escapade in Paris, reminds one of a Balzac novel, where love, money, ambition, and propriety become hopelessly entangled. Woolf does masterfully evoke the experience of reading a Dostoevsky work for the first time. She never addresses, however, the experience of rereading his stories, which leads one to suspect that she herself did not return to the texts.

Though she can see no evidence of artistic shaping, Woolf does discern previously unrecognized patterns of the mind itself: "When the speed is thus increased and the elements of the soul are seen, not separately in scenes of humour or scenes of passion as our slower English minds conceive them, but streaked, involved, inextricably confused, a new panorama of the human mind is revealed." Dostoevsky's novels explode traditional notions of personality and force his English readers to accept a more complex model of the human psyche: "The old divisions melt into each other." Moralistic and static conceptions of the self are thus dissolved: "Men are at the same time villains and saints; their acts are at once beautiful and despicable. We love and hate at the same time. There is none of that precise division between good and bad to which we are used." His works even overturn our usual emotional affinities: "Often those for whom we feel the most affection are the greatest criminals, and the most abject sinners move us to the strongest admiration as well as love." After Dostoevsky, the old absolutes of human character can no longer be applied.

Dostoevsky prompts the realization that English narrative traditions mirror the customs of an entire nation grounded in materialism and a restrictive social hierarchy.

If we wished to tell the story of a General's love affair (and we should find it very difficult in the first place not to laugh at a General), we should begin with his house; we should solidify his surroundings. Only when all was ready should we attempt to deal with the General himself. Moreover, it is not the samovar but the teapot that rules in England; time is limited; space crowded; the influence of many points of view, of other books, even of other ages, makes itself felt. Society is sorted out into lower, middle, and upper classes, each with its own traditions, its own manners, and, to some extent, its own language.

Besides challenging the literary traditions of England, Dostoevsky's works oppose its social traditions, its history, and its fixed social boundaries, an opposition that explains why he was such a welcome visitor in the iconoclastic neighborhood of the Bloomsbury circle.

What matters most about Dostoevsky, according to the "Russian point of view," is his cultural and literary *difference*. In his alleged obliviousness to form and tradition, Woolf finds hope for the future. She contrasts the "constant pressure upon an English novelist to recognize [social and literary] barriers" with the absence of "such restraints" on Dostoevsky. The surging tides of his primitive, spontaneous genius help to topple the reign of the English teapot: "The novels of Dostoevsky are seething whirlpools, gyrating sandstorms, waterspouts which hiss and boil and suck us in." With tidal force, they overwhelm the safe and false conventions of English literature, setting the stage for new creations which may emerge after the flood waters recede. In his destruction of outworn forms, Dostoevsky brings the novel closer to where Woolf thinks it should go. "Nothing is outside of Dostoevsky's province; and when he is tired, he does not stop, he goes on. He cannot restrain himself. Out it tumbles upon us, hot, scalding, mixed, marvellous, terrible, oppressive – the human soul."[27]

A COOLING OF ENTHUSIASM (1926–1941)

The final stage of Woolf's response is marked by long intervals of silence; only once during this time does she offer extended comments about him. In her 1929 essay, "Phases of fiction," Woolf discusses *The Possessed*, her first and last analysis of a major Dostoevsky novel. Unlike her previous statements, this essay offers no praise of Dostoevsky's freedom from novelistic conventions, and it finds his psychology often impenetrable. No longer can Woolf address his work as a liberating force; instead, she voices fear that content separated from form can lead only to an inartistic and uncivilized terminus. Later comments about Dostoevsky in her diary are perfunctory, far removed from earlier excitement.

Her "Phases of fiction" essay is important for two reasons. First, it deals extensively with Dostoevsky in terms of his *resemblance* to other writers; second, it negates much of her earlier praise. Where previously she viewed him as a writer apart from all others, she now classifies him as one of the prototypical "Psychologists," grouping him with James and Proust as a writer whose foremost concern is the analysis of consciousness. Though Dostoevsky seems to inhabit a fictional universe entirely remote from Proust's, Woolf recognizes their shared preoccupation with "the mind at work." The reader needs to move beyond Dostoevsky's "glaring oppositions" and his "crude and violent emotions" to discover that he "lays bare regions deep down in the mind where contradiction prevails." Despite Woolf's uneasiness with his fictional world, where "the mesh of civilization is made of a coarse netting" with "holes" that "are wide apart," and her embarrassment about his characters who "are free to throw themselves from side to side, to hiss, to rant, to fall into paroxysms of rage and excitement," she praises his illumination of mental complexity.

In her analysis of the distinctive features of *The Possessed*, Woolf touches upon an important formal technique, the reliance on tumultuous, scandal-ridden group scenes as a means of unmasking truths about the individual participants. The depth of Dostoevsky's characters,

not depend, as Woolf contends, on the portrayal of unfiltered emotion; indeed, most of the emotions result from pretense and theatrical posing because virtually every one has something to hide. Rather, the narrative impetus is carried by the tension between what is known and what is not known. At this point, Stavrogin's marriage is not a certainty, clouded as it is with conflicting reports and interpretations. In fact, nearly all of the relationships among the major participants are marked by deceptions or secrets that will only be revealed as the movement of the plot carries the reader from unexplained mysteries to tragic knowledge (implied by "The subtle serpent"). In the context of the *entire* novel, the scene provides a brilliant distillation of major conflicts, a foreshadowing of the scandalous anarchy of later group scenes with their far more disastrous consequences, and a memorable dramatic introduction of the two most important protagonists (Stavrogin and Pyotr Stepanovitch). Every detail contributes to the artistic whole.

Woolf, however, cannot discern an underlying pattern because she interprets all emotional excesses in his works as evidence of impaired authorial judgment. As Alex Zwerdling has noted, Woolf "distrusted her own anger," and she connected "violent emotion of any kind with distortion and self-deception." She repeatedly insisted, according to Zwerdling, that "the direct expression of anger is fatal to art."[35] When Woolf found violent emotion in Dostoevsky, she assumed that he was out of control, perhaps even verging towards the same madness that afflicted her. Indeed, her descriptions of the manic moods of his novels, their raw emotional spontaneity, and their defiance of all conventional restraints bear an important resemblance to descriptions of her own bouts of madness. Perhaps Woolf's attraction to Dostoevsky and her eventual pulling away may be partially explained by her own personal experience of the mind's passionate disorder.[36] The Russian novelist may have played the role of a Septimus Smith, the pathetic madman in *Mrs. Dalloway*; like Smith, Dostoevsky challenged all certainties and proprieties, but he also brushed aside all the order and art of civilization. Despite her lifelong attraction to anarchy, Woolf sensed that too much disorder led to death, not liberation.

Not unexpectedly, she prefers the subtle nuances of Proust, finding his quiet rendering of emotions a welcome relief from Dostoevsky.

We have, if we turn to Proust, more emotion in a scene which is not supposed to be remarkable, like that in the restaurant in the fog. There we live along a thread of observation which is always going in and out of this mind and that mind; which gathers information from different social levels, which makes us now feel with a prince, now with a restaurant keeper . . . so that the imagination is being stimulated on all sides to close slowly, gradually, without being goaded by screams or violence, completely round the object.

Proust succeeds in avoiding the violence of Dostoevsky as he lucidly brings the reader "every piece of evidence upon which any state of mind is founded." The French novelist proves himself amenable to the reflective demands of art.

Woolf favorably contrasts the emotional and intellectual clarity of Proust to Dostoevsky, who abandons "the intellect," allowing the mind to be "always and almost at once overpowered by the rush of feeling; whether it is sympathy or anger." She cannot detect a residing intellectual presence in his fiction that can resolve contradictions or illuminate motives: "There is something illogical and contradictory often in the characters, perhaps because they are exposed to more than the usual current of emotional force. Why does he act like this? we ask again and again, and answer, rather doubtfully, that so perhaps madmen act."[37] In her eyes, Dostoevsky could *present* the activity of consciousness but could not *explain* it. His strong emotions produced memorable creations, but such volcanic passion can only flow when the intellect is held in abeyance and the artistic will kept in subservience to passion. As Woolf notes later in the essay, "the first sign that we are reading a writer of merit is that we feel his control at work on us," a control she never experienced with Dostoevsky.[38]

Woolf focuses almost exclusively on the chaos of the individual voices within *The Possessed*, misled by what Bakhtin identifies as "the plurality of independent and unmerged voices and consciousnesses."[39] Incapable of understanding the dialogical nature of Dostoevsky's art, Woolf assumes that he could not fuse the plurality of perspectives represented in his novels into a coherent whole. She saw everywhere abundant use of heterogeneous and incompatible material and judged it as evidence of artistic deficiency, failing to recognize that in the combination of disparate materials, in the chaos of dialogic oppositions, in the polyphony of contending voices, and in the whirlwind movement of events, Dostoevsky was working out his own distinctive aesthetic design. Artistically, Woolf approached Dostoevsky as Clive Bell approached the Impressionists: he was to be admired for dissolving old standards of realism, yet his work is marked by an absence of formal significance. The subject-matter was allowed to dominate the novels at the regrettable expense of "significant form."[40]

The comparison with Bell's perception of the Impressionists falls short in one crucial area. Bell, at least, recognized the Impressionists as working within artistic traditions, even faulting them for subscribing too readily to the untenable assumptions of the old masters that visual perception can be "translated" to the canvas. Woolf, however, persistently regards Dostoevsky as one who remained oblivious to all literary traditions. One might imagine that he simply gazed into his soul and began to write. On one hand, Woolf's perception can be explained in terms of literary history. Readers of the Garnett translations did not have the advantage of the Dostoevsky notebooks, diaries, and essays that give ample evidence of his literary concerns; nor did they have detailed information about Dostoevsky's literary education. On the other hand, it seems evident that Woolf's failure to do justice to the literary nature of Dostoevsky's work can also be traced to her own insufficient knowledge of the novel's traditions. If she had had more knowledge about writers such as Balzac, Hugo, Cervantes, Sand, Hoffman, Gogol, Poe, and others, she might have been able to recognize Dostoevsky as an experimenter who self-consciously reshaped the conventions of novel writing. Innumerable echoes of other writers can be found in his works.

Woolf's inability to perceive artistic form in Dostoevsky can also be connected to her methodological concerns as a novelist. While contemporary criticism, especially the work of Alex Zwerdling and Lucio Ruotolo, identifies the limitations of separating Woolf's work from her critique of society, she still can be approached as a writer who defined herself, in Zwerdling's words, as a "poetic novelist interested in states of reverie and vision, in mapping the intricate labyrinth of consciousness."[41] Her work, especially *The Waves*, *Jacob's Room*, and *To the Lighthouse*, can be regarded as an attempt to move the novel from a prose sensibility to a poetic sensibility, to merge novelistic expansiveness with the lyric rendering of the mind's interior.[42] Woolf sought to raise the novel above its lowly origins and attain a concentration of language, beauty of style, and subtle clarity of form that she identifies as belonging to the domain of poets. In the end, Dostoevsky, like Joyce, offends Woolf's sense of literary decorum, and her condemnation of *Ulysses* as "unbred" can also be applied to the Russian author.

Bakhtin's discussion of carnivalized literature provides a useful means of explicating her sense of decorum. In key respects, Woolf supports carnivalization, as defined by Bakhtin, because it breaks down the same barriers that she and her fellow moderns fought against. Its "joyful relativity of all structure and order" serves a liberating cause.[43] Bakhtin's analysis of Dostoevsky helps to explain her earlier reaction to his work, where she was attracted to his use of carnivalized oppositions that reveal a new panorama of the mind itself: "Everything in his [Dostoevsky's] world lives on the very border of its opposite. Love lives on the very border of hate, knows and understands it; and hate lives on the border of love and also understands it."[44] Woolf's previous essays show that she was impressed with the carnivalized inclusiveness of Dostoevsky's *subject-matter*, which she viewed as an antidote to the conventions of English restraint. But she did not discern the carnivalized nature of Dostoevsky's *literary craft*. In his deliberate mixture of styles, with the multiplicity of tone, the juxtaposition of the high and low, the serious and the comic, the sacred and profane, Woolf only found an absence of artistry. Where literary style is concerned, she espouses Augustan values of clarity and decorum, insisting that matters of high importance be treated in a style of high importance, keeping the likes of Flush and Orlando always at a safe distance from the worlds of the Ramseys and the Dalloways. While Woolf sometimes reached for a carnivalistic inclusiveness of subject matter, perhaps best illustrated by *The Years*, her work achieves a unity of tone and a narrative distance from its subject that proves her resistance to the stylistic influences of the carnivalized.

Woolf's final comments about Dostoevsky reinforce the distance between them. In a diary entry of 1933 (August 16), Woolf contrasts Dostoevsky to Turgenev: "Form, then, is the sense that one thing follows another rightly. This is partly logic. T.[Turgenev] wrote and rewrote. To clear the truth of the unessential. But D.[Dostoevsky] would say that everything matters. *But one can't read D. again* [emphasis mine]". Woolf does admit that Dostoevsky achieves some kind of form when she asks herself, "How do we know if the D. form is better or worse than the T." But she never attempts to describe that form. Her entry concludes by comparing the two novelists in terms of their ability to exclude. In contrast to Turgenev, who "states the essential and lets the reader do the rest," Woolf finds that Dostoevsky "supplies" the reader with every possible help and suggestion."[45]

Five days later, Woolf wrote to S. S. Koteliansky, rejecting his idea that she write a preface to their collaborated translation of *Stavrogin's Confession*, a previously unpublished segment of *The Possessed*, which had been suppressed by the czarist censors. In this episode Stavrogin makes a confession to Tikhon, a monk legendary for his holiness; the tormented but proud young wastrel admits to the violation of a young girl and her subsequent suicide. Though Stavrogin makes repentant gestures, a part of him still insists that no distinctions can be made between good and evil and that he can free himself from the prejudices of moral codes. In response to Kot's request, Woolf says: "I think it is an interesting document. But I do not think that I can write an introduction, because in order to say anything of interest about these notes one would have to go deeply into the questions of novel writing and into the whole question of Dostoevsky's psychology as a writer." Considering her previous extensive comments about Dostoevsky, her admission of ignorance seems suspect: "I do not feel I know enough about him." Perhaps Woolf claimed ignorance simply to mask her growing disinterest. To write about Dostoevsky, she tells Kot, would require too much thought, for "he is such an extraordinary case as a writer" that she would "feel silly to hazard guesses about him."[46] Woolf only made two more recorded comments about him in her lifetime. In 1934, a diary entry notes that Dostoevsky, one of the great satirical writers in the history of the novel, does not satirize.[47] In 1940, her diary records an indecipherable comment about keeping Dostoevsky to herself "in a selfish way."[48]

Her final lack of interest provides a provocative contrast with Lawrence's response to Dostoevsky in his last years. Unlike his Bloomsbury counterpart, Lawrence accepted a similar request from Koteliansky and wrote his memorable and misguided introduction to *The Grand Inquisitor* in 1930. He ransacked that excerpt to find evidence of Dostoevsky's perverse misdirection and to show the reader how his morality obscured the potentially liberating vision of his art. Like Woolf, Lawrence assumed that Dostoevsky was merely transcribing his own inner turmoil. Unlike Woolf, however, he did not find fault in any perceived absence of artistic form; instead, he laid the blame on the vision of life that emerges. He judged Dostoevsky's failure in terms of his diseased vision of life and his corrupt will; the failure of the artist can only be explained by the failure of the man.

Woolf, however, perceived his failure as an artistic one. In her view Dostoevsky was incapable of form because he was too overcome by his passionate subject matter. Where the freely expressed rage of Lawrence's final comments shows that he recognized his Russian rival as a writer who had the potential to proclaim Lawrencean truths, the reticence of Woolf's last comments shows her sense of unbridgeable dissimilarities. Though Lawrence could never forgive Dostoevsky for voicing the wrong prophetic message, he at least recognized him as a fellow novelist. Woolf, in the end, found him to be an interesting alien whose

monstrous creations helped loosen the chains of novelistic convention
and probe the labyrinths of consciousness, but whose absence of design
led ultimately to a fictional cul-de-sac.

THE POETICS OF PARTIES: A LITERARY COMPARISON

Perhaps the best way of measuring the distance between Dostoevsky
and Woolf can be found by comparing their party scenes. The social
gatherings of Clarissa Dalloway, Mrs. Ramsey, and Delia Pargiter, as
well as the two dinner parties of *The Waves*, function as symbolic and
structural centers of their novels. Dostoevsky's parties, exemplified by
Marmeladov's funeral feast, Nastasya's birthday party, and the literary
fête in *The Possessed*, serve equally important functions. Both writers
relied on such scenes to bring together dissimilar characters and contending points of view. Their parties loosen the hold of social convention
and provide an opportunity to reveal interacting characters in a setting
that is free from many of the ordinary restraints of daily life. Yet such
gatherings, regardless of surface similarities, provide the clearest evidence of the differences between the two writers.

In Woolf's parties most of what is important happens beyond the
reach of shared, public language. The author finds her subject chiefly in
the interior monologue of private consciousness because the characteristic state of the self, in her view, is one of meditative isolation, an
impregnable privacy which can only be temporarily overcome by so-
cializing efforts. On his way to the Dalloway festivity, Peter Walsh
reflects on "the truth about our soul," a meditation that seems to
embody Woolf's own views: "our self, who fish-like inhabits deep seas
and plies among obscurities threading her way between the boles of
giant weeds, over sun-flickered spaces and on and on into gloom, cold,
deep, inscrutable," occasionally "shoots to the surface and sports on the
wind-wrinkled waves; that is, has a positive need to brush, scrape, kindle
herself, gossiping."[49] The private self provides a refuge from the judgment of others; at one point, in the midst of Ramsey-party chatter about
government, the rights of fishermen, and other male concerns, we catch
a rare collective glimpse of dinner guests: "All of them bending themselves to listen thought, 'Pray heaven that the inside of my mind may not
be exposed.'"[50] That prayer could be the epitaph of many a Woolf
character.

Dostoevsky, by contrast, frequently dissolves the barriers between the
public and private self because in his fictional world such barriers are

not as intimidating or controlling. The inhibition that prevents Lily Briscoe from offending Charles Tansley, that pulls Peggie back from her verbal attack on North, and that maintains Clarissa's politeness to Hugh Whitbread does not operate in Dostoevsky; his characters can more easily defy social restraint, in part because they are so desperate to vindicate their own tenuous standing. Marmeladov's wife, for example, approaches the funeral feast as a final opportunity to assert her own respectability among the disorderly and drunken lodgers and her unsympathetic landlady. The brute despair of her life may be temporarily assuaged if the feast meets her standards of bourgeois civility, an impossible task. Once the affair unravels, Katerina Ivanovna loses all control; amid such disruption and humiliation, no retreats to private consciousness are possible. The barriers between public and private no longer hold.

The inhibitive barriers that typify Woolf's parties may be attributed to their class-bound restrictions. Her parties are dominated by people from similar social backgrounds who allow their actions and words to be restrained by a shared sense of propriety. Rose Kliman and Septimus Smith, as Alex Zwerdling has noted, would never be invited to a Mrs. Dalloway party because of their inferior class status.[51] Mrs. Ramsey's party in *To The Lighthouse* slightly expands Woolf's class boundaries due to the presence of one guest from working-class origins, the unlikable Charles Tansley. The young scholar, however, recognizes the rules of middle-class propriety, for he is a middle-class aspirant with solid academic credentials.[52] Only *The Years*, where the hostess Delia announces her pride in her ability "to mix people" from different classes and "do away with the absurd conventions of English life," can be seen as an attempt to stretch class lines. Yet Delia's efforts are satirized by Woolf, who chides the hostess's self-congratulatory "complacency" in looking round "the crowded room": "There were nobles and commoners; people dressed and people not dressed; people drinking out of mugs, and people waiting with their soup getting cold for a spoon to be brought to them."[53] Even in this party, the reader is not privy to the thoughts of any characters below the middle class, and North can find only "Dons and Duchesses" among the crowd, despite Delia's alleged social "promiscuity."[54] When the children of the caretaker are introduced near the party's end, they sing an unintelligible song that seems merely to confirm and support class differentiation. Their song is described by the implied narrator in a manner that betrays the author's class-bound perception: "There was something horrible in the noise they made. It was so shrill, so discordant, and so meaningless."[55]

Woolf's descriptions of parties are characterized by a quiet, reflective tone and an absence of serious disruption. When news of the suicide of Septimus Smith arrives, Clarissa does not allow it to impede the leisured activities of her guests. She vacates the room to come to terms with such black news in private. Lily Briscoe, unlike Clarissa, possesses serious disruptive impulses, feeling far more constrained by her Victorian female role and its false expectations. But she suppresses impulse throughout the party and maintains a veneer of respectability. While disruptions temporarily surface in Delia's party, as evidenced by Brown's attempt at speech-making, Peggy's insult of North, and the odd song of the caretaker's children, such disruptions do not pose a serious threat; laughter and party chatter eventually restore outer harmony and propriety. If *The Years* is more tolerant of eccentric behavior – one cannot imagine the Victorian-bred Mrs. Ramsey or the Edwardian-bred Mrs. Dalloway allowing a prominent guest to fall asleep – such eccentricity does not challenge social foundations. Eleanor Pargiter may indeed be Woolf's anarchist hero, as Lucio Ruotolo suggests, but her anarchy is private, cerebral, and emotive, posing no threat, undermining no external order.[56]

Of course, anarchy is everywhere in Dostoevsky. In *The Possessed*, the literary fête begins in drunken disorder as an unruly crowd surges through the doors; the "savages" are expecting a free lunch, only to learn that readings of poetry have replaced the meal, news that provokes vociferous displeasure. When the governor and his wife enter, the orchestra fails to produce the expected triumphant march, offering a mocking flourish instead. Scandal escalates when a "hopelessly drunk" Captain Lebyadkin reads a bawdy poem; the figurehead of the celebration, Karmazinov (a parody of Turgenev) declaims an interminable, derivative poem that provokes open hostility from the unkempt audience. Following that embarrassment, Stepan Trofimovitch attacks the pampered young radicals for the "stupidity" of their beliefs. Inevitably, the forces of chaos mount, until the culminating disaster of widespread arson and the murders of Captain Ledyadkin and his sister that evening. Looking back on the day's disasters, the narrator wonders, "How was it that everything, including the police, went wrong that day?"[57] The literary fête offers a comic nightmare of a world in the throes of disintegration, the ultimate product of radical ideology.

Nastasya's birthday party is another quintessential Dostoevskian occasion, a scene of tempestuous disorder with participants who cannot be restrained by social decorum. In this episode, Nastasya's suitors are engaged in a bidding war for her affections, awaiting her promised decision of marriage. Totsky, her guardian–seducer, has arranged for 75,000 rubles to be given to Ganya when the latter marries her, in effect, buying his own freedom to marry General Yepanchin's eldest daughter. Upon a suggestion by the calculatingly depraved Ferdyshenko, the partygoers agree to a most unusual parlor game: each man present must confess his most despicable deed. Though the game is aborted after only three confessions, which all flatter the teller's ego, the travesties set the tone for what follows. As if by whim, Nastasya asks Myshkin if she should marry Ganya; his negative response threatens the mercenary schemes of most of those present. A desperate Rogozhin, accompanied by a dozen ragged, drunken followers, then enters with a last-minute bid of 100,000 rubles wrapped in newspaper. Depressed by the night's sordidness, Nastasya turns against herself, only to be buoyed by Myshkin's frank declaration of love and offer of marriage. The party ends with a spellbinding scene in which Nastasya throws the newspaper-rolled money into the fire, challenging Ganya to degrade himself to fulfill his greed. After his vanity triumphs over avarice, Ganya faints, his body paying the price for a Herculean struggle. Tragically divided, Nastasya runs off with Rogozhin.

In such a world there can be no escape to the leisured exploration of private consciousness. Indeed, private consciousness can only become known in a *public* forum; only in dialogue or dispute can the self become known, and the self is never far removed from public issues. Nastasya's vacillation among suitors, for example, reflects contending views of the world that are vying for supremacy within her; self and other are bound in a Gordian knot. Her party reflects a profound cultural crisis that penetrates every aspect of human behavior and thought, both collective and private.

To defend himself against the charge that he had depicted unrealistic characters in *The Idiot*, Dostoevsky elaborated his aesthetic credo of "fantastic realism" in a letter to A. N. Maikov:

I have a totally different conception of reality and realism than our novelists and critics. My idealism is more real than their realism. God! Just to narrate sensibly what we Russians have lived through in the last ten years of our spiritual development – yes, would not the realists shout that this is fantasy! And yet this is genuine existing realism. This is realism, only deeper; while they swim in the shallow waters . . . Their realism – cannot illuminate a hundredth part of the facts that are real and actually occurring.

This statement, as Joseph Frank points out, reveals "Dostoevsky's own conception of what he was striving to achieve: an illumination of all the heights and depths of the moral crisis of Russian life as he saw it at present."[58]

The sense of crisis affects how the story is told. As readers, we first see events through the perspective of the uninvited Myshkin, but before long we are caught up in the whirlwind of events with no single perspective to guide us.[59] The narration often moves hurriedly to scan the reactions of many participants; it is as if the reader has stepped onto a crowded stage in the midst of a contentious, improvised scene. Because Rogozhin, Nastasya, Myshkin, and others have set themselves free from any inhibiting social rules, either positive or negative, the reader is immersed in an arena where the choices for human action are virtually unlimited and hence impossible to predict. The anarchy that Woolf romanticizes through the thoughts of Eleanor Pargiter and her snoring disregard for convention here represents a serious threat to life.

Dostoevsky's riotous party reflects a conception of the self that challenges Woolf's perspective. Her favorite method as a novelist is to isolate her subject, even in a party's midst, in order to probe the layered complexities of individual consciousness, of private unspoken thoughts. Of course, the interior self is never completely free from the pressures of the other. Mrs. Ramsey's thoughts still suffer from the confinement of Victorian roles; Lily Briscoe cannot mentally flee all the socially determined restrictions of her sex; and Mrs. Dalloway remains imaginatively bound by her middle-class manner. Still, Woolf implies that the self must strive for liberation from the contamination of the other, that we are children of Rousseau who can learn to forge a self radically singular and unrepeatable, that we can hope to break the Promethean chains of society. Nastasya's party, in a sense, shatters Woolf's romantic epistemology of the self because Dostoevsky insists, with post-romantic sociological wisdom, that individuals must be comprehended within the human collective that shapes each person's language, actions, dreams, and desires and that renders dubious any claim of pure originality or any vision of a self immune from the other, any model of wholly private interiority. The crisis of modern life makes a truly private self impossible.

The irrational and frenzied disorder that characterizes Dostoevsky's portrayal of modernity does not give evidence, as Woolf herself assumed, of impaired authorial judgment. Rather, the precipitancy of *The Idiot* and other novels is symptomatic of a world in the midst of apocalyptic crisis that thoroughly permeates all aspects of the form and content. The novel, in Dostoevsky's hands, must strive for a "new word" that would do justice to the moral dissolution of his epoch. It should be the most inclusive of all art forms, for it needs to comprehend the most complex and urgent issues of the day – political, social, moral, and religious – while meeting the exacting, if hard to define, standards of novelistic art. Dostoevsky, one might imagine, would never have been engaged by Woolf's novels because they exclude too much, and they are too far removed from the disorder that characterizes modernity. Yet, in fairness, Woolf was not alone in her judgment that Dostoevsky's very inclusiveness is what seems to lead him beyond the bounds of art. Ultimately, her inability to recognize his artistry can be traced to their radically different expectations of what art can and should include. To her, Dostoevsky's monstrous subject matter prevented the achievement of art. In his view, one may infer, Woolf wrote with the same nostalgic yearning for order and beauty, the same romantic simplification of contemporary turmoil, that characterized two other gentry novelists, Tolstoy and Turgenev.[60] To achieve novelistic poetry, she excluded most of modernity's violent, rude, and graceless chaos – the very subject matter of Dostoevsky's novels.

CHAPTER 4

Sympathy, truth, and artlessness: Arnold Bennett

It is popularly assumed, especially in the United States where few read his novels and fewer still his criticism, that Arnold Bennett deserved what he got. The novelist whose earnings enabled him to keep three residences, a mistress, and a steam yacht has always been an easy target for those who judged him a Philistine in the house of fiction. Ezra Pound caricatured him with savage brilliance in "Hugh Selwyn Mauberly," where Bennett served as the model for Mr. Nixon, who bestows advice on royalties and income and the selling of literature.[1] Virginia Woolf repeatedly attacked Bennett as an obstacle to the liberating experiments of modern fiction, a patriarchal voice of outmoded values and fictional techniques. Her attacks reflect her profound ideological differences with Bennett about the appropriate means of revealing and defining human character. Woolf's tireless and eloquent opposition, however, cannot be separated from her class-bound snobbery: she sought to protect Mrs. Brown from the middle-class vulgarity of Bennett and his Edwardian counterparts. How could a man who stammered with the broad accent of the Potteries (the district in west-central England named for its manufactured products), whose thick lips, coarse presence, and daily word counts gave evidence of his "shopkeeper's view of literature," be expected to appreciate the subtle, anarchic movements of conscious-ness?[2] Mrs. Brown, in such hands, would never be freed from the unimaginative restrictions of her class.[3]

Those who seek evidence of Bennett's mercantile values and literary compromises will not be disappointed. By his own admission, the man who once called himself an "engine for the production of fiction" wrote plays for money alone. Bennett was the best-paid writer and reviewer of his age because of his shrewd contract negotiations and his equally shrewd sense of what an audience would like. He lived lavishly well, dressed in the finest lace shirts, drove a Rolls Royce, and became the most visible literary figure in London. So powerful was the lure of his celebrity that people often stopped and stared when he walked the streets. His popularity was aided, no doubt, by the use of his name on London billboards to sell papers. With seemingly little effort, he could change gears from serious creative effort to popular dross. The bibliography of his works includes practical philosophies (*How to Live on Twenty-Four Hours a Day, How to Make the Best of Life*, etc.); plays; works of commercial advice (*Journalism for Women* and *How to Become an Author*); and serious novels. He apparently saw no contradictions among his various roles, as evidenced by his question to a magazine editor: "Do you want me to do my best and most serious work, or do you want me to adopt a popular standard?"[4]

While Bennett may be justly criticized for his Edwardian limitations, he was by no means typical of his age. Bennett's best fiction, such as *The Old Wives' Tale* (1908) and *Clayhanger* (1910), combines a sensitive rendering of small-town English life – the subtle nuances of his sense of place can be profitably compared to the works of Hardy and Lawrence – with a French concern for novelistic structure and technique derived from his readings of Balzac and Maupassant. His most successful work revolves around mundane characters, a world of shopkeepers and matrons circumscribed by the slowly moving patterns of habit, propriety, and social convention, all subject to the erosions of time. Bennett cared passionately about his subject and its literary form, and he succeeded in creating some enduring works of art. As a critic, his literary and artistic tastes were cosmopolitan and catholic, his judgment of new talent often uncanny (ranging from Gide to Hemingway, Dreiser to Evelyn Waugh), and his defense of artistic freedom in the face of England's stifling and archaic censorship laws admirable and even courageous. In the words of his most capable critic, Samuel Hynes:

Like James and Conrad and Ford he was a "good European" in a time of English insularity; he lived for several years in France (*The Old Wives' Tale* was conceived in Paris and written near Fontainebleau), married a French wife, and had a wide acquaintance among French intellectuals, including Gide and Ravel. His knowledge of modern French writing, painting, and music was extensive, and his responsiveness to new movements was quick and generous. In all this (except perhaps the wife) he was very much the Edwardian avant-garde artist.

He not only wrote major novels; he worked for "three decades," according to Hynes, as "the best literary journalist in London."[5]

Bennett in his role as journalist did more to promote Dostoevsky's works in England than anyone else, with the possible exception of the translator Constance Garnett. He insistently pushed for the publication of a complete Dostoevsky, even naming the desired translator and publishing house, at a time when virtually none of his works were available. He wrote frequently and avidly of Dostoevsky's merits in a span that covered more than twenty years (1910–31), and he raised his works as the standard by which books old and new could be judged. Bennett helped to "Europeanize" English reading habits and spurred the educated public to pay serious attention to Dostoevsky and his fellow Russians, Tolstoy, Turgenev, Gogol, and Chekhov. Throughout his career he advocated the merits of Continental novels – Russian, French, German, Italian, and others – often at the expense of English novels. And the greatest novelist of all the Europeans was Dostoevsky.

Unfortunately, Bennett's advocacy eventually became inseparable from the dispute with modernism that characterized his later criticism. Dostoevsky and other Russians were used as weapons against modernist writers, such as Woolf and Joyce, whom Bennett regarded as proponents of a sterile preoccupation with artistic form. In his earlier essays on Dostoevsky, Bennett viewed him as working within the traditions of the European novel. In fact, he was the only major English novelist of his age who placed Dostoevsky squarely within such traditions, though he always judged him a flawed artist. Bennett's later essays, however, removed Dostoevsky from the realm of literary art, insisting that his works were on the side of "morality" and "life." Bennett retreated to an oversimplified life-versus-art dichotomy as a means of defending himself against Woolf's attacks. But his choice of position had unfortunate consequences, for Bennett used his position as the most powerful reviewer of his age as a pulpit to sound virtues that have little to do with the Russian writer's artistic and moral vision. In the end, Bennett distorted Dostoevsky just as thoroughly as Lawrence and Woolf did.

BENNETT AS PUBLICIST FOR TRANSLATION (1899–1911)

The first stage of Bennett's response to Dostoevsky needs to be understood in terms of his role as an opponent of English cultural insularity. His earliest comments on Russian literature dealt with Turgenev, not Dostoevsky, but they are useful because they show Bennett's commitment to translation and his concern for art. His comments appear in one of his first publications, an essay entitled "Ivan Turgenev" (1899). Bennett praises the novelist for his stylistic control and craftsmanship: "What Ibsen did for European drama, Turgenev did for European fiction; he uttered the last word of pure artistry."[6] The essay shows Bennett's familiarity with the entire range of Turgenev's works, as well as his knowledge of the major French critical works about him. Bennett notes the quality of the English translations that were produced by Constance Garnett and compares them favorably to the French translations supervised by Turgenev himself. He reveals himself to be a strong proponent of translation who saw such efforts as a means of overcoming English provincialism: "The decade now drawing to a close has been rather remarkable for newly translated and worthily produced editions of great foreign novelists. We have had Dumas, Balzac, Victor Hugo, Björnson, and d'Annunzio."[7]

Bennett maintained a lifelong interest in issues of the literary marketplace. In a 1909 essay, "The novel reading public," he severely criticized the English literary climate, lambasting the scarce availability of good books and the limited audience for serious literature. Too often, he complained, the English middle class allowed respectability and sentimentality to pass for "literary merit." The reading public was typically indifferent or hostile to true literary art, for such art often undermined comfortable middle-class assumptions.[8] As a result, English literature tended to be long on entertainment and short on art. In a 1910 review, Bennett praised Sturge Moore's *Art and Life* for leading the English away from their stifling traditions. Moore's value, in Bennett's judgment, "is that he could make the English artist a conscious artist." Implicitly, Moore unmasks in "the most startling way the contrast between . . . the English artist and the Continental artist," exemplified by the difference between Flaubert's correspondence, with its continual attention to literary craft, and the correspondence of Dickens and Thackeray. The reviewer complains that he has "been preaching on this theme for years" and insists that he "shall continue."[9]

One week after his Sturge Moore essay, Bennett again had an opportunity to advance literary art in his *New Age* column (31 March 1910), this time by reviewing Maurice Baring's *Landmarks in Russian Literature*, a popular introduction to Russian literature, written by an Englishman who knew the language and the people. The historical importance of Baring's study lies in its emphasis on Dostoevsky. "About half of the book," as the review notes, "is given to a detailed, straightforward, homely account of Dostoevsky, his character, genius, and works."

Bennett praises the book as a means of furthering interest in Dostoevsky. Towards that end, he recounts his own experience with his works:

I thought I had read all the chief works of the five great Russian novelists, but last year I came across one of Dostoevsky's, *The Brothers Karamazov*, of which I had not heard. It was a French translation, in two thick volumes. I thought it contained some of the greatest scenes that I had ever encountered in fiction, and I at once classed it with Stendhal's *Chartreuse de Parme* and Dostoevsky's *Crime and Punishment* as one of the supreme marvels of the world.

Like Woolf and Lawrence, Bennett first read Dostoevsky in French, but his early interest was apparently even stronger than theirs, and he completed his readings of the novels before the Garnett translations were available.

Bennett's review judges him as a great but flawed writer, a masterful dramatist and seer into the human soul whose novels lacked form, perfection, and "exquisite soft beauty." The famous scene of the Karamazovs' visit to Zossima's cell is cited as an example of Dostoevsky's unparalleled power: "These pages are unique. They reach the highest and most terrible pathos that art has ever reached. And if an author's reputation among people of taste depended solely on his success with single scenes, Dostoevsky would outrank all other novelists, if not poets." But Dostoevsky could not, in Bennett's judgment, extend his mastery of single scenes to a mastery of an entire novel. His "works – all of them – have grave faults. They have especially the grave fault of imperfection, that fault which Turgenev and Flaubert avoided." As a result, the novels are "tremendously unlevel, badly constructed, both in large outline and in detail."

Bennett follows a line of reasoning first popularized by Melchior de Vogüé in France and finds in the Russian writer a Christ-like sympathy for humanity. Dostoevsky's stature as a novelist is achieved, in large part, because of the combination of his moral virtues with his tragic vision. According to Bennett, "nobody, perhaps, ever understood and sympathized with human nature as Dostoevsky did": "Indubitably, nobody ever with the help of God and good luck ever swooped so high into tragic grandeur." Yet Dostoevsky, as an author, "had fearful falls": "He could not trust his wings. He is an adorable, a magnificent, and a profoundly sad figure in letters. He was anything you like. But he could not compass the calm and exquisite soft beauty of *On the Eve* or *A House of Gentlefolk*." Assuming an attitude that had become commonplace in France, Bennett explains Dostoevsky's deficiencies in terms of the extraordinary pressures under which he worked. As both a human being and a novelist, the Russian author is to be loved and pitied.

At the end of his review, Bennett makes a request of great significance: "And now, Mr. Heinemann, when are we going to have a complete Dostoevsky in English?"[10] Heinemann was the publisher who had been responsible for the complete translations of Turgenev published in the 1890s; on the basis of the quality of those translations Bennett chose him as the most appropriate publisher for Dostoevsky.

Within three months after his call for translation, Bennett compared his own fiction to Dostoevsky's while working on *Clayhanger*, a novel that was to become one of his most acclaimed. On 12 June 1910, he noted with workmanlike honesty: "Yesterday, wrote complete chapter of *Clayhanger*, 2,400 words. But I had to work at the thing practically all day. I finished about 5:30 after 12 hours off and on. I really doubt whether, as a whole, the book is good. It assuredly isn't within 10 miles of Dostoevsky."[11] Like Virginia Woolf, Bennett used Dostoevsky to measure his own value.

As a novelist Bennett never tried to respond creatively to Dostoevsky, perhaps because he realized that his own strengths were incompatible with the psychological intensity and pressurized narrative condensation achieved by his Russian counterpart. Dostoevsky's novels typically focus on a few pivotal days, where temperaments and ideologies collide with explosive force; Bennett's finest productions, in contrast, reflect the slow rhythms of provincial life. The characters in *Clayhanger*, for example, lead unremarkable lives; they endure the loss of their dreams and the confining routines of their life, seldom giving voice to great passions, heroic visions, or violent controversies. Edwin Clayhanger, the central character, dutifully abandons his youthful hope of becoming an architect to take the reins of his father's printing business. He is rendered a victim of time's unending toll; like his oldest sister Maggie, a spinsterish soul of great patience, his life is a minor triumph of endurance. In *The Old Wives' Tale*, Constance Povey, facing death, tallies her own life: "She was not discontented with herself. The invincible common sense of a sound nature prevented her, in her best moments, from feebly dissolving in self-pity. She had lived in honesty and kindliness for a fair number of years, and she had tasted triumphant hours." Though Constance "had many dissatisfactions," including the premature death of her husband and a thirty-year separation from her beloved sister, "she rose superior to them." "When she surveyed her life, and life in general, she would think, with a sort of tart but not sour cheerfulness: *'Well, that is what life is!'*"[12]

Bennett at his best wrote with great compassion and understanding, the two qualities that he admired most in Dostoevsky, about ordinary people in ordinary circumstances. Even in the midst of extraordinary events, such as the Siege of Paris and the murder of Daniel Povey's wife in *The Old Wives' Tale*, Bennett's characters keep a steadfast eye on the exigencies of the routine. Constance's sister, Sophia Baines, frets about rising prices in Paris: "If she did not sleep well, it was not because of distant guns, but because of her preoccupation with finance."[13] When confronting the corpse of his cousin's wife, Samuel Povey can only see her alcoholic disarray. He is not so much disturbed by Daniel's desperate act as he is by the knowledge that a wife and mother has failed to meet her responsibilities. Even in death, "She was vile. Her scanty yellow-gray hair was dirty, her hollowed neck all grime, her hands abominable, her black dress in decay. She was the dishonour of her sex, her situation, and her years. She was a fouler obscenity than Samuel had ever conceived."[14] In such fashion, Bennett's fiction gives voice to the shopkeeper who insists that all daily rounds be met and the landlady who refuses to let a war interfere with the business of providing supper. Ironically, Bennett is joined with his rival Virginia Woolf in the valorization of uneventful lives, especially the domestic lives of women.

In February of 1911, nearly a year after the Baring review, Bennett's call for translation had not yet been answered, prompting him to use his *New Age* column more forcefully to shame the London publishers into action. He began by reviewing the major Russian translations that had been completed to date: "We now have an admirable though incomplete Tolstoy in English. We also have an admirable and complete Turgenev . . . [and] two volumes of Chekhov." All of which pointed to Dostoevsky, "the crying need of the day, in the translation department." Bennett's admiration for Russian fiction seems to have grown in the interim, for he now finds it to be "the greatest fiction in the world."

He reiterates his praise – "I cannot too often repeat that the finest scenes in all fiction are to be found in Dostoevsky's novels" – but this time he offers a practical, trans-Atlantic publishing scheme: "I do not suggest that there would be a great deal of money in a complete Dostoevsky. But I do suggest that, in collaboration with a publisher in the United States, it might be done without loss, and that it ought to be done; and that it is the duty of one or other of our publishers to commission Mrs. Garnett to do it." Bennett's moral argument on behalf of translation even takes a satirical turn. Where previously he concluded with a gentlemanly request, he now mocks the scandalous irresponsibility of English publishers. If one of Bennett's wealthy publishers can afford to keep "twenty gardeners," "it is a complete scandal that there should exist no complete good English version of Dostoevsky."[15]

Bennett again refers to Dostoevsky in a column written in March of the same year, while commenting on the work of the French novelist Marguerite Audoux. His column gives the following report of an interview he had with her: "It was my reference to Dostoevsky that first started her talking. In all literary conversations Dostoevsky is my King Charles's head [a reference presumably to the comic preoccupation of the mad Mr. Dick in *David Copperfield*] . . . She had read Dostoevsky and was well minded to share my enthusiasms. Indeed, Dostoevsky drew her out of her arm-chair and right across the room. We were soon discussing methods of work."[16] Even in conversation, Bennett used the Russian novelist as an instrument for measuring literary value.

Later that month, he returned to Dostoevsky in his *New Age* column, announcing Heinemann's plan to publish Constance Garnett's translations. While disclaiming any influence in the decision, Bennett takes obvious delight in his role as agitator: "I feel like a social reformer who has actually got something done." Viewing the impending translations as a great boon to English novelists, he hopes that Dostoevsky will expand English literary horizons: "And those English writers who cannot read Russian and who are too idle or too insular to read either French or German, will at last have an opportunity of studying the greatest scenes in fiction written by anybody. I hope they will profit by the opportunity." Continuing his role as publicist, he identifies those writers as the appropriate buying public: "If all the well-intentioned novelists in England buy the new edition of Dostoevsky, the success of Mr. Heinemann's venture is assured."

Bennett's column can be seen as an attempt to secure a market for Heinemann's books. The publisher's plan for a complete Dostoevsky was contingent upon the sales of the first six volumes to be released: a two-volume edition of *The Brothers Karamazov*, *Crime and Punishment*, *The Idiot*, *The Possessed*, and a combined edition of *The House of the Dead* and *The Insulted and Injured*. The remaining works, according to Bennett, would only be published if the series met with financial success. Indeed the prospects were so uncertain that Constance Garnett felt compelled to agree to a flat rate instead of the usual royalty arrangement. Perhaps because so much depended upon the sales of Dostoevsky's first six texts, Bennett makes virtually no comments here about the author's failings. With an advertiser's enthusiasm, he ranks *The Brothers Karamazov* with

Stendhal's *Chartreuse de Parme*, a work which would be familiar to many of his *New Age* readers, as "the most heroical novel in European literature." Dostoevsky's work is praised for containing "about a dozen absolutely colossal figures. It is fiction raised to the highest power." While Bennett admits that "Stendhal is perhaps more even and more easily comprehensible and more urbane," he insists that "Dostoevsky goes deeper and rises higher."

In Bennett's view, success is imminent. He promises that the audience will experience "a tremendous sensation" in reading *The House of the Dead* and *The Possessed*, confidently predicting a surge of interest in Dostoevsky, who "will soon loom much larger in the literary heavens than he presently does. His turn is emphatically coming."[17] These are the words of a man who had a masterful sense of England's literary market and who realized the limitations of unread or unpublished art. In this column, the two sides of Bennett's personality converge. As a creative writer he supported the cause of a fellow artist; as a literary businessman he adeptly promoted that cause, knowing that business interests would largely determine the fate of Dostoevsky in England.

CHANGING FICTIONAL VALUES (1912–1920)

During the years in which the Garnett translations were released, 1912 to 1920, Bennett did not have as much to say about Dostoevsky as one might expect. Most likely, this can be explained by his relative inactivity as a reviewer during this period and the wartime hiatus of his literary efforts. It should also be noted that Dostoevsky no longer needed a publicist; Heinemann's venture succeeded beyond expectations, achieving sales that ensured the completion of Garnett's translating efforts. Yet Bennett's comments reveal the consistent hold that Dostoevsky exerted over his literary thought. His 1913 essay, "The author's craft," helps to place Dostoevsky within the context of Bennett's own fictional values. His other comments show that he continued to celebrate Dostoevsky as a standard of literary merit. Evidence also points, however, to Bennett's changing literary values and his gradual disengagement of Dostoevsky from considerations of novelistic art.

"The author's craft" represents the most coherent statement of Bennett's literary principles and indirectly contributes to an understanding of his fascination with Dostoevsky. Like the famous version of Woolf's "Mrs. Brown" essay, Bennett begins with an anecdote to illustrate the difficulties of fiction writing. He imagines a street scene involving action and sentiment: a motor bus accident that kills a puppy and the subsequent crowd scene, complete with a man in brass buttons, a policeman, a puppy-loving boy, and others. Enlarging on this accident to address the author's role, Bennett prefigures Woolf's comments about Mrs. Brown: "The one condition is that the observer must never lose sight of the fact that what he is trying to see is life, is the woman next door, is the man on the train – and not a course of abstractions. To appreciate this is the first inspiring preliminary to sound observation."[18] Observation may be the starting point of fiction, but it is not simply, despite Woolf's later charges, a focus on material details: "You have looked at the tens of thousands of policemen, and perhaps never seen the hundredth part of the reality of a single one. Your imagination has not truly worked on the phenomenon."[19]

Though Bennett strikes some of the same chords later sounded by Woolf, the dissimilarities are far more apparent. Woolf freely admits that her attempts to reveal the true character of Mrs. Brown are impeded by the difficulty of deciphering the abundant and incongruous details of her presence, as well as by the difficulty of drawing a clear distinction between the object of perception (Mrs. Brown) and the subject (Woolf herself). Her narrative, as a result, is clouded by doubt and indeterminacy, guesswork and conjecture. Mrs. Brown's reality, an emblem of all human identity, must be recognized as always more complex, mysterious, and mutable than the language that can describe it. All narrative techniques, Woolf insists, must be derived from the complex reality of the human subject rather than the needs of the narrator or the reader for order, coherence, and clarity. Bennett, however, operates with more conventional and confident assumptions. As an author–observer, he scans the external world for its unambiguous and indisputable evidence of internal realities. He assumes that careful, imaginative observation will reveal unassailable truth about his subject, and, unlike Woolf, recognizes no doubt or impediments to narrative knowledge. The author maintains a privileged epistemological position. He or she can know all that is essential in a character and fully communicate that knowledge to the reader.

"The author's craft" lists the requirements of an author's worldly education, all of which are designed to improve the writer's observational skills. A writer, in Bennett's view, first needs to observe geographical conditions. To understand an English inhabitant, for example, one needs to be cognizant of the nation's island topography. The writer also needs to observe roads and architecture, for such material constructs provide insight into character: "every street is a mirror, an illustration, an exposition, an explanation, of the human beings who live in it. Everything in it is valuable, if the perspective is maintained."[20] Like Balzac, his hero, Bennett assumes a natural symmetry between external and internal realities. One can often know Bennett's characters simply by knowing where they live and how they surround themselves. His drawing rooms and shops reveal as much about their inhabitants as Balzac's descriptions of the Maison Vauquer in *Père Goriot.* Samuel Povey, the embodiment of capitalist enterprise, can be defined by the huge signboard boldly erected to identify his draper's business. The miserly bookseller, Henry Earlforward, the protagonist in *Riceyman Steps,* can likewise be defined by his choice of a wedding present for his spouse – a safe. The romantic and dreamy nature of Hilda Lessways can be easily discerned from the book given the most prominence on her bookshelf, Tennyson's *Maud,* for her "a source of lovely and exquisite pain."[21]

The artifacts and abodes of human life are crucial for Bennett because they disclose our innermost realities. Even a Victorian factory, if penetrated by a skillful writer, can manifest essential truths. Bennett's own description of Henry Mynor's pottery works in *Anna of the Five Towns* (1902) illustrates his aesthetic assumptions. The workshop perfectly reflects Henry's shrewd managerial character and his utilitarian values: "He found his satisfaction in honestly meeting public taste. He was born to be a manufacturer of cheap goods on a colossal scale." In such a place, the transmutation of clay becomes a celebration of human labor: "One instant the clay was an amorphous mass, the next it was a vessel perfectly circular . . . the flat and apparently clumsy fingers of the craftsman had seemed to lose themselves in the clay for a fraction of time and the miracle was accomplished." The factory's efficient operations impose a rational unity on the stray stuff of the world: "Neither time nor space nor material was wasted." When Anna first sees the warehouse, she is overwhelmed by the magnitude of the final product, "the total and final achievement towards which the thousands of small, disjointed efforts . . . were directed." For better or worse, the pottery works, in all of its material activities, proclaims the values of the Five Towns: efficiency, profit, and pride in one's labor.[22]

For the novelist, that most astute and sympathetic observer, the world comes equipped with remarkably clear mirrors. And the clearest mirror of all, according to Bennett, can be found in the human face. The author–observer can learn all he needs to know about the people of London simply by walking the streets and studying the faces. Of course, Bennett is never content to limit his observations; the London *flâneur* should take in as much as possible if he is to make sense of the inhabitants: "It is true that the face is a reflection of the soul. It is equally true that the carriage and gestures are the reflection of the soul."[23]

Bennett's essay proposes three standards of novelistic construction that all focus on a novel's effect upon its readers. First, the novel must have a clear center of attention: "a novel must have one, two, or three figures that easily overtop the rest. These figures must be in the foreground, and the rest in the middle-distance or in the back-ground." Second, a novel must have sympathetic leading characters: "These figures – whether they are saints or sinners – must somehow be presented more sympathetically than the others." Finally, "the interest must be maintained," by which he means "the interest of the story itself, and not the continual play of the author's mind."[24] Bennett's traditional standards can be applied to many kinds of novelists, from Fielding to Tolstoy, Richardson to Flaubert. According to what Bennett has to say elsewhere, Dostoevsky met all three standards but found his greatest success in the creation of sympathetic characters. His works are to be valued because they represent the culmination of the novel's traditions.

Dostoevsky's greatness, however, cannot be explained by adherence to principles of novelistic construction. Indeed, in "The author's craft" Bennett once again notes failed craftsmanship: "What a hasty, amorphous lump of gold is the sublime, the unapproachable *Brothers Karamazov*! Any tutor in a college for teaching the whole art of fiction in twelve lessons could show where Dostoevsky was clumsy and careless." Presumably, Dostoevsky's greatness can only be explained by the expansiveness of his sympathies and the compelling interest of his stories. As if to defend his favorite, Bennett downgrades the importance of technique: "With the single exception of Turgenev, the great novelists of the world, according to my own standards, have either ignored technique or have failed to understand it."[25]

Bennett offers more detailed comments on Dostoevsky in his 1916 essay "Some adventures among Russian fiction," which provides a capsulated history of his encounters with Russian literature. It begins with his praise of the translating efforts of Mrs. Garnett: "honest, courageous, and capable translators have begun to appear; at any rate one has appeared, and the glory [of Russian fiction] is seen more brightly." Bennett goes on to recount his first encounter with Russian literature in the pre-Garnett days of the early 1890s, when he read an unremarkable English translation of some Dostoevsky short works: "That he was a novelist of the first rank assuredly did not occur to me . . . I dropped Dostoevsky, and thought no more of him for many years." His appreciation of Russian literature was revitalized by his reading of *War and Peace*, though it is not clear whether he read that novel in an English or a French translation. Then came his reading of Turgenev, through the translations of Constance Garnett, in the midst of the "Turgenev vogue" around the turn of the century.

On the Eve was, for eager young Englishmen of letters [such as Bennett himself], the greatest novel ever written, and Bazarov, in *Fathers and Children*, the most typical character ever created by a novelist . . . We knew the Russians put Dostoevsky first and Turgenev third of the three, but we had no hesitation in deciding that the Russians did not thoroughly understand their own literature and that we did.

Like so many of his contemporaries, Bennett regarded Turgenev as the master craftsman of the novel.

The English writer's "perusal of *The Brothers Karamazov* in French – there was no English translation" – left him a "changed man." He judged the novel, "even in its shorn and unfaithful French version," as "both more true and more romantic than any other whatsoever." Unfortunately, Bennett's essay proceeds to formulate a simplistic defense of Dostoevsky's failed craftsmanship. If Stendhal "cured [Bennett] and many others of Flaubertism," Dostoevsky served as an antidote to "Turgenevism." Both writers "were free of that perverse self-consciousness of the artist which at bottom is the cover for a lack of inspiration and of interest in life itself. Both were too far interested in life to be unduly interested in art." Bennett now wholeheartedly pushes Dostoevsky away from all conventions of novelistic art.

He creates a vivid portrait of a primitive and virtuous storyteller, a noble savage among novelists. Such a portrait has only one flaw – it contains no truth.

Dostoevsky in particular wrote hurriedly; he tumbled the stuff out of himself pell-mell. He excelled in sheer impressiveness because he had a more universal and authentic sympathy and deeper comprehension of human nature than anybody else. *Dostoevsky abhorred artifice, if he ever thought about artifice.* He never tried for effects. He did not know what it was to be "literary." He wrote novels as if he was eagerly talking to you, neither artlessly nor artfully, but in full bursting possession of his subject. Some novelists perform as though they were conjurers in evening-dress. *Dostoevsky worked like a skilled workman with his sleeves rolled up and his hairy forearms showing.* Or he may be likened to a master of a great sailing ship. He will bring a novel safely to a climax and close amid terrific stresses as a Scotch captain rounds Cape Horn in a gale – and you are on board! (Emphasis mine)[26]

There is something painfully cheap about Bennett's facile characterization, as if he were trying to create from the spinning of his populist imagination a working-class hero as novelist, one who came from the uncultured hinterlands bearing the coarse marks of his heritage, not unlike Bennett himself. His fictionalized portrait may have stimulated innocent musings about a romantically primitive Dostoevsky, but it also set up a regretfully simple dichotomy between "art" and "life" that typified much of Bennett's later responses to Dostoevsky as well as a good deal of the dispute that was to emerge between Bennett and Woolf.[27]

Ironically, his next known reference to Dostoevsky raises him as a standard of civility and high culture. In recording his impressions of Elizabeth Asquith in a journal entry of 13 May 1917, he notes her "deep ignorance of literature": "she didn't know that the French translations of Dostoevsky are incomplete and the English ones complete." Asquith had committed the egregious faux pas of reading the Russian novelist in French, and, for this reason, she could not be taken seriously.[28]

Despite Bennett's depiction of Dostoevsky in rolled shirtsleeves, with hairy forearms and a mystic obliviousness to art, he continued to use him as a standard of excellence. While writing to the young novelist Frank Swinnerton, he notes, in a moment of self-criticism, the only failing of his recent novel: "I think the emotional power might have been stronger . . . This is of course to apply the highest standard to my book, by which I mean the Dostoevsky or Balzac standard."[29] In his correspondence with André Gide, Dostoevsky is mentioned as a shared measure of excellence. Bennett discusses his own inadequacies as a novelist in a 1920 letter to Gide, where he notes that "the greatest difficulty is to write the truth. It always escapes." While Bennett takes pride in having "learned something about construction and . . . ornamentation," which he "could have taught both Dostoevsky and Stendhal," he realizes that "these two men had a faculty of getting so near the truth, and getting there beautifully, that I always say to myself when reading them: No! I could never do anything equal to that."[30] The "truth" of Dostoevsky and Stendhal is presumably a truth of human life, not novelistic art. Perhaps the post-war decline in the quality of

Bennett's work, a decline widely acknowledged, can be attributed to his reductive separation of art from life.

BENNETT AS MORALISTIC ADVOCATE, 1921–1931

The last stage of Bennett's response centers around his friendship and support for André Gide and his literary essays for London's *Evening Standard* newspaper. In the history of Bennett's "Books and persons" articles, one can trace the movement of his literary reputation. In the first phase of columns, 1908 to 1911, Bennett's column appeared in the *New Age*, a periodical under the leadership of the remarkable A. R. Orage that often represented the cutting edge of modernism in England's literary and cultural life. In the second phase of his columns, 1926 to 1931, the column appeared in a mass circulation newspaper, the *Evening Standard*. Though Bennett commanded a readership of far greater numbers in the second phase, his influence and standing among London's literary elite, especially those writers who came into prominence after the war, had fallen precipitously.

During these years, Bennett maintained enormous popularity as a novelist, playwright, and reviewer. The "good European" who had defended modernist literature and art and chastised English insularity now found himself subject to attacks from the younger generation. His opinions no longer swayed the most talented writers. In the post-war world of London, the voices of Woolf, Eliot, Joyce, and others made Bennett appear to be an old-fashioned writer, an anachronism who was too willing to compromise with public taste, too eager to display the materialistic rewards of his labor. Bennett's literary power base now resided in the same middle class that he had once criticized for lack of taste. His advocacy of Dostoevsky during the last years of his life reflects the moralistic values and resistance to artistic innovation of that class.

In 1923 Bennett read a book of essays about Dostoevsky that his friend Gide had written in France. Eventually the English writer managed to have the work translated and published in his own country. Though interest in Dostoevsky had not ebbed in France since the 1880s, Gide's essays are notable for their modern, post-Nietzsche slant, a far remove from Vogüé's essays of the 1880s. Gide is drawn to Dostoevsky's presentation of the contradictions and discords within the self: "each character never relinquishes consciousness of his dual personality with its inconsistencies."[31] He reads the Russian writer in terms of Nietzsche, though he is astute enough to recognize their many differences: "Nietzsche advocates the affirmation of personality . . . Dostoevsky postulates its surrender. Nietzsche presupposes the heights of achievement where Dostoevsky prophesizes utter ruin."[32] Where Vogüé approached the novels through the conventional beliefs of Christianity, Gide takes a more Blakean direction, with Dostoevsky seen as a proponent of energy, delight, and contraries, a romantic prophet of affirmation and eternity-in-a-moment.

In Gide's view, Kirillov from *The Possessed* is an exponent of Dostoevsky's religious philosophy. The young man commits suicide to test his theory that his death will usher in a new era of human freedom. By dying, Kirillov, a triumph of Feuerbach's atheistic humanism, hopes to deify himself in a move that will free human beings from dependence on the transcendent, giving birth to the Man-God. What Gide admires here is the renunciation of the self for the good of humanity, even though he recognizes in Kirillov a "moral bankruptcy," presumably because the romantic youth is so thoroughly duped by the radicals who plan to exploit his death in the cause of destruction.

In a 1923 letter, Bennett offers praise, mixed with regret that Gide is silent about matters of technique: "Your book on Dostoevsky (for which many thanks) has made a very considerable impression upon me. And yet you say almost nothing about his technique, which interests me considerably . . . (If he had any technique!) Of course Dostoevsky is *your* author. His moral foundations suit yours." The letter informs Gide that Bennett has already "suggested to Chatto and Windus that your book ought to appear in English," because "it is by far the best thing on Dostoevsky I ever read."[33] Bennett's effort to have Gide's work translated finally met with success in 1925 when J. M. Dent published a translation, with an introduction by Bennett himself. Here, Bennett makes a tantalizingly vague claim about the foundation of their friendship: "I first met Gide in the immense field of Dostoevsky. He said, and I agreed, that *The Brothers Karamazov* was the greatest novel ever written."[34]

Bennett's introduction promotes both Gide and Dostoevsky. He favorably compares the French writer, whose own novels did not find decent English translations until the publication of Dorothy Bussy's works starting in 1927, to Balzac, Maupassant, Paul Bourget, and Zola for his "moral basis": "scarcely one of his books . . . but poses and attempts to resolve a moral problem." In Bennett's judgment, "it was natural and even necessary that such a writer as Gide should deal with such a writer as Dostoevsky. They were made for each other." The introduction lavishly praises Gide's critical study, judging it as far

superior to that of Melchior de Vogüé. The French count had praised
Dostoevsky for his compassion and moral insight, regarding him as a
psychologist of the abnormal, a night laborer in the fields of fiction who
portrayed only dismal and mangled souls. Gide's work exonerates
Dostoevsky from charges of morbidity and for this earns Bennett's
admiration: "All the conventional charges against the greatest of the
Russians – morbidity, etc. etc., fall to pieces during perusal. They are
not killed; they merely expire."[35]

It is difficult to understand how the author of *The Old Wives' Tale* and
the author of *L'Immoraliste* could have found agreement in their respective readings. Bennett's Dostoevsky is a Christ-like hero, protected by an
indefatigable morality from the swirling tides of passion and contradiction. He maintains his purity and sympathy in the midst of the world's
corruption, and his Christian beliefs would not be likely to offend a
vicar. Gide envisions a Dostoevsky who could thrive only by preserving
the "discordant elements" and "extraordinary wealth of antagonisms"
within himself. Though he sees the Russian novelist as humbling himself
before Christ, his view of the submission owes more to an artist's need to
overcome self-torment by self-denial and surrender to a higher power
than it does to Christian humility.[36] For Gide, Dostoevsky's religion
serves as a cathartic means of self-preservation, having little connection
to traditional beliefs. Bennett apparently never commented on such
differences or even acknowledged their existence.

Despite the opposing content of their views, Bennett and Gide both
assumed Dostoevsky to be incapable of irony. They believed that he
simply poured his own views into his works, largely oblivious to formal
concerns of art. The two friends shared an attraction to the vision of life
that they discerned in the novels, even though the visions they found
seem mutually exclusive. Bennett, like Gide, regarded Dostoevsky as a
moral teacher and exemplum. His introduction concludes by advising
the reader to turn to Dostoevsky for "his humanity and his wisdom,"
which is "derived from the man Jesus who delivered the Sermon on the
Mount."[37]

Bennett returned to the topic of Russian literature in a 1927 "Books
and Persons" essay written for the *Evening Standard*, entitled "The 'cowardice' of Thackeray." According to Bennett, Thackeray stands as a
representative English novelist who could not squarely face the most
difficult issues of life. Though in *Vanity Fair* he often veers towards a
situation "whose solution will demand honesty and bravery," he always
"curves away from it, or he stops dead" because of a cowardly fear.

"Perhaps his cowardice springs from a good motive – his fear of disgusting you with human nature. But he is a coward all the same."

As a corrective, Bennett advises English readers to study the merits of the Russian novelists, who "handsomely excel in the best sort of realism – namely the realism which is combined with a comprehending charity of judgment." He also praises the heroic stature of their works, which he traces to their absorbing interest in "individual psychology." Again, Bennett frames his analysis in dualistic terms. "Unquestionably deficient" in "artistic discipline," the Russian novelists "appear to despise form – except Turgenev, who could assuredly have taught even Henry James how to 'organise' a novel;" "The Russians as a rule are far too prodigal and far too excited about the particular page which they happen to be writing, to the neglect of the main outline of the work." But once artistic expectations are put aside, the reader will discover in their works essential truths about human life.

Bennett, echoing the judgments of Vogüé before him, favorably compares the Russians with the realism of Zola, who is blamed for his lack of "sympathy." He contrasts the French naturalist's clinical morbidity, his "certain chill, disillusioned hostility toward human nature," with the Russians who "are more generally sympathetic" and "are not frightened by any manifestation of human nature, as, for example, Thackeray was." Their fiction may focus on unseemly events, but the authors "have no qualms about disgusting you with human nature, for they are not themselves disgusted with it." Bennett values their fiction for its moral effect: "They understand; they forgive; they love. They compel you to do the same. There is a Christ-like quality in the finest Russian fiction."[38]

In Bennett's portrait, such novelists emerge as unwashed and unlearned monks. It is sadly ironic that a man with such broad knowledge of English and French novels no longer seemed capable of detecting echoes of those traditions in Russian literature. Bennett became so enamored with the moral lessons of Russian literature that he became blinded to its similarities and debts to Western traditions. He helped to perpetuate a stereotype that still persists today, one that portrays the Russians as primitive icons whose power and truth is solely derived from non-literary sources, a stereotype that invites readers to expect no ironies or literary complexities from their texts.

The essay continued with a second part published one week later, boldly entitled "The twelve finest novels." Bennett had often alluded to his judgment that the twelve best novels were Russian, first on a lecture tour in New York and subsequently in claims made in the *Evening Standard* columns. Now he supports his claims. *The Brothers Karamazov* is ranked first, with the "lovely" *Idiot* placed second: "its closing pages are the summit of simple majesty." In third place, one finds the "still lovelier" *House of the Dead*, which Bennett, like many of his generation, read as strictly autobiographical: "It is, in my opinion, the most celestial restorative of damaged faith in human nature that any artist ever produced. The most successful and touching demonstration of the truth that man is not vile." Bennett's praise is noteworthy because few of his contemporaries showed interest in *The House of the Dead*, and no other novelist bothered to comment about it, though critics now regard it as one of Dostoevsky's finer creations. Finally, Bennett ranks *Crime and Punishment* as the world's fourth best, "a novel which cannot possibly be omitted from the dozen."

What interests Bennett is the vision of life presented. He focuses on the character of the author himself, as one might focus on a Socrates, Confucius, Jesus Christ, or other moral teacher: "The objectors to Dostoevsky say that he was an epileptic. Well, he was! And what of it? They also say he was morbid. This I deny. He was an imperfect person; he made a mess of his life; he suffered terrible trials; he was continuously hard up for a hundred rubles." Bennett concludes that "none of these things made him morbid; his outlook upon the world was always sane, undistorted, and kindly."

When Bennett moves on to discuss Tolstoy, whose *Anna Karenina, War and Peace*, and *Resurrection* hold down the fifth through seventh places in the novel's pantheon, his perspective on Dostoevsky comes into sharper focus.

The mind of Tolstoy is harder, less sympathetic, less exquisitely compassionate than that of Dostoevsky. But his regard for truth was not inferior; the general level of his creative power was perhaps slightly higher . . . also he had a better sense of form and far more discipline than Dostoevsky. After a course of Dostoevsky you may be inclined to think that Tolstoy is relatively common-place, banal, vulgar, material. But go back to Tolstoy, and you will once more be his helpless and contented victim.[39]

Sympathy. Truth. And, one might add, comprehensiveness. Such are the qualities for which Bennett admires Dostoevsky's work. He never doubts his grip on the moral values of the Russian novelist, and he consistently finds clear and uncomplicated support of those values in his works.[40]

Bennett's last recorded comments on Dostoevsky appeared in a 1930 essay entitled "Books that make one see." The essay marks a return to his earlier interest in the artistic issues of fiction. Here, Bennett makes the Conrad-like point that "imaginative literature is negligible which does nothing to make the reader see people, places, and phenomena as freshly as though he had never set eyes on them before." Bennett goes further, stating that "a first-class book or play must have something more even than this quality. It must give an effect of beauty. No matter how sordid, squalid, ugly, repulsive its raw material, it must give an effect of beauty." In other words, Bennett is calling for a union of form and content, art and morality. He cites Dostoevsky's *The House of the Dead* as a supreme achievement of such unity: Dostoevsky succeeds in "turning into beauty" the "horrors of prison life." The essay represents an anomaly of Bennett's later career, for it shows him still capable of acknowledging the link between artistry and moral impact. Perhaps if Bennett had not felt so compelled to act as a public moralist, he might have contributed more substantially to the literary debates of the 1920s.[41]

An interesting parallel can be drawn between Bennett's advocacy of Dostoevsky and Melchior de Vogüé's celebration of the major Russian novelists. According to F. W. J. Hemmings, "the significance of Vogüé's masterpiece cannot be grasped unless it is seen as an attempt at utter demolishment of the naturalist aesthetic theory: it can be viewed . . . as a counter-blast to Zola's *Roman Experimental,* which had come out only a few years previously." The French critic called upon his fellow citizens to turn away from the impassive and pitiless depravity of "experimental" writers to the revitalizing tonic of Russian fiction.[42] While it would be unfair to characterize Bennett as an enemy of all forms of modernism, his support of Dostoevsky was based upon a similar moral position. Bennett praised Dostoevsky and other Russian novelists for qualities that he found largely absent in his contemporaries.

His views on current English fiction often showed discomfort, as exemplified in his 1929 essay, "The progress of the novel." To judge a novelist as "serious" Bennett had to discern a clear moral: "Scratch a serious novelist and you will find a preacher with a moral message. I doubt whether there is any exception to this rule." Morality for Bennett is based on sentiment, and the greatest of all sentiments is sympathy, for it establishes a level of shared humanity and acknowledges mutual responsibilities. The novel, because of its unusual capacity to elicit sympathy, could and should become a means of moral instruction;

perhaps it is even the best means. The standard of judging a novel, then,
is derived from its moral function. The test of novelistic worth also
becomes a test of the author's personal moral worth: "As a rule, but not
always, the greatest novelists have become the greatest sympathizers.
The greatest sympathizer of all was Dostoevsky, whose nature had for
human imperfections that Christ-like, uncondescending pity which
should be the ideal of all novelists."

"The progress of the novel" singles out two modernist adversaries for
their moral failures: James Joyce and Virginia Woolf. While Bennett
recognizes Joyce as a "genuine innovator," admitting the "considerable" influence of *Ulysses*, he judges him to be a "wall builder" who lacks
"discipline and decency." He labels Joyce as "the noble savage of the
novel" because of his perceived failure to attend to the needs and
sensitivities of his audience. Joyce alienates the general literary audience, according to Bennett, and thus denies the moral function of his
art. Readers cannot learn sympathy if they cannot understand what
they read. Bennett also finds fault with Virginia Woolf, though he seems
to evade a moralistic criticism by focusing on her "absence of form" and
"her psychology," which is seen as "an uncoordinated mass of interesting details."[43] If one turns to other Bennett comments, however, it is
clear that all of his complaints about Woolf's "psychology" can be
explained in terms of his position on sympathy. As Bennett reported in
an earlier 1926 essay, the people in Woolf's novels "do not sufficiently
live, and hence they cannot claim our sympathy or even our hatred;
they leave us indifferent." Speaking of *Mrs. Dalloway*, he noted that he
"failed to discern what was its moral basis."[44] Though Bennett often
complained about Woolf's insufficiencies in matters of plot, theme, and
"logical construction," all of his criticism can be subsumed within his
larger concern for the novel's moral impact. As a reader, he could not
sympathize with the characters of Woolf, Joyce, and others; he interpreted his absence of sympathy as evidence of the author's abdication of
his or her moral authority.

Bennett presented himself as a moral advocate at a time when
literature had seemed to be oblivious or indifferent to moral issues, or,
worse still, seemed to be promoting its own set of values, antithetical to
those of the general public. Like Vogüé, Bennett hoped to rescue
literature from the elitist concerns of the "wall builders," so unrelenting
in their assaults on the middle-class and traditional sources of authority.
For his French predecessor, that meant liberation from the scientific
determinism of Zola and from an aesthetic theory grounded in natural-

ism. For Bennett, that meant liberation from the complexities of a Joyce or a Woolf. Both men hoped for the resurgence of a literature that would be more approachable and more humane, engendering values which coincided with their own. They used Dostoevsky as a weapon in their battle to return literature to the main currents of society, where it could serve as a bulwark against the tides of changing morality and beliefs. Literature, at its best, could be a haven from the chaos and dissonance of modernity.

Bennett may be viewed as rightly insistent in his focus on the essentially conservative nature of Dostoevsky's moral values, at a time when readers often blithely distorted those values. At least in the early stages of his response, he addressed the Russian writer in the context of European traditions, counterbalancing those who romanticized and sensationalized him as a monster in the house of fiction. As a publicist, Bennett consistently kept Dostoevsky in the foreground of the public arena; his role in promoting the Garnett translations, from inception to sale, cannot be overvalued. His performance as a literary critic, however, proved less satisfactory; by opposing life and art, he strips away the complexity of Dostoevsky. The novelist can only be made a preacher by the destruction of his art, for, unlike most preachers, Dostoevsky always strove, as Robin Feuer Miller has noted, to "avoid the direct expression of his thoughts."[45] While it would be foolish to deny the paramount importance of moral and religious issues in Dostoevsky's work, it would be even more foolish to separate, as Bennett did, moral themes from the artistic forms that gave them power. Perhaps the shrill moralism and resistance to experimental fiction that marked Bennett's later responses can be best understood as a desperate refusal to acknowledge the uncertainties and disruptions of the modern world.

CHAPTER 5

Keeping the monster at bay: Joseph Conrad

Malcolm Arbuthnot's photograph of Conrad, taken in 1924, shows the novelist as he would like to be remembered. Dressed in a well-tailored jacket and cravat with a gold fob looping from his pocket, he appears guarded and composed, bearing the refined manner of a landed aristocrat. The photograph conveys the image of Conrad that he himself cultivated throughout his essays, prefaces, and letters. The artist, with unswerving dedication, asserts control over everything he touches, creating order from disorder and achieving, with "precise intention," a "perfect blending of form and substance."[1] This image of artist as fastidious god seems far removed from the violent tumult of Dostoevsky's artistic world, distant from the "soothing" voice of authorial style so admired by Conrad.[2] Yet the eyes in the photograph belie the image of Artist in Control. The photograph confirms Lady Ottoline Morrell's first impression of Conrad: "His eyes under their pent-house lids revealed the suffering and the intensity of his experience . . . yes, it was a tangled, tortured, and very complex soul that looked out through those mysterious eyes."[3] In these mysterious and suffering eyes, one finds subtle evidence of a hidden kinship between the two writers.

Conrad, however, vehemently denied any affinity with Dostoevsky. He consistently sought to distance himself from the writer who epitomized all that he hated about the country that oppressed his homeland and brought his parents to a premature death. To avoid any association with things Russian, Conrad even claimed that he knew "practically nothing" about the Russian people, though he lived under the yoke of the czarist reign until he was a young man.[4] As a child he had lived with his parents in a remote Russian province, sharing the bitter consequences of their political deportation for revolutionary activities, an exile which eventually left Conrad an orphan. Though evidence points to a probing, if not necessarily extensive, reading of Dostoevsky, Conrad recorded only one comment about his fiction, where he dismissed *The*

Brothers Karamazov as "fierce mouthings from prehistoric ages" and complained that Dostoevsky was "too Russian for me."[5] His relative silence about him needs to be interpreted in terms of repression, not disinterest, for the reticent Pole's lived experience and the subject matter of his art brought him closer to Dostoevsky than any other novelist writing in English.

A careful examination of various sources will show the bitter subterranean depths of Conrad's relationship with the Russian novelist. Quite simply, he hated what Dostoevsky represented, politically, morally, and artistically. The depth of his hatred can be compared to Lawrence's soulful antagonism towards his Russian rival: no other writer was capable of eliciting such persistent and vitriolic disdain from the two aliens on the shores of English fiction, one from the working class, the other from the mysterious, "Slavic" East. Where Lawrence condemned Dostoevsky as an intellectualizing moralist whose works emanated from a diseased consciousness that suppressed the quick life of passion and instinct, Conrad denounced him as a writer who had been caught up within the vortex of his passionate and chaotic subject matter. Dostoevsky's complete failure as an artist in Conrad's judgment was the result of his equally complete failure to assert control over the dark, brimming underworld within and without. In Conrad's view, the Russian writer failed to adhere to the boundaries of art that were dependent upon the ability of the artist to select, refine, and control.

To understand Conrad's relationship to Dostoevsky, it will be helpful to enlarge the scope of inquiry by first examining his artistic relationship to Turgenev and his personal friendship with Edward and Constance Garnett. Conrad's admiration for the works of Turgenev, the writer whom he regarded as a model antithesis to Dostoevskian excess, illuminates his own values as a writer and helps to explain his disdain for Dostoevsky. His personal and professional relationship to the couple who introduced Turgenev's works to the English-speaking world, Constance and Edward Garnett, provides further insight. Though both Garnetts were early champions of Conrad's fiction, their enthusiasm, especially that of Edward, was a mixed blessing. Edward's influential reviews of his friend's work, with their persistent "Slavic" comparisons, unsettled and eventually enraged the novelist who wanted to be perceived as a writer in the Continental tradition of cool restraint and aloofness represented by Flaubert and Maupassant.

Conrad's personal and political views of Russia need to be understood in order to explain the depth of his rage. Unlike all the other

English writers discussed in this study, he experienced first-hand the crushing power and tragedy of "monstrous" czardom. Because of his lived experience, he was the only novelist who paid serious attention to the political, ethnic, and religious contexts of Dostoevsky's novels. Conrad, like his contemporaries, may have heard a primitive, undisciplined voice in the Russian novelist, but he always heard echoes of the czarist, Russian, and Orthodox institutions that shaped Dostoevsky's voice. That voice always remained inextricably linked to Conrad's most bitter and painful memories.

The vehemence of Conrad's response can perhaps best be understood within the context of their similarities. Conrad's hatred, like Lawrence's, was fueled by a recognition of similar novelistic territory. As Irving Howe points out, Conrad recognized and repressed Dostoevskian elements within his own personality and art. That repressive effort represents a central tension in Conrad's life and work.[6] Despite his antipathy, Dostoevskian themes resonate throughout Conrad's fiction. His literature slowly evolved towards a direct confrontation with his Russian rival, as evidenced by the progression of *The Sisters* (an unfinished fragment), *Nostromo*, and *The Secret Agent*. Confrontation finally occurred with the writing of *Under Western Eyes*, the culmination of Conrad's creative response to Dostoevsky. It stands as a work that could not have been written without its Dostoevskian antecedents and may be judged as a systematic reworking of *Crime and Punishment*. Though Conrad condemned Dostoevsky as a monster, he felt compelled to grapple with both the author and his subject, fighting with the vehemence of one who seeks to protect what is most loved.

TURGENEV AS REFUGE FROM DOSTOEVSKIAN STORM

Conrad's admiration for Turgenev, a writer whom he regarded as safely removed from the barbaric excesses of Russia's politics and its literary emotionalism, never wavered. According to his own reports, his boyhood readings included *Smoke* (in a Polish translation) and *House of the Gentlefolk* (in French), works which he liked "purely by instinct."[7] Conrad's earliest recorded comment about Turgenev surfaces in a letter to Edward Garnett in 1897, which renders effusive praise to both the writer and his translator: "The reader does not *see* the language – the story is alive – as living as when it came from the master's hand." Though Conrad "knew and remembered the stories before," they evoke "the delight of reveling in that pellucid flaming atmosphere of Turgenev's life

which the translator has preserved unstained, unchilled, with the clearness and heat of original inspiration."[8] This letter was written in a
crucially formative time of Conrad's own career, just after the publication of *The Nigger of the "Narcissus,"* the first sustained artistic success of his
early years. The letter suggests that Conrad was already quite familiar
with Turgenev before Constance started her translation project and
renders questionable his later claim that "Turgenev for me is Constance
Garnett and Constance Garnett is Turgenev."[9] Yet both Garnetts,
Edward as critic and Constance as translator, contributed to Conrad's
appreciation of the writer whom he regarded as a master.[10]

Constance responded warmly to her friend's praise by comparing his
own work to that of Turgenev's. Her comments show that she found a
strong affinity between the two novelists: "I feel, as I have always told
Edward, that your brain does not think English thoughts, – as Turgenev's own, – it is more delicate, more subtle, richer and more varied
than ours. Your use of adjectives – so chosen, fastidious, often ironical –
reminds me again and again of Turgenev's manner." Constance concludes by noting that Conrad himself "ought to have had the task of
translating him."[11]

Her praise calls to mind some of Conrad's own statements about
fictional art in his famous preface to *The Nigger of the "Narcissus,"*, which
was also written in 1897. The preface invokes those values that gave
impetus to his work and stirred his appreciation of Turgenev. Conrad
could judge a work as art only if he saw "its justification in every line."
In every word, phrase, and sentence, he had to find the imprint of the
controlling artist who worked with "unswerving devotion to the perfect
blending of form and substance." Art required what Constance Garnett
had found in his own fiction – evidence of chosen, fastidious, ironical
language.[12] Conrad also insisted that art be defined in terms of its
sensory appeal: "All art, therefore, appeals primarily to the senses, and
the artistic aim when expressing itself in written words must also make
its appeal through the senses."[13] By all such measures, Conrad judged
Turgenev as a successful artist. Yet when applying the same measures to
Dostoevsky, he would find only evidence of failure. Fifteen years after
his correspondence with the Garnetts about the Turgenev translations,
he wrote to Edward about the first volume of Constance's Dostoevsky
translations, *The Brothers Karamazov*: "But indeed the man's art does not
deserve this good fortune. Turgenev (and perhaps Tolstoy) are the only
two really worthy of her."[14]

Both Constance and Edward Garnett saw Conrad and Turgenev as writers following the same path to artistic excellence. Edward, who wrote many of the introductions to Constance's translations, even dedicated a collection of Turgenev stories to his friend. *A Desperate Character Etc.*, published in 1899 and translated by Constance, was dedicated "to Joseph Conrad whose art in essence often recalls the art and essence of Turgenev."[15] Conrad seemed genuinely touched by the Turgenev dedication.

Is it possible that I should deserve to stand so close to the great creator, to his great interpreter and to the man who, in this country, alone had penetrated the Master . . . When you send me that [Turgenev] volume ask your dear wife to write her name in it for me. I almost think I understand better than anyone all the perfection of her finished task. That is why I said Interpreter and not translator. She is in that work what a great musician is to a great composer – with something more, something greater. It is as if the Interpreter had looked into the very mind of the Master and had a share in his inspiration.[16]

Though many critics and biographers have noted Conrad's tendency to praise his friends excessively – at times, he is embarrassingly obsequious in his letters – Conrad was almost always a sober and uncompromising judge of literary quality. His assessment here is unquestionably the product of his own conviction.

In 1904 Conrad wrote an important essay that remained unpublished until 1926. Ostensibly, "A glance at two books" reviews John Galsworthy's *The Island Pharisees* and W. H. Hudson's *Green Mansions*. Yet the essay also reflects Conrad's own literary values and shows his appreciation of Turgenev's craft. Conrad begins by lamenting that the "national English novelist seldom regards his work – the exercise of his art – as an achievement of the active life." Instead of aiming for "certain definite effects upon the emotions of his readers," the writer regards his work "simply as an instinctive, often unreasoned outpouring of his own emotions." Conrad regrets that English authors do not regard a novel as an aesthetic deed, "that writing it is an enterprise as much as the conquest of a colony." With a "full heart" and "no such clear conception of his craft," the English novelist "liberates his soul for the satisfaction of his own sentiment; and when he has finished the scene he is at liberty to strike his forehead and exclaim: 'this is genius.'"[17]

Conrad goes on to portray Thackeray as representative of those writers who neglect "to use their powers of selection and observation," contrasting his work with the achievement of Turgenev's. Swayed by the lure of popular sentiments, the writer of *Vanity Fair* could not create a heroine who could live in the real world. "He was in love with the sentiments" represented by his heroines. "He was in fact, in love with what does not exist – and that is why Amelia Osborne does not exist, either in color, in shape, in grace, in goodness." Turgenev, by contrast, is praised as a writer capable of distancing himself from his creations. Lisa, the sympathetically portrayed young woman in *The House of the Gentlefolk,* is loved "disinterestedly, as it were, out of pure warmth of heart, as a human being in the tumult and hazard of life. And that is why we must feel, suffer and live with that wonderful creation. That is why she is as real to us as her stupid mother, as the men of the story, as the sombre Varvard, and the others."[18] Turgenev does not allow himself to be overwhelmed by either the pathos of his subject matter or the heat of his own imagination; he never loses sight of the desired effect upon the reader.

Conrad favorably compares Hudson to Turgenev and praises his work for adhering to those values defined in the preface to *The Nigger of the "Narcissus,"* always bearing the mark of an artist in control.

The innermost heart of *Green Mansions* . . . is tranquil, is steeped in that pure love of the external beauty of things that seems to breathe upon us from the pages of Turgenev's work. The charming quietness of the style soothes the hard irritation of daily life in the presence of a fine and sincere, of a deep and pellucid personality. If the other's book's gift [i.e., Galsworthy's] is lyric, *Green Mansions* comes to us with the tone of elegy.

Conrad quotes from the novel to show his appreciation. The excerpt reveals the narrator's discovery of a spider in hunt of its prey: "I noticed a small spider with a flat body and short legs creep cautiously out on to the upper surface of a small leaf. Its pale colour, barred with velvet black, first drew my attention to it; for it was beautiful to the eye." The style is "soothing like a soft voice speaking steadily amongst the vivid changes of a dream."[19] Conrad admires the Turgenev-like virtues of the passage: its language, aesthetically distant from its brutal subject, creates an effect of beauty and tranquillity.

In the spring of 1917, Edward Garnett asked Conrad for an introduction to his soon-to-be-published study of Turgenev. Conrad responded with a long letter that outlined his lack of qualifications for the job, only to conclude by saying: "But my dear Edward if you say definitely I've to do it – well I'll try. I don't promise to bring it off tho'!" The letter begins with a confession of ignorance: "The trouble is that I don't know Russian; I don't even know the alphabet." Some critics, most notably Frederick Karl, have disputed Conrad's claim, reasoning that his residence in the Russian empire probably led to some knowledge of Russian vocabulary and grammar. Given Conrad's talent for acquiring languages – he was, after all, a novelist writing in his third language – and his father's apparent knowledge of Russian, it is possible that Conrad knew more about the language than he admitted.[20] He may have feigned ignorance, fearing that if he claimed any knowledge he would only be supporting the tendency of the English audience to judge his novels as Slavic excrescences. Conrad never wanted to be tagged as a Slavic writer, for he insisted that his work could only be understood within the proud lineage of the English language and French novelistic artistry. No evidence has yet surfaced either to prove or to disprove Conrad's assertion of ignorance of Russian.

The letter shows Conrad's reluctance to present himself as a qualified judge of Russian literature. Though he acknowledges that he first encountered Turgenev through French and Polish translations, he claims that his judgment of Turgenev's value was dependent on the work of Constance and Edward Garnett, and he defers to Edward's critical judgment: "The truth of the matter is that it is you who have opened my eyes to the value and quality of Turgenev." Of Conrad's sincerity here there can be little doubt, yet his deference to the Garnetts also helps to distance himself further from any hint of expertise in Russian, with its possible implications of his own literary indebtedness to Russian sources or to the Slavic temperament that the English readers presumed shared by all Eastern Europeans. Near the end of his letter he admits to Edward: "To be frank I don't want to appear as qualified to speak on things Russian."

The letter reveals Conrad's ambivalence about the relationship between Turgenev's nationality and his literature. On one hand, he suggests that the paragon of literary merit should *not* be read as a Russian author: "I admire Turgenev but in truth Russia was for him no more than a canvas for the painter." His characters are judged "very much like Shakespeare's Italians. One doesn't think of it" (i. e., their nationality). Turgenev should be read, it may be implied, as Conrad should be read, as an international artist who has transcended national boundaries and ethnic origins. On the other hand, Conrad admits that Turgenev still needs to be understood in the distinctively Russian context of his times, and he praises Edward Garnett for recognizing this: "As far as I know you are the only man who had seen T. not only in his relation to mankind but in his relation to Russia. And he is great in both."

He proceeds to contrast Turgenev with Dostoevsky, drawing a portrait of the former as a gifted artist "cursed" by the magnitude of his gifts and plagued by the tragic discrepancy between the scope of the artist's vision and the limits of what an audience will accept or understand.

But to be so great and at the same time so fine is fatal to an artist – as to any other man for that matter. *It isn't Dostoevsky the grimacing haunted creature who is under a curse*; it is Turgenev. Every gift has been heaped on his cradle. Absolute sanity and the deepest sensibility, the clearest vision and the most exquisite responsiveness, penetrating insight and unfailing generosity of judgment, and unerring instinct for the significant, for the essential in human life and in the visible world, the clearest mind, the warmest heart, the largest sympathy – and all in perfect measure! *There's enough to ruin any writer.* (Emphasis mine)

The contrast between Turgenev and Dostoevsky is crucial for it shows how Conrad viewed one as a pure artist tragically caught between his apollonian gifts and the mire of the world, while he viewed the other as a grim, graceless writer who lacked all that Turgenev possessed.

This letter was written at the height of Dostoevsky's popularity in England. Conrad seems to condemn as mindless both Turgenev's Russian audience and contemporary England – the kind of audience that preferred Dostoevsky to Turgenev. Here Conrad betrays his own frustrations in garnering a large audience. Even if he and Edward Garnett were to catch Marcus Aurelius, that exemplar of stoic wisdom, "and exhibit him in a booth of the world's fair, swearing that his life was as perfect as his form," they "wouldn't get one per cent of the crowd struggling next door to catch sight of the double-headed Nightingale or of some weak-kneed giant grinning through a collar."[21] The lament about heroic souls who go unappreciated by the crowd resonates deeply. The emperor at the world's fair represents both the Polish and the Russian novelist.

Conrad never fully overcame his reluctance to emerge as a public judge of Turgenev's merits, though he did write a published introduction to Garnett's work. To do so, he simply revised and expanded his letter. The revision pays far more attention to the national context of Turgenev's work, recognizing Russia's growing political turmoil in the watershed year of 1917. Conrad's introduction notes that Turgenev's fiction reflects "the deep origins" of "social and political events in Russia" that have come to pass since the author's death, and he recognizes the author as a profound "national writer."

The introduction is more strident than the original letter in its attacks, both direct and implied, on Dostoevsky. When discussing whether

Turgenev's literary fame will endure, Conrad does not miss a chance to attack the current tastes, as he places Turgenev on the side of truth and an unnamed Dostoevsky on the side of monsters: "Fashions in monsters do change, but the truth of humanity goes on for ever, unchangeable and inexhaustible in the variety of its disclosures." Turgenev is praised for offering an alternative to Dostoevsky's darkly oppressive world, but again Conrad refuses to name the target of his anathema.

In the larger, non-Russian view what should make Turgenev sympathetic and welcome to the English-speaking world is his essential humanity. All his creations, fortunate and unfortunate, oppressed and oppressors, are human beings, *not strange beasts in a menagerie or damned souls knocking themselves to pieces in the stuffy darkness of mystical contradictions.* They are human beings, fit to live, fit to suffer, to win, fit to lose in the endless and inspiring game of pursuing from day to day the ever-receding future. (Emphasis mine)

When Conrad finally names Dostoevsky, at the same juncture as in the original letter when Turgenev is identified as a tragic writer, his loathing seems complete. Where the original dismissed Dostoevsky as a "grimacing haunted creature," he is now "the convulsed terror-haunted Dostoevsky."[22]

Two quotations from Conrad's letters help to further illuminate his standards for literature. Writing to his publisher, Blackwood, in 1902, he confidently predicted that "my work shall not be an utter failure because it has the solid basis of definite intention."[23] For Conrad, restraint was a necessary, though not sufficient, condition for art. An author needed to suppress his passion, his indignation, and even his own moral beliefs to write effectively. Conrad took considerable pride in his ability to exercise such control. In a 1908 letter to Edward Garnett, he wrote with satisfaction: "The fact is that I have approached things human in a spirit of piety foreign to those who would like to make of life a sort of Cook's Personally Conducted Tour – from the cradle to the grave. I have never debased that quasi-religious sentiment by tears and sighs. I have neither grinned nor gnashed my teeth. In a word I have behaved myself decently."[24]

Throughout his life Conrad judged Turgenev as an artist to be "one of us," and refused to allow Dostoevsky admission to the ranks. Yet in key respects, which will later be explored in depth, this opposition hides more than it reveals. In the astute words of Morton Dauwen Zabel:

whatever Conrad's repugnance or disclaimers, the "turmoil and darkness" of Dostoevsky's vision evidently had as much to say to the Pole's experience of excess and contradiction as Turgenev's classic balance did; and if a novel like *Under Western Eyes* is to be referred to a Russian precedent, it is as much to that of the "terror-haunted" Dostoevsky as to that of the "impartial lover of *all* his countrymen."[25]

THE RUSSIAN CIRCLE OF THE GARNETTS

Conrad's relationship with Edward and Constance Garnett parallels that of Lawrence. Both novelists formed a personal bond with the Garnetts, especially Edward, who immeasurably assisted them in their literary careers. They admired the translating efforts of Constance and recognized her works as literary creations in their own right. But where Lawrence ended by breaking off the friendship, as he did so many others, Conrad continued as a lifelong friend. To understand his view of Dostoevsky, one must understand his relationship to the fascinating world of the Garnetts, whose Surrey cottage, the Cearne, often served as refuge to revolutionaries, exiles, and literati.

Constance and Edward were enamored with leftist political and social causes and befriended Russian exiles who shared their interests. As a young man, Edward, according to his biographer, George Jefferson, imbibed "the rousing revolutionary influences of Wagner, Ibsen, Whitman, William Morris, and Tolstoy . . . and above all, Nietzsche."[26] Like her husband, Constance was a professed atheist; she was also a socialist whose political activities brought her in contact with a remarkable spectrum of people, from George Bernard Shaw to Lenin. In the view of Jefferson, the husband and wife exemplified their era, "a period when diverse groups although united in opposition to the old order of things followed many different paths in their rebellion – socialist, Fabian, Nietzschean, Bergsonian, Theosophist and others." While Constance expressed her rebellious beliefs through action, Edward remained "sceptical of organized movements."[27]

Notable and incendiary Russian exiles, such as Felix Volkhovsky, Peter Kropotkin, and Sergei Stepniak, found sympathy and friendship at the home of the Garnetts. As reported by Jefferson, "These exiles were regarded as heralds against the old order of society which liberals viewed as riddled with prejudice, insincerity, and hypocritical conventions." One of them, Volkhovsky, "had escaped from Siberia and suffered from deafness, the consequence of seven years in the Peter and Paul fortress" in St. Petersburg where Dostoevsky himself had been detained while on trial. Volkhovsky "became a great friend and earned the lasting gratitude of Constance by suggesting she should learn Russian." He gave her "a grammar, a dictionary, and the first story she attempted to read in Russian."[28] Through him, she also came to know Stepniak, the self-described nihilist who, according to one account, "had fled Russia in 1880 after knifing a general who had ordered two girls associated with the revolutionary movement to be arrested and flogged."[29]

Apparently, Stepniak, a man of many talents and indisputable charm, did admit to assassinating the cruel Russian Chief of Police, General Mezentsev, in 1878, but the exact circumstances of the murder, as well as the confession, are far from clear, and his deed was long kept secret from his English friends. After settling in London in 1883, Stepniak became a political writer; the editor of *Free Russia*, a periodical sponsored by The Society of the Friends of Russian Freedom; a literary author, translator, and lecturer. Thomas Moser builds an interesting case to show that Stepniak probably influenced Conrad's creation of both Razumov and Haldin in *Under Western Eyes*. Though Haldin is the assassin of a hated czarist official, Moser finds that Razumov, the unwilling accomplice, bears even greater resemblances to Stepniak in his physical attributes, melancholy temperament, loneliness, the burden of his secret past, and the comfort that he finds in writing. Stepniak, like Razumov, confessed to his crime even after the false accusation of another appeared to exonerate him.[30] In 1895, the Russian exile was killed while crossing a railroad track, hit by a train that he seemingly did not hear. According to David Garnett, Stepniak had always been able to "shut out exterior sounds when he was thinking," a facility that might account for his accidental death.[31] Razumov, it should be remembered, was similarly hit by an unheard tramcar.

The personal relationship between Stepniak and Constance had interesting literary and political consequences. He encouraged her to become a professional translator and assisted her efforts to learn the language. A beloved friend of the Garnetts, as well as Edward's younger sister, Olive, Stepniak wrote the prefaces to the first five of Constance's Turgenev translations, and he motivated her subversive, cloak-and-dagger adventures. Constance traveled to Russia by herself and participated in a "scheme to arrange means of communication between exiles such as Stepniak and secret revolutionary organizations in Russia."[32] She eventually earned the respect and friendship of many Russian exiles, including Vera Zasulich, who had attempted to assassinate another Russian general, and Vera Figner, who had been jailed for plotting the assassination of Alexander II.[33]

Conrad may have learned more about Russian revolutionaries – and Russian despotism – from his association with the Garnetts than he did from his own experience in Russia. The influence of Russian exiles was prevalent at the Garnetts' home, and a number of *émigrés* lived nearby in a group of bungalows known as "Dostoevsky's corner."[34] While visiting the Cearne, Conrad met Ford Madox Ford, who became a patron, collaborator, and friend. Ford's brother-in-law, David Soskice, was a highly influential revolutionary *émigré*, born in Conrad's birthplace, the Ukrainian city of Berdichev, and had spent three years in St. Peterburg's Peter and Paul fortress. According to Thomas Moser, Soskice knew the "inside story of contemporary Russian revolutionary and secret police activities." Moser argues the likelihood that Ford, in his collaborative role, would have passed along Soskice's knowledge to Conrad.[35] Though Stepniak died before Conrad's first visit to the Cearne, the novelist doubtlessly heard a great deal about him. Conrad might also have met Stepniak's widow, Fanny, who lived nearby and was also a close Garnett friend. Perhaps there were times when Conrad felt as isolated at the Cearne as Razumov did at the mansion of Madame de S–, for philosophically and politically he was far removed from the values that found expression there. Yet his experience with the exiles and the tales of their exploits helped to shape *Under Western Eyes*.

In addition to providing raw material for his fiction, Conrad's relationship to the Garnetts also had an impact on the reception of his works. Edward Garnett was the most influential early critic of Conrad's work. From 1898 through 1911, the year that *Under Western Eyes* was published, Edward published laudatory and perceptive reviews of his friend's work. He paid careful attention to the psychological depth of Conrad's fiction, and urged that it should be ranked among the world's finest. Though Conrad appreciated the sympathetic and often penetrating remarks, the reviews eventually disturbed the friendship of the two men, for Conrad saw them as part of Edward's long-standing campaign to "russianize" the tastes of the English reading public. Garnett, as might be expected, frequently compared his friend to the great Russian novelists, and he insisted on addressing Conrad as a "Slav" novelist, thereby offending both his Polish and his English sensibilities.

Edward Garnett first publicly praised Conrad's art in 1898. Using terms that call to mind Virginia Woolf's comments about Dostoevsky, he found in Conrad a "new world," a new insight into the "darkness of human nature." He notes that "the blank solid wall of the familiar . . . has melted before this artist [who has connected] . . . this tangible world with the vast unseen ocean of life around him." Conrad's work displays "the poetic realism of the great Russian novels"; his art "seems to be on the line that divides East and West." Though Garnett recognizes his technique as "modern in the sense that Flaubert and Turgenev are modern," he also finds "a luxuriance" and "an extravagance . . . of phrase which leads us towards the East."[36]

Subsequent reviews increasingly drew comparisons to Dostoevsky and emphasized Conrad's Slavic background. In 1902 Garnett testified to the compelling power of "Heart of darkness" by comparing it to Dostoevsky: "The weirdness, the brilliance, the psychological truth of this masterly analysis . . . is conveyed with a rapidly rushing narrative . . . the pages of the narrative are as enthralling as the pages of Dostoevsky's *Crime and Punishment*."[37] When *The Secret Agent* was published in 1907, Garnett seemed to push Conrad further away from Western European traditions: "He [Conrad] makes clear to his English audience those secrets of Slav thought and feeling which seem so strange and inaccessible in their native language." The review stresses Conrad's Slavic origins, ignoring, in a manner that must have been painful to Conrad, any distinctions between the Russians, Poles, or other Slavic peoples: "Mr. Conrad . . . is to us as a willing hostage we have taken from the Slav lands, in exchange for whom no ransom could outweigh the value of his insight and his artistic revelation." Garnett's Slavic enthusiasms lead him to ignore the English subject matter of the novel, whose main characters – Verloc, Winnie, Stevie, the Assistant Commissioner, and Chief Inspector Heat – are all English citizens. The review concludes by finding in *The Secret Agent* "the profound and ruthless sincerity of the great Slav writers mingled with the haunting charm that reminds us so often of his compatriot Chopin." All literary and artistic comparisons here fall east of the Elbe.[38]

Garnett reviewed *Under Western Eyes* in 1911 just seven months before the release of his wife's translation of *The Brothers Karamazov*. Once again, he drew attention to the psychological power and intensity of Conrad, this time comparing him explicitly to Dostoevsky: "The study is very special, and to the English reader, who knows nought of Dostoevsky, and is touchingly ignorant of his own soul's dark places, may seem a nightmare of hallucinations, but in fact, within its narrow lines, it is illuminating in its psychological truth." The review pays considerable attention to the distinctive Russian character of Conrad's fictional world. Garnett praises Natalia Haldin, the sister of the assassin and the love interest, as an "exquisite type of Russian womanhood," and Sophia

Antonovna as "a woman Nihilist of the old school, who recalls the heroines of the early 'eighties.'" He recognizes the novel as a profound expression of Russian nationality, with its "frustrated and blighted generations" and its "mournful internal history."

Yet the novel also evokes some uncharacteristically harsh judgments: "This merciless picture . . . would seem vindictive art, had not the author introduced into the group the admirable figure of Sophia Antonovna." Conrad's unmasking of "autocracy's pretensions" does not disturb Garnett nearly as much as his unsparing portrait of the revolutionists. Though obviously moved by the dark power of the novel, the critic felt uncomfortable in his admiration, for Conrad probed the cynical origins and futile results of an insurgent underworld that had captured the imagination and sympathy of Garnett and many of his English contemporaries. He had difficulty admitting to his admiration for a work that challenged his own political beliefs and sympathies: "There is something almost vitriolic in Mr. Conrad's rejection of the shibboleths of humanitarian lovers of their kind, and we confess to an enjoyment, positively indefensible, in such perfect little scenes as the one on the little islet, 'a perfection of puerile neatness,' where stands the exiled effigy of Jean Jacques Rousseau."

On balance, however, the review shows Garnett to be a loyal and discerning advocate of the novel's merit. It concludes by ranking Conrad among the masters: "Many of his pages may be placed by the side of notable passages in Turgenev and Dostoevsky, to both of which masters Mr. Conrad bears affinities and owes a debt."[39]

Conrad's response to Garnett's critical judgment, an anomaly amid their polite and deferential correspondence, attacks his friend with a sarcasm reminiscent of Lawrence's denunciatory letters. He denies that his work reflects personal hatred for the Russians: "Subjects lay about for anybody to pick up. I have picked up this one. And that's all there is to it." He then proceeds to lambaste one of his most loyal friends.

You are so russianised, my dear, that you don't know the truth when you see it – unless it smells of cabbage-soup when it at once secures your profoundest respect. I suppose one must make allowances for your position of Russian Embassador to the Republic of Letters. Official pronouncements ought to be taken with a grain of salt and that is how I shall take your article in the *Nation*.

Though Conrad attempted to mask his feelings with humorous barbs about cabbage soup and Garnett's role as a protector of all things Russian, the letter reflects deep personal hurt.

Garnett had unintentionally attacked the ground of Conrad's existence as a novelist, his ability to maintain ironic distance from his subject
matter and his creative sympathy with fictional characters who in real life
would have been distasteful to him – the criminal, the outlaw, the
revolutionist. What pained Conrad the most was his friend's inability to
realize just how much personal antipathy was *prevented* from entering the
novel. Considering his political and personal views of Russia, which were
an expression of perhaps the greatest suffering in his life, *Under Western
Eyes* represents a triumph of the creative imagination that enabled the
Polish patriot to depict such Russian characters as Razumov, Natalia,
Sophia, and Tekla with understanding, empathy, and even warmth.

The act of writing the novel certainly must have involved a fierce act
of discipline, which helps to explain the heat of Conrad's response to
Garnett.

But it is hard after lavishing a "wealth of tenderness" on Tekla and Sophia, to
be charged with the rather low trick of putting one's hate into a novel. If you
seriously think that I have done that then my dear fellow let me tell you that you
don't know what the accent of hate is. Is it possible that you haven't seen that in
this book I am concerned with nothing but ideas, to the exclusion of everything
else, with no *arrière pensée* of any kind. Or are you like the Italians (and most
women) incapable of conceiving that anybody ever should speak with perfect
detachment, without some subtle hidden purpose . . . with no desire of
gratifying small personal spite – or vanity.

The letter's conclusion bitterly accuses Garnett of pandering to current
tastes: "And anyhow if hatred were there it would be too big a thing to
be put into a 6/- novel. This too might have occurred to you, if you had
condescended to look beyond the literary horizon where all things
sacred and profane are turned into copy."[40]

In fairness to Garnett, it should be pointed out that part of Conrad's
anger resulted from his desire to maintain a public image of one who
knew virtually nothing about Russia. He apparently wanted his English
audience to believe that any convincing evocations of that country were
simply the result of a novelist's imagination and careful reading of the
English newspapers. Russia, according to his pose, existed no more for
Conrad than Italy did for Shakespeare. In a letter to Olive Garnett,
written on the same day as his tirade against her "russianised" brother,
Conrad claimed "to know extremely little of Russians."[41] His letter to
Edward may have been the result of long-simmering resentment over
Edward's constant habit of comparing him to the Russians, especially
the hated Dostoevsky.

THE CZARIST BLIGHT AND DOSTOEVSKY

Before addressing the literary parallels and divergencies between Conrad and Dostoevsky, especially those found in *Under Western Eyes*, it will be helpful to focus on the former's political attitude towards czarist Russia. Conrad published his most explicit and forceful statement in "Autocracy and war," a 1905 essay that was prompted by the ongoing war between Russia and Japan. Here, Conrad paints an utterly black picture of the Russian autocracy, one that reflects his experience as its victim. The language in the essay is that of a Jeremiah who denounces the oppressors of his people.

The touch of czarist Russia, according to Conrad, blights everyone unfortunate enough to encounter it. The Russian people, a people more dead than alive, are identified as the first casualties of czarist power. "For a hundred years the ghost of Russian might, overshadowing with its fantastic bulk the councils of Central and Western Europe, sat upon the gravestone of autocracy, cutting off from air, from light, from all knowledge of themselves and of the world, the buried millions of Russian people."[42] Yet the essay predicts that the war with Japan will lead ultimately to the destruction of Russian tyranny, for the "gravestone of autocracy" is "already cracked." One can find "in the blood-soaked ground" of battle "the first stirrings of a resurrection." Conrad warns, however, that the Russian autocracy, despite its precarious state, ominously threatens Europe. He urges all Europeans to use the war as an opportunity to penetrate into Russia's bleak truth: "Never before had the Western world the opportunity to look so deep into the black abyss which separates a soulless autocracy posing as, and even believing itself to be, the arbiter of Europe, from the benighted, starved souls of its people." The war's "real-object lesson," Conrad tells his audience, resides in "the unforgettable information" that it provides the West.[43] Using nineteenth-century history as his justification, he judges the "Russian influence in Europe" to be "the most baseless thing in the world."[44]

Conrad refuses to see any merit in Russian culture and social institutions: "An attentive survey of Russian literature, of her Church, of her administration and the cross-cultures of her thought must end in the verdict that the Russia of today has not the right to give her voice on a single question touching the future of humanity." That is "because from the very inception of her being the brutal destruction of dignity, of truth, of rectitude, of all that is faithful in human nature has been made the imperative condition of her existence."[45] This sweeping denunciation, as Zdzislaw Najder has pointed out, immediately follows an allusion to Dostoevsky, who, in Conrad's view, abandoned youthful rebellion in exchange for a slavish devotion to despotism: "Some of the best intellects of Russia, after struggling in vain against the spell, ended by throwing themselves at the feet of that hopeless despotism as a giddy man leaps into an abyss."[46]

Conrad's Russia is the diametrical opposite of the Russia that Dostoevsky embraced. Where Dostoevsky saw his country, at least in its visionary potential, as a beacon of Christian hope and enlightenment, Conrad saw it as "a bottomless abyss that has swallowed up every hope of mercy, every aspiration towards freedom, towards knowledge, every ennobling desire of the heart, every redeeming whisper of conscience."[47] Where Dostoevsky heralded his native land as the potential salvation of Europe, the one possible source of affirming, unifying truth that could steady a confused, despairing continent, Conrad condemned Russia as a disruptive monster, and he found it "impossible to believe" that no one had yet "penetrated the true nature of the monster."[48] The Russia of Dostoevsky's mystic yearnings embodied his best dreams for the future. In a letter to his friend Apollon Maikov, he revealed his hopes: "I fully share ... your patriotic feeling about the *moral* emancipation of the Slavs. This is the role Russia must play, our great magnanimous Russia, our holy mother ... Yes, I share with you the idea that Europe and her destiny will be fulfilled by Russia."[49] Conrad viewed the same country as "the negation of everything worth living for."[50] Both writers held their beliefs with absolute, prophetic conviction, at least in those moments when they were not writing fiction and exploring worlds rich in contradiction.

Ironically, Conrad's own political beliefs, once separated from the issue of Russian autocracy and nationalism, probably bear a strong resemblance to Dostoevsky's own. Two of Conrad's most distinguished critics, Morton Dauwen Zabel and Albert J. Guerard, both judge Razumov's credo in *Under Western Eyes* as a reflection of Conrad's own political values:

History not Theory
Patriotism not Internationalism
Evolution not Revolution
Direction not Destruction
Unity not Disruption[51]

Certainly that credo would not be alien to the beliefs of the author who wrote *The Possessed* and *Crime and Punishment*, two penetrating studies of what happens when humanity submits to the contagion of the false values of theory, revolution, and destruction.

EVOLUTION OF AN UNWONTED RIVALRY

The most forthright evidence of Conrad's antagonism towards Dostoevsky comes from the personal reminiscences of those who knew him. Richard Curle, a close friend and admirer, reported that "there was no name in literature that Conrad detested more than that of Dostoevsky, and usually the mere mention of it drove him into a fury."[52] Though the Polish exile once told Galsworthy that Dostoevsky was "as deep as the sea," Curle interpreted that comment as an allusion to "the depth of an evil influence": "Dostoevsky represented to him the ultimate forces of confusion and insanity arrayed against all that he valued in civilization. He did not despise him as one despises a nonentity, he hated him as one might hate Lucifer and the forces of darkness." In Curle's judgment, Dostoevsky was Conrad's "most formidable antagonist." He offered the following explanation of this antagonism: "It is true that Conrad had a hereditary dislike of Russians and that, moreover, Dostoevsky makes contemptuous references to Poles, but I have an idea that his real hatred for Dostoevsky was due to an appreciation of his power."[53]

Curle's testimony may have been slanted somewhat by his own admitted enthusiasm for Dostoevsky, which provoked Conrad's disdain on more than one occasion. Yet other reliable sources also noted Conrad's antagonism. Bertrand Russell recounted his own conversations: "His dislike of Russia was that which was traditional in Poland. It went so far that he would not allow merit to either Tolstoy or Dostoevsky. Turgenev, he told me once, was the only Russian novelist whom he admired."[54] E. M. Forster similarly commented on his "Russophobia" though he does not specifically address his dislike of Dostoevsky: "Conrad's passions are intelligible and frank: having lived thus, thus he feels, and it is idle to regret his account of Russians as it would be to regret Dostoevsky's account of Poles in *The Brothers Karamazov*." Forster excused Conrad's vitriolic disdain for Russia on the grounds of his personal suffering.[55]

Based on the evidence presented thus far, Conrad's disparaging remarks about *The Brothers Karamazov* – his only recorded comments about any specific work of Dostoevsky's – should come as no surprise. A letter to Edward Garnett written soon after the publication of Constance's translation serves to measure the distance between the two authors.

I do hope you are not too disgusted with me for not thanking you for the *Karamazov* before. It was very good of you to remember me; and of course I was extremely interested. But it's an impossible lump of valuable matter. It's terrifically bad and impressive and exasperating. Moreover, I don't know what D. stands for or reveals, but I do know that he is too Russian for me. It sounds like some fierce mouthings from prehistoric ages. I understand the Russians have just "discovered" him. I wish them joy.[56]

Conrad's glib assumption of literary superiority, however entertaining, hides more than it reveals, for he was far more affected by his reading of Dostoevsky than his letter suggests. To discover the true complexity of his response, one has to turn to Conrad's fiction.

Conrad's knowledge of Dostoevsky's literature preceded the Garnett translations. Like Woolf and Lawrence, he probably first read the novels in French because the previous English translations were out of print and difficult to obtain.[57] Unlike the two younger writers, however, Conrad's judgment of Dostoevsky was unaffected by his readings of the Garnett translations. By the time Constance Garnett's version of *The Brothers Karamazov* was published in 1912, he had already made up his mind; more importantly, he had already creatively responded to Dostoevsky through his fiction, especially *Under Western Eyes*. Unfortunately, he covered the tracks of his reading, and no record is available of what works Conrad did or did not read. Though the evidence of his creative response to his Russian rival is necessarily circumstantial, a compelling case based on similarities of subject matter, plot, theme, and language can be made to show the impact that Dostoevsky had on Conrad's fiction.

In the winter of 1896 Conrad wrote a fragment of a novel, *The Sisters*, that was never completed, though Ford Madox Ford reports that his friend had often thought of returning to the work. The first part of the fragment sympathetically depicts a Russian character, a meditative, idealistic painter named Stephen, in search of "the august world of the infinite, the Eternal."[58] Stephen abandons his parents and his beloved homeland to "set off on his search for a creed . . . From Berlin to Dresden, from Dresden to Vienna . . . he travelled on trying to read a meaning into all the forms of beauty that solicited his admiration."[59] But like a latter-day Rasselas, Stephen's quest for meaning always ends in disappointment. The disillusioned artist finally settles in Paris, living in a building owned by a Spanish merchant, José Ortega, and his domineering wife. The fragment then changes focus to tell the story of Ortega's orphaned nieces, Theresa, who is brought up by another uncle, a "mystical fanatic" priest, and Rita, who is brought up by José's family with the help of another family.[60] According to Ford, Conrad intended to bring the two plot strands together by having the Russian artist marry the younger sister, Rita; after his marriage, Stephen would then meet the elder sister, Theresa, "fall beneath [her] gentler charm," and end by fathering her child. Ford reports that "the story was to end with the slaying of both the resulting child and the mother by the fanatic priest." At one time Conrad thought about "transporting the characters both to Spain and to Russia so as to get the last drop of contrast out of opposed race natures."[61]

Given Conrad's hostility towards virtually all things Russian, the fragment represents a puzzling choice of subject matter and tone. Not only is the Russian artist a sympathetic character, but there are no criticisms of any aspect of Russia; no negative word about its people, its politics, or its religion. Even though Stephen's father, a peasant merchant, cannot understand his son's artistic quest, he too is drawn sympathetically, even in his ignorance, and so is his wife. The novel praises the immense and overpowering beauties of the Russian countryside in passages worthy of Turgenev. Perhaps the elegiac tone, with its quiet and genteel dignity, represents Conrad's imitative tribute to Turgenev. But the question remains: how could Conrad have written a work so completely removed from the pain and tragic loss of his own experience of Russia, not to mention the collective experience of the Polish people? In no other place does Conrad ever offer such unmixed praise of what is distinctively Russian.

Unless other evidence emerges, Conrad's reasons for adopting such an attitude in this work will remain unexplained. There remains, however, the possibility that *The Sisters* reflects a time of his life when he was enamored with Russia, or at least a time when he possessed hope in its potential. This explanation, though seemingly far-fetched, has some historical support. Eloise Knapp Hay has found in one of the letters from Conrad's uncle, Tadeusz Bobrowski, evidence that "Conrad had embraced for a time [about 1880–81] certain aspects of the Russian mystique. It may have been during this period that he first read Dostoevsky . . . who may have transmitted some of his Slavophilism to Conrad."[62] The letter, which is also cited by Avram Fleishman, shows the uncle's attempt to correct the naive and idealistic Pan-Slavic hopes of the nephew.

Pan-Slavism represented the most potent political movement spanning Eastern and Central Europe in the ninteenth-century. Its goals were powered by diverse and sometimes contradictory nationalistic and cultural agendas, based on romantic dreams, as Fleishman has noted, of the "union of all Slavic peoples" and usually dependent on Russia's potential role as liberator and unifier. From Napoleon's re-mapping of Europe to the Serb rebellions against the Turks, Pan-Slavism permeated nineteenth-century politics. The power of the Pan-Slavic ideal is memorably portrayed in Book 7 of *Anna Karenina,* where Levin's brother, Koznyshev, dedicates himself to "our co-religionists and brother Slavs"; the Serbian war "aroused in the whole nation [i. e., Russia] a desire to help their brothers not only with words but by deeds." That sense of Slavic unity filled trains with young men, including the despairing Vronsky, who left Russia to join their Serb brothers.[63] Apparently, Conrad's own hopes for Poland were linked to that ideal. According to Fleishman, "even in the first years of his self-imposed exile, Conrad continued to indulge himself in certain of the mystical theories of Polish national revival, namely those which go under the heading of 'Pan-Slavism.'"[64] In Hay's judgment, Conrad, during this period, "seems to have entertained a notion that Poland might become the leading Slavic nation in the Panslavonic movement."[65] Though his hopes were those of a Polish patriot, they apparently remained tied to a belief in Russia's Pan-Slavic destiny, as Bobrowski's letter indicates:

What you write of our hopes based on Panslavism is in theory both splendid and feasible, but it meets great difficulty in practice. You don't take into account the significance which actual numbers have in the affairs of the world. Each of the more influential nations starts by relying apparently on the Panslavic ideal and by forgetting its own interests – but secretly and almost unconsciously relies on some aspect of its existence that will ensure its leadership.

Bobrowski warned his nephew that "Russia does not interpret Panslavism otherwise than as a means of russifying all other nations."[66]

Conrad may have retained elements of that belief in the Pan-Slavic mystique while writing *The Sisters.* His decision not to return to the novel may have been influenced by a violent rejection of his former beliefs. Perhaps *The Sisters* came so close to his youthful Slavic enthusiasms that he could never find the distance he needed in order to write about the subject; the novel is, after all, the story of a young Slavic artist who leaves country and family to pursue romantic dreams and artistic truth, an artist who finds no certitude for his mystic yearnings and who feels oppressed by the memories of all that he left behind. That, of course, is an argument built upon suppositions that cannot be proven either true or false. As an argument, however, it has potentially great explanatory power. If Conrad, as Hay supposes, once embraced a Russian mystique, that youthful embrace may help to explain the depths of his hatred for Dostoevsky. Hatred often flourishes in soil enriched by the decayed matter of love, and Conrad may have hated the Russian novelist who epitomized his own naive, youthful, and rejected dreams. Perhaps admiration preceded Conrad's disdain for Dostoevsky.

Ford's preface to the 1928 publication of *The Sisters* draws provocative comparisons to Dostoevsky that may have been derived from Conrad himself. The preface reports that Conrad shared Ford's own belief that novels "should usually concern themselves with the life of the great cities." Ford claims that his friend and collaborator at one time "wished to be what I have called a straight writer, treating of usual human activities in cities and countrysides normal to the users of Anglo-Saxon or Latin speech. *He desired in short to be a Dostoevsky who should also be a conscious artist* writing in English or preferably in French [emphasis mine]." Interestingly, no mention is made of the writers most admired by Conrad and Ford – Flaubert, Maupassant, and Turgenev, though all of them wrote about urban subjects. Later in the preface, Ford again compares his friend to Dostoevsky when he discusses Conrad's "two great novels dealing with city life" and acknowledges *Under Western Eyes* as Conrad's "finest achievement." "Here – again I say 'it seems to me' – you have Conrad appearing in the role of a Dostoevsky who is also a conscious artist."[67] Considering Ford's relative lack of interest in Dostoevsky, a novelist whom he seldom even mentions in his voluminous writings about literature, one may conjecture that the comparisons did not originate with Ford but with Conrad himself.

Ford judged Conrad's abandonment of *The Sisters* in 1897 for *The Nigger of the "Narcissus"* as evidence that "he bowed his head to his friends and the inevitable. Readers might be found for books about the sea; it was unthinkable that they would support Slav introspections passing in Paris."[68] Though *The Nigger of the "Narcissus"* "definitely established Conrad as a sea-writer," Ford, while admitting that few critics were likely to agree with his judgment, regretted his friend's choice of nautical subjects because he found them inherently less interesting than "the misty problems of the Slav soul amidst the more complicated, strained and subtle psychologies of city streets."[69]

Conrad's seafaring fiction does seem far removed from the confining, sunless spaces of Dostoevsky's St. Petersburg or the earth-bound, gossipy provincialism of his Russian small towns. Yet similarities between the two novelists surface even in Conrad's stories of the sea. Works such as *The Secret Sharer* and *The Shadow Line*, for example, can be profitably analyzed in terms of their Dostoevskian use of doubles. Albert Guerard, in his justly acclaimed study of Conrad, found that he, "like Dostoevsky, finds the best way to dramatize the schisms of the spirits: to objectify in a physical outsider a side of the self we sympathize with yet condemn."[70] Like Dostoevsky, Conrad returned again and again to studies of tragic isolation and romantic pride, of characters such as Jim and Kurtz who by self-will or fate perceive themselves as beyond the reach of ordinary moral or social standards. Like his Russian counterpart, Conrad focuses on characters in the face of catastrophe who have to make choices between crime and fidelity, despair and faith, evasion and commitment, individual and collective standards. One has to move to his land-bound novels to find the most provocative similarities between the two novelists.

Conrad's political novels – *Nostromo*, *The Secret Agent*, and *Under Western Eyes* – can be seen as stages in an evolution leading to a Dostoevskian meeting ground, one that was hinted at in *The Sisters* but never achieved. Without diminishing the purpose and integrity of *Nostromo* and *The Secret Agent*, they can be judged as necessary antecedents to the writing of *Under Western Eyes*. In contrast to Lawrence, Conrad had to wait until he was well established and secure in his reputation before he could write about life in the dark, blighted land of his childhood. For temperamental and artistic reasons he needed to distance himself from his subject matter, and he may have abandoned *The Sisters* because of that need. Yet with each successive political novel, he came a step closer to the tragedy of his family and his childhood. He stepped closer to the brutal effects of political repression and the reactive dreams of regeneration through revolution that were responsible, however indirectly, for destroying the lives of both his parents, leaving him an orphan and exile.

Nostromo, published in 1904, stands as his most ambitious political novel, an attempt to depict an entire society; yet the novel also stands at the furthest distance from Conrad's personal experience. Here, he created with convincing detail a world far removed from his own life. To achieve the verisimilitude and "felt life" of *Nostromo*, he relied heavily on knowledge drawn from his readings and his friendship with R. B. Cunninghame Graham, the writer, socialist politician, and Latin American expert.[71] That the novel brims with a Dickensian abundance of characters and represents a remarkable cross-section of Sulaco, from the aristocracy to the Indian miners, from hotel-keepers to the outlaw peasants, is a tribute to Conrad's imaginative power. Though he deals with issues that will continue to preoccupy him throughout his political novels – revolution, repression, political idealism, and political cynicism – he does so only by keeping the subject matter at a safe distance. However convincing the details, Costaguana and Sulaco are purely fictional worlds, the powerful result of an impressionist and symbolist imagination.

With *The Secret Agent*, published in 1907, Conrad moved a step closer to his own experience. Unlike *Nostromo*, the plot hinges on an actual incident that occurred in the capital of Conrad's adopted homeland. The London anarchists in the novel may be seen as his composite and satiric rendering of the anarchist world that he encountered through the Garnetts, if not through personal meetings then at least through the stories and reminiscences he heard at their home. The creation of the fat, charming, idealistic Michaelis who is celebrated by the upper strata of society may have been partly a result of stories that Conrad had heard about Stepniak.[72] The plot's political intrigue brings the author closer to his own experience as a victim of czarist politics. Yet Conrad is purposely indirect about the national identity of the embassy that plays such a crucial role in the novel, naming it with typical Conradian indirection. After Mr. Vladimir tells the Assistant Commissioner, "I've always felt that we ought to be good Europeans," the Assistant Commissioner replies, "Yes . . . Only you look at Europe from its other end."[73]

Perhaps Conrad was reticent about explicitly naming the embassy because he wanted the novel to have an English center, not a Russian one. Though his story is framed by the immoral and dehumanizing politics of czarist Russia, the center of attention remains consistently English, from Verloc, the English citizen, shopkeeper, and complacent seeker of middle-class comfort, to his stoic English wife, Winnie, who does not question her husband until it is too late. Conrad does not allow the narration to bring us very close to the one character (Vladimir) whom we know for certain is Russian; the other characters in the novel are either English or of uncertain nationalities. Such evidence suggests that Conrad intended his work to come across as a novel about an essentially English subject written from an English point of view.

The Secret Agent brings Conrad closer to Dostoevsky's world, however, than he had ever come before. The unsparing examination of anarchists, revolutionaries, and reactionaries and the unmasking of their petty motives, their intellectual shallowness, and their moral lethargy call to mind Dostoevsky's fiction. The dark, ironic tone of *The Secret Agent* is especially reminiscent of *The Possessed*. Both novels are dominated by a black vision of a world where goodness is either too powerless or too naive to contend with the forces of despair and destruction. In both novels the elements of order and disorder are caught in the same treacherous web of sham and deceit. Their plots hinge on the gradual revelation of dark secrets (Stevie's death, Stavrogin's marriage, the plot to kill Shatov and incite incendiary rebellion), yet revelations bring further destruction rather than a cleansing truth. In each, political subversion has tragic domestic consequences; the activities of revolution and counter-revolution tear apart domestic relationships, those between husband and wife, parent and child, and brother and sister. Characters representing varying degrees of impaired judgment, such as Verloc, Shatov, Winnie, and Marya Timofyevna, are entangled in events beyond their control, yet each pathetically believes in his or her own illusive control of destiny. Pyotr Trofimovitch and the Professor, the fearless and chillingly extreme sources of physical, moral, and social destruction, remain free and uncontrolled at the end of the novels, implying that the worst evil has yet to occur. Both novels end with suicides (Stavrogin's and Winnie's) that are more pathetic than tragic. Finally, the characters who seem most deserving of our sympathy, Stepan Trofimovitch and Stephie, are victims of evil that they can sense but cannot comprehend.

The character of Stevie also brings to mind two other Dostoevsky novels. Like Prince Myshkin in *The Idiot*, Stevie abounds with intuitive sensitivity and compassion for suffering, but he has an enfeebled understanding that renders him incapable of living in a morally ambiguous universe where good and evil are often inextricably mixed. Stevie's most memorable experience of evil is brought about by witnessing the senseless beating of a horse, an incident that recalls Raskolnikov's haunting dream of his boyhood self in *Crime and Punishment*. Stevie, like the young Raskolnikov, suffers intensely with the horse, but he too is powerless to alter the outcome. *The Secret Agent*, the character of Myshkin, and Raskolnikov's dream all present visions of innocence rendered helpless before evil.

Irving Howe finds that "Dostoevsky is everywhere to be seen" in the novel, "though more or less as a force to resist than an influence to absorb." "To Conrad the Dostoevskian milieu seemed barbaric, lawless, Eastern, an enemy of the 'sanity and method' he clung to"; yet Howe asserts that Conrad could not "turn his back" on this milieu, "perhaps because he sensed that in this . . . was to be found the most highly charged experience of his time."[74] Given the similarities of subject matter, how can Conrad be said to "resist" the "force" of Dostoevsky? The resistance lies partly in his choice of an English context but mainly through his choice of narrative method. Conrad's disrupted chronology and his impersonal, ironically aloof narrative style (which compounds the ironic effects of the disrupted chronology) are not only means of controlling the reader's response; they also serve to keep an aesthetically controlled distance between the author and his "barbaric" subject. Such distance contrasts sharply with Conrad's view of Dostoevsky. He mistakenly saw the Russian novelist as incapable of artistry because he was so thoroughly and passionately immersed in his subject matter. Conrad believed that Dostoevsky failed to create a literary discourse, that his narratives lacked the classical virtues of unity, restraint, and radiance, making no effort to achieve an elevated diction and euphonious beauty, negating all hope of dispassionate exposition. Conrad would define a novel as art only if he could find evidence of an objective construct, a structure seemingly vacated by the author, a triumph of a depersonalized aesthetic. Though Conrad might write about anarchists he could not cease to be a gentleman abiding by civilized standards of decorum and restraint.

Under Western Eyes maintained Conrad's standard of narrative civility, but it also enabled him to contend more directly with the Russian ghosts of his own past. He announced in a 1908 letter to Galsworthy that his intention for the novel was to "capture the very soul of things Russian."[75] The finished work shows that Conrad was indeed able to transcend his hatred for things Russian. Edward Garnett, in a retraction of his earlier comments, judged it as a sympathetic response to the country and the people who were the source of his friend's deepest suffering: "All that he [Conrad] had known and all that his family had known and suffered at Russian hands, all that he had read and brooded deeply over, he put together without artistic prejudice."[76]

Conrad's preface to the novel, written nine years after its 1911 publication, calls attention to the heroic efforts of detachment needed to write it.

My greatest anxiety was in being able to strike and sustain the note of scrupulous impartiality. The obligation of absolute fairness was imposed upon me by the peculiar experience of my race and family, in addition to my primary conviction that truth alone is the justification of any fiction which makes the least claim to the quality of art or may hope to take its place in the culture of men and women of its time. *I had never been called to a greater effort of detachment: detachment from all passions, prejudices, and even from personal memories.* (Emphasis mine)

The statement shows the melding of Conrad's artistic aims and his need for personal detachment. Even though he admits that the subject matter of *Under Western Eyes* comes perilously close to his deepest antipathies and suffering, the admission is only partial, for a disclaimer of sorts immediately follows. Conrad claims that "no special experience" was necessary to create "the various figures playing their part in the story," and that he only relied on a "general knowledge of the conditions in Russia." The novel, his preface suggests, was simply the result of an applied formula, the "formula of senseless desperation provoked by senseless tyranny" that explains the "moral and emotional reactions of the Russian temperament."[77] Conrad implies that he had no need or cause to draw upon his own unique experience of Russian tyranny. If that were true, however, he never would have had to struggle so hard to detach himself.

His ambivalence towards his Russian subject may be partially explained by the spirit of Dostoevsky that hovered so near the topic. According to Jessie Conrad, no other work proved as difficult to write: it was the only book "which, from a few words which he [Conrad] dropped at different times, I think he regretted having begun at all." Jessie goes on to explain her husband's fear of Russian comparisons: "He told me once that this work, which he considered to be intensely personal in its views and its style, would inevitably be pronounced by certain critics as derivative! *'They will be trying to drag in comparisons with Russian writers of a certain kind'*, he said. The mere thought of this was odious to him [emphasis mine]."[78] *Under Western Eyes* can be viewed as a literary struggle with Conrad's greatest rival – the author he feared as one who would "deny everything for which I stand."[79] The novel may be interpreted, as Jocelyn Baines has observed, as a "challenge to Dostoevsky on his own ground" which renders the psychology of Russia "through a Western European perspective."[80]

The thinly veiled allusions to Dostoevsky in the author's note hint at the rivalry. Conrad takes pains to remind his audience that "Nobody is exhibited as a monster here, neither the simple-minded Tekla nor the wrong headed Sophia Antonovna." Even the "perfect flower of the terrorist wilderness," Nikita (who, along with Tekla, could be easily transplanted to Dostoevsky's fictional universe), is best described in terms of "banality," not "monstrosity."[81] Conrad suggests that his characters are more comprehensible and more humanely drawn than the monstrous creations of his rival. Yet he borrowed extensively from the writer whom he perceived as the embodiment of Russian evil and excess. While *Under Western Eyes* owes a heavy debt to Dostoevsky, as will become evident, it also functions as a creative retort.

"The plot of *Under Western Eyes*," as Irving Howe maintains, "is inconceivable without Dostoevsky."[82] While comparisons can be drawn between this novel and virtually any of Dostoevsky's, for Conrad's predecessor shared his interest in the fevered passions, distorted hopes, and brutal contradictions of revolutionary and counter-revolutionary worlds, *Crime and Punishment* alone exerts a direct and controlling influence. Ralph Matlaw even suggests that the "patent similarity" of the two novels is "unique" in the annals of Western literature.[83]

Similarities of plot between the two works have been noted by many; perhaps the most succinct statement was offered by the Polish critic Wit Tarnawski:

Poleska [another Polish critic] quotes the fundamental resemblance, that the heroes of both novels are students psychically shattered by a crime they committed. To this we may add that love is a factor arousing the consciences of both and leading them to the confession of guilt. Resemblances in detail are still more striking: the roles of mother and sister in both novels, the mental derangement of both mothers at the end of the novels, the curious illness of both heroes after committing the crime, the identical roles played by the sledge-driver Ziemianitch and the house-painter, both suspected and at the same time relieving the hero of suspicion. Finally, both writers create a similar final situation so that their confessions may arise from their own free will.[84]

Frederick Karl also notes the striking resemblances btween the Mikulin–Razumov and the General–Razumov interviews in Conrad's work and the Porfiry–Raskolnikov interviews in Dostoevsky's: "Razumov's mental playing with his secret is similar to Raskolnikov's temptation to divulge his crime; the need for spiritual cleansing is common to both 'sinners'; the tensions of a pathological condition affect the sanity of both men." Karl also points out that "Razumov and Raskolnikov consider themselves superior to other men and destined for some calling in which their worth will be realized."[85] Much of what happens in each novel takes place on landings, staircases, and hallways as if to underscore the sense of life in flux, where change and movement are signs of impending catastrophe, where thresholds seem to lead only from bad to worse.

Similarities of language are perhaps even more striking. Jocelyn Baines notes the following verbal echoes.

Razumov's "Do you conceive the desolation of the thought – no one – to – go – to?" recalls Marmeladov's "Do you understand, sir, do you understand what it means when you have absolutely nowhere to turn?" Razumov calls Nathalie Haldin a "predestined victim" just as Raskolnikov calls Sonia Marmeladov an "eternal victim." Nathalie Haldin says "It is impossible to be more unhappy," and Sonia says to Raskolnikov: "There is no one – no one in the whole world so unhappy as you." Then Razumov's "it was myself, after all, whom I have betrayed" recalls Raskolnikov's "I murdered myself, not her!"[86]

Eloise Knapp Hay found another curious connection when examining the Conrad's original manuscript for the novel: "From the page where . . . [Sophia Antonovna] is first introduced until 232 pages later, she is Sophia Semenovna. Conrad may have realized only then that he was naming her after Sonia, the very different heroine of *Crime and Punishment*."[87] Despite the substantial differences between Conrad's Sophia Antonovna and Dostoevsky's Sophia Semenovna, the similarities between them go far beyond their names. The two Sophias are both historical victims, the prostitute of poverty and drunkenness, the revolutionary of the forces of repression. Both retain hope that the future may bring regeneration, and their suffering does not diminish their capacity for compassion, even for a murderer or a betrayer.

Hay also points out that Razumov's name is "a sort of epithet, from the Russian *razumet* (to understand), meaning 'the man of reason.'"[88] She might have followed her analysis a step further. The name Razumov calls to mind the name Razumikhin in *Crime and Punishment*, similarly related to the Russian term. Though Razumov may seem far removed from his impetuous and passionate "namesake" in Dostoevsky's novel, the two characters share important attributes. They are men of ordinary talent and unoriginal minds who work with diligence and common sense to pursue career goals. They resist the extremes of thought represented by their youthful contemporaries, remaining aloof from the stridently voiced aims of revolutionaries. Conrad's choice of Razumov as his main character, whom he regards as an "ordinary young man, with a healthy capacity for work and sane ambitions," seems to be repudiating Dostoevsky's emphasis on the "extraordinary"

Raskolnikov.[89] Conrad took what was a counterpoint in Dostoevsky's novel – the ordinary man of good sense – and made it the ironic center of his novel. Unlike Razumikhin, however, this ordinary man reflects the phlegmatic temperament of the English; he is described as "collected – cool as a cucumber. A regular Englishman."[90] Interestingly, Razumov and Raskolnikov seem to move in opposite directions as their respective stories progress: Razumov's imagination becomes inflamed and his passions fevered; Raskolnikov realizes that his extraordinary pretensions cannot be sustained.

Other similarities of plot and character can be identified. Conrad's depiction of the student Kostia, for example, has the characteristics of a Dostoevskian buffoon such as Lebezyatnikov in *Crime and Punishment*. The two characters are essentially weak and foolishly enamored with revolutionary rhetoric, yet each is capable of a kind of heroism. One acts to save the honor and well-being of Sonya Semenovna, the other acts to save Razumov's life, though Kostia's heroism is ironically undercut by the absence of any real danger to Razumov. Another minor character also evokes comparison to Dostoevsky. As Albert Guerard has noted, Conrad's Tekla is a "Dostoevskian figure of compassion."[91] Not unlike the pawnbroker's sister, Lizaveta Ivanovna, she is a pathetic figure oppressed by the ruthlessness of those with whom she lives. Finally, the two novels include striking similarities in their depiction of savagely brutal acts. The graphic account of Razumov's beating of the peasant sledge driver Ziemianitch bears a strong resemblance to the beating of the horse in Raskolnikov's dream. Horse and peasant alike are beaten senselessly into oblivion, and the act of violence itself becomes a source of pleasure for the person administering the beating.

Despite the many similarities between the two novels, their differences must be given at least equal weight. Jocelyn Baines finds "the aim, tone, and form of the two books" to be "absolutely opposed."[92] Irving Howe identifies the essential difference as one of tone: "But what is quite alien to Dostoevsky is the tone of cool detachment – of willed detachment – in which most of *Under Western Eyes* is composed. Dostoevsky looks at the political world as a reactionary, Conrad as a conservative . . . Conrad shares Dostoevsky's contempt for radicals, but he also indulges a condescension toward them that would be impossible to Dostoevsky."[93] Frederick Karl similarly relates differences in tone to narrative distance: "Dostoevsky continually moved in and out of his characters, whereas Conrad had already taken a firm position outside them. He had decided before he wrote that he would reject whatever his characters might say to him, whereas Dostoevsky allowed his characters to gain his sympathies even as he criticized their actions." While Karl neglects the considerable sympathy that Conrad showed for Razumov and others – and the enormous effort that such sympathy required – his comments are nonetheless useful. Karl notes how "Conrad moderated his materials by observing them through the eyes of a Westerner, the language teacher, thereby restraining his presentation of Slavic 'haunted creatures' as well as negating the 'fierce mouthings' that would have resulted from direct confrontation with anarchists and socialists."[94]

Karl's insight, though essentially correct, fails to distinguish among the tonal variations in the novel. In the first part, the narrator is wholly dependent on the information provided by Razumov's diary, in contrast to subsequent parts where he is also a direct observer and a participant in events. At times the action in the first part reaches a Dostoevskian pitch of intensity because the reader is drawn directly into the thoughts of Razumov; for long stretches it is even possible to forget the presence of a narrator. As a result, we are allowed to empathize more completely with Razumov. When the events move away from St. Petersburg to Geneva, the narrator becomes significantly more obtrusive, partly due to his own emotional involvement; his intrusions serve to expand the distance between the reader and the characters. We become more aware that these events are being *told* to us.

Dostoevsky, by contrast, sought to maintain a consistently close proximity between the reader and Raskolnikov. Though he wisely turned away from the use of first-person narration after drafts proved unworkable, he was still able to sustain a "first-person" immediacy throughout the novel, or at least until the epilogue. The reader intimately shares the thoughts of Raskolnikov and is only allowed infrequent glimpses into the thoughts of other characters. In effect, the reader participates in the activities of Raskolnikov's consciousness and encounters, with a sometimes painful directness, the contradictions, confusion, and suffering that he experiences. Such a narrative method does not ask for a suspension of the reader's moral judgment, but it does elicit an active sympathy for the protagonist that would be difficult to achieve through other forms of narration. In the darkest moments of his evil – the scenes leading up to and including the murders of the pawnbrokers – the reader only knows what Raskolnikov knows, and the narration depends upon our identification with him. Through the process of reading, we learn what it is like to think and feel as a murderer; the narrative method implicates us in Raskolnikov's guilt. For the sake of the story, and the theology that informs it, the reader must share the sense of guilt in order to experience the regeneration and redemption that will eventually follow.

Both novels tell of events that have occurred in the past, but only in *Under Western Eyes* are we constantly reminded of the distance of time. We are also reminded of the profound and unbridgeable differences of nationality, belief, style, and temperament that separate the narrator from the characters he is describing. As readers, we know that the story represents the narrator's choice of what can and should be told; we also know that some information, such as that contained in Razumov's diary, is only being partially disclosed. Though we may readily sympathize with Razumov, especially in the first part of the novel, as well as with characters such as Nathalie Haldin and Tekla, we are never allowed to forget that this is a story that is already closed. Conrad's fictional world always carries with it the markings that define it as fiction, in contrast to Dostoevsky's where narrative immediacy makes it sometimes possible to lose sight of the distinction between fiction and life, especially during first readings.

Irving Howe judges Conrad's choice of narrator as a sign of his own need "to be aligned with the orderly West, to be insulated from all that Russia implies." But "this Russia cannot be avoided" because "it is a bloated image of our own world. That the novel was written at all shows that Conrad knew this; that the English narrator so often blocks our view of things shows how deeply he needed to resist his knowledge."[95] Howe's statement links Conrad too closely to his narrator, for the narrator's judgment should not be construed as always reliable nor always immune to ironic undercutting. The narrator can be judged as an embodiment of the Bobrowski side of Conrad's family lineage – the voice of a sane, practical, and rational vision, not unlike the voice of Conrad's uncle and guardian. But there is another voice that must also be recognized as Conrad's, one representing the romantic, artistic, passionate, and doomed heritage of his father: Razumov, especially in the latter part of the novel, embodies the tragic Korzeniowski family line. The ironic interplay between the perspectives of Razumov and of the narrator mirrors the author's internal conflict. The Bobrowski-like narrator seeks to assert control over Korzeniowski disorder and passion, just as Conrad sought, with intermittent success, to master the disruptive impulses within his own psyche.

Howe's statement suggests a larger truth about the differences be-tween the two novelists. Conrad may write about the contentious forces of revolution, anarchy, and dissolution, but his style of writing never becomes grounded in the chaos he describes. The world may be heading to apocalyptic doom but his sentences seldom suffer for it. Nothing in Conrad can approach the frenzied chaos of the narration of Marmeladov's funeral feast or the pressurized cacophony of Nastasya's birthday party in *The Idiot*. The balanced cadence and elegance of his prose resists the intrusion of carnivalized stylistic elements just as thoroughly as it is resisted in Woolf's prose. Though Conrad experimented with many narrative styles throughout his career, the narrative voice of whoever is telling the story never loses control.

Dostoevsky, by contrast, seems to write from within the whirlwind. His consciously chosen artistic style represents one of the modern era's most ambitious attempts to reflect the disruption, turmoil, and conflict of the modern world. Robert Louis Jackson has admirably documented Dostoevsky's commitment to a new way of writing that would do justice to the complexity of his epoch. Jackson has drawn attention to the crucial importance of the distinction between *obraz* (form/image/beauty) and *bezobrazie* (the imageless, or, more suggestively, the monstrous) in Dostoevsky's aesthetics.[96] The artist's style, the Russian author insisted, must include the monstrous as well as the beautiful; only the combination of such opposites would enable the artist to render the "tragedy of the underground" that characterized his age.[97] Though Dostoevsky was capable of varying his style – his short fiction, drafts, and notebooks show how incessantly he experimented – he always had to write in a voice, or, more precisely, in multiple voices, that reflected the strain, mockery, and contrapuntal dissonance of his era. When Conrad heard such voices, he could not hear the artist. That does not mean, as some Conrad enthusiasts would have us believe, that he was a greater artist, but it does serve to measure the difference between the two writers.

Because of Dostoevsky's efforts to render the complexity of his contemporary society, his characters are always emblematic of larger social and historical forces. To a far greater extent than Conrad, Dostoevsky uses characterization to illuminate sociological typology. Joseph Frank and numerous others have stressed that he needs to be understood as an ideological novelist:

His creative imagination was stimulated primarily by the problems of his society and his time rather than by his personal problems and private dilemmas. Or, to put the point the other way around, he was always able to project these private dilemmas in terms that linked up with the sharp conflict of attitudes and values occurring in the Russia of his time.[98]

Dostoevsky wrote to render, in the words of Robert Louis Jackson, "man and society in movement, in a state of social upheaval."[99] Perhaps that explains the Russian novelist's well-known refusal to identify himself as a psychologist: the parameters of psychology, however defined, are too narrow to do justice to the social complexities that shape the human psyche. As an artist and man, he spent his life battling against reductive tendencies – whether of idealistic or materialistic origin – that would distort or oversimplify the human spirit.

Perhaps the truest measurement of the distance between Conrad and Dostoevsky can be found on a moral rather than aesthetic ground, one perhaps best illustrated by the opposing situations of their two protagonists. Razumov's crime of betrayal is not a simple moral wrong as many critics have too readily assumed. When a young man who holds no sympathy for revolutionary causes is asked by a student whom he hardly knows to risk his life and his future to help a political assassin go free, his situation can hardly be identified as clear-cut. The consideration that Haldin's request is at least partially motivated by Razumov's isolation, which ensures that if the latter gets caught he will have no family to implicate in his crime, deepens the level of complexity. Razumov does end by betraying Haldin, and the betrayal is regarded by all as heinous. But all the mitigating circumstances surrounding the betrayal need to be recognized: Razumov's choice was never obvious. If he had helped Haldin escape, he would have still been guilty of betrayal, for he would have violated his own convictions to support a cause that he disdained. The moral context of his decision, therefore, is charged with ambiguity. When Haldin entered his room, Razumov became enmeshed in an impossible dilemma, because there was no choice that would have morally exonerated him.

Yet the novel drives Razumov inexorably to a realization of his guilt. Like Oedipus, he has to accept the terrible consequences of his actions even though his crime seems more a result of a malevolent fate than a moral flaw. Though he accepts his guilt and confesses his crime, there is never any possibility for expiation or forgiveness in this dark, Hardyesque universe. Unlike Raskolnikov, Razumov can never free himself from his criminal burden. Conrad's flinty refusal to admit the possibility of forgiveness is explained in an earlier letter to Marguerite Poradowski, where he vehemently denounced the belief in the efficacy of suffering as a "fallacy . . . carried over from religious doctrines." He judged such belief as an "infamous abomination," "a product of savage minds." Conrad's universe, as his letter indicates, does not allow for second chances: "Each act of life is final and inevitably produces its consequences in spite of all the weeping and gnashing of teeth and the sorrow of weak souls who suffer as fright grips them when confronted with the results of their own actions."[100] Consequences of moral choices are irreversible for Conrad because there can be no faith in a forgiving God, no trust in a compassionate humanity. In a sense, Conrad's characters cannot be forgiven because their actions, their fates, are ultimately not the product of free will but the result of chance. Fate so thoroughly circumscribes human life that individuals are given few opportunities for moral choice: one wrong decision, itself often dictated by circumstance, virtually guarantees doom. Conrad's stern morality, built upon the debris of the Christian moral tradition, evokes the austere temperament of the ancient Stoic moralists.

Dostoevsky also perceived the collapse of Christian traditions, and his fiction depicts a psychic and social underworld that seems vacated by God. But his darkest and most despairing vistas point to the need for God, and every major issue in his fiction is ultimately a religious one. Raskolnikov's crime is more serious than Razumov's, both in intention and consequence; it was the result of a freely made choice, not a choice that was thrust upon him. Yet Raskolnikov can be forgiven for his crime, and his suffering does indeed lead to atonement, though critics have long disputed the artistic success of the novel's epilogue. Raskolnikov embodies one of Dostoevsky's most cherished beliefs: the image of the divine can never be entirely effaced from the human soul, even though it may be disfigured, as Jackson notes, in "cruelty, violence . . . and sensuality."[101] Though few novelists have so thoroughly explored the negation of God, Dostoevsky in the end identifies himself as an artist of religious affirmation. His religious beliefs inform every aspect of his writing, from choice of subject matter to aesthetic values.

Two documents provide invaluable evidence about Dostoevsky's religious beliefs. Shortly after being released from a Siberian prison camp in 1854, he wrote about his own faith to a sympathetic correspondent, Madame Fonvizina. While describing himself as "a child of this century, a child of doubt and disbelief" and admitting that his "thirst to believe" had cost "terrible torment," he offered a statement of his creed "in which all is simple and clear," a product of his rare moments of "great tranquillity": "to believe that there is nothing more beautiful, more profound, more sympathetic, more reasonable, more courageous, and more perfect than Christ . . . More than that – if someone succeeded in proving to me that Christ was outside the truth, and that if *indeed*, the truth were outside Christ, I would sooner remain with Christ than with the truth."[102] In the disjunction between faith in Christ and truth, Joseph Frank finds a resemblance to Kierkegaard's theology, which "separates off faith entirely from human reason."[103]

In 1876, Dostoevsky wrote an article, "The peasant Marey," for his *Diary of a Writer*, in which he recalled a conversion experience that occurred during his imprisonment. During an Easter-week holiday, he had been overwhelmed by the drunken and barbarous behavior of the peasant inmates, who had nearly beaten a Tartar to death merely to quiet him. Such actions filled Dostoevsky with disgust and intensified his feelings of isolation. To escape from the hellish din, he mused about impressions from his past life, a habit that enabled him to escape imaginatively. This time, he was flooded with a long-forgotten memory from his youth. While wandering on his father's rural estate as a nine-year-old boy, he had imagined that he heard the cry of a wolf. In his terror he ran to the peasant Marey, who was nearby plowing a field. The peasant gently assured his master's son that all was well, blessed him, and sent him back home. The recollection of this small gesture, suffused with tender compassion, abruptly changed Dostoevsky's attitude towards his fellow prisoners: "I remember when I got off the plank bed and gazed around, that I suddenly felt I could look on these unfortunates with quite different eyes, and suddenly, *as if by miracle*, all hatred and rancor had vanished from my heart." Even the "despised peasant with shaven head and brand marks on his face . . . why, he may be that very Marey; after all, I am not able to look into his heart."[104] Joseph Frank offers an insightful account of this article, which he sees as pivotal in explaining the "regeneration of [Dostoevsky's] convictions." As a result of this transformative memory, Dostoevsky "believed that he could at last see through the surface of the worth to a beauty hitherto concealed from the eyes of his moral sensibility."[105]

Conrad's struggle with Dostoevsky needs to be understood within this religious context. The Polish novelist, in the words of Edward Said, was "the restless seeker after normative vision and his solutions always had one end in view – the achievement of character."[106] But his search for moral standards never included a religious dimension; he apparently had disallowed the validity of religion early in his life. Conrad believed that religious quests diminished the dignity of the individual and cheapened life. No wonder he was so impatient with Dostoevsky; the Russian novelist was obsessed with questions that he regarded as illegitimate. *Under Western Eyes* can be seen as a kind of moral treatise about Dostoevskian issues with this important difference: all questions about God and religion have been omitted.

Despite the profound differences between the two authors, Conrad's indebtedness to Dostoevsky must be recognized. He may have hated his Russian counterpart, but his fictional responses show that he understood Dostoevsky's power far better than any other writer in English. If he turned his back in abhorrence of "monstrous" style, I believe he did so because he feared that if one followed the path of Dostoevsky the novel could not become an object of beauty. Perhaps more importantly, Conrad also feared Dostoevsky for personal reasons; he saw him as one who stared directly at the heart of darkness within himself, only to recoil in a shameless and public display of emotion. Conrad could grant Dostoevsky his black visions, but he could not forgive his excessive emotions, because they were the same emotions that Conrad struggled with and heroically sought to repress. And he could not forgive Dostoevsky's religious faith, for Conrad saw religion as a cowardly and evasive refusal to face life's most intractable dilemmas.

The writing of *Under Western Eyes* reveals Conrad's answer to Dostoevsky; it represents his attempt to combine the power of the Russian's monstrous subject matter with the beauty of Conrad's style. At the same time, the novel confronts the horrors of his own Russian past and his personal, political, and moral antipathy to what Russia represented. With *Under Western Eyes*, Conrad sought to exorcise the oppressive demons of both his life and his art. The struggle of this exorcism through writing led to a devastating aftermath immediately following the completion of the manuscript, described by Jeffrey Berman: "Conrad fell into a feverish delirium, during which he mumbled incoherently in Polish except for reciting portions of the English burial service, as if he were presiding over his own funeral."[107] He was bed-ridden and incapacitated for the next three months, reeling from the effects of what would now be described as a complete nervous breakdown. No other novel exacted such physical and emotional costs, because no other work brought Conrad closer to his own personal heart of darkness. Appropriately, only Conrad knows whether or not the exorcism of his own worst demons was successful.

Conrad's wrestling with the "demonic" Dostoevsky may help to explain the diminished intensity and literary quality of the fiction that followed *Under Western Eyes*. In writing his Russian novel, he came perhaps too close to a despairing abyss – and to the writer whom Frederick Karl has named as Conrad's *bête noire*.[108] Conrad's subsequent fiction prudently backed away from the confrontation that had been so costly. Interestingly, the only work, after *Under Western Eyes*, that is generally acknowledged as among Conrad's best, *The Shadow Line* (published in 1916), marks a return to his earlier nautical subject matter. Conrad never again wrestled with a Dostoevskian subject.

CHAPTER 6

Dostoevsky and the gentleman–writers: E. M. Forster, John Galsworthy, and Henry James

In 1924 the self-exiled D. H. Lawrence described his ambivalent attitude towards E. M. Forster in a letter to the author: "To me you are the last Englishman. And I am the one after that."[1] While the comment shows an appreciation of Forster's role as the gentle humanist, it also marks the distance between his sense of cultural and social continuity and Lawrence's modernist alienation. Forster's world of Cambridge and its classical education, of assured incomes and comfortable (though rented) estates, of kindly manners and cultivated conversation was one that Lawrence perceived to be in its death throes. The genteel tradition of liberal humanism that Forster represented could not address the perpetual crisis of the modern, or so Lawrence was convinced.

Lawrence's "last Englishman" designation can also be extended to John Galsworthy. Educated at Harrow and Oxford, groomed, as a gentleman's son, for the law, and skilled in the games of the ruling elite, Galsworthy wrote novels to condemn the smug sins of his peers. Like Forster, he realized that his social standing opened doors inaccessible to those less fortunate. Even more so than Forster, he possessed a sensitive social conscience that registered innumerable oppressions and cruelties, often at the expense of turning his novels and plays into social treatises rather than art. Yet Galsworthy's heated social criticisms never threatened to jeopardize his own secure social position. In fact, the tragic limitations of his life and art may be found in his inability to free himself from the guilt and responsibilities of his privileged status. His last words expressed his class-bound despair: "I've enjoyed too pleasant circumstances."[2]

Though not born in England, Henry James benefited from the legacy of English traditions transplanted to American soil. Schooled by tutors and governesses, and later enrolled at Harvard, James grew up in a rarefied social stratum, one that allowed him to move effortlessly from the Boston of William Dean Howells to the Paris of Flaubert and

Turgenev to the London of Tennyson and Gladstone. James defined himself as a writer who worked within a continuous tradition; he saw his innovations as the fine tuning of a venerable instrument rather than the creation of a totally new art form. By the time he became an English citizen near the end of his life, he was secure in his English loyalties and gentrified habits, though his citizenship was more a formality than an act of conscience or renunciation. Great Britain awarded him the Order of Merit, the same award – the highest in the realm – that was given to Forster and Galsworthy (the latter also received the Nobel Prize for literature). Lawrence, Woolf, Bennett, and Conrad never accumulated such honors in their lifetime because they were writers who, for reasons of social origin (Lawrence and Bennett), sex (Woolf), or nationality (Conrad), were never granted full membership in England's cultural elite.

Forster, Galsworthy, and James belonged metaphorically to the same exclusive club of humanistic gentleman–writers. When Dostoevsky, that most ungenteel of writers, was introduced to that club the reactions were mixed, yet all three authors shared an inability to recognize him as an artist in control. Forster, despite early misgivings, welcomed him because he upset the club's furniture and challenged its assumptions. Forster shared the excitement felt by his Bloomsbury compatriot Woolf as he experienced the emotional intensity of Dostoevsky's novels and their explorations of the inner recesses of consciousness. He acclaimed the Russian as a prophet whose work pierced the veil of the phenomenal world to give the reader a rare glimpse of mystical truths. The elements of Dostoevsky's world – its frank exploration of passion, its quest for transcendent truths, its moral sentiments, its suspicion of the intellect, and its probing of interior lives – appealed to many sides of Forster. Yet however much he appreciated the power and pathos, he was unwilling to abandon the cultural tradition of his class, with its emphasis on restraint, balance, and rationality. Forster could endorse Dostoevsky as a stimulus but not as a model: gentleman-writers should read his works but not follow in his ways.

Galsworthy was far more explicit and argued that the doors of the gentleman-writers' club should not be opened to Dostoevsky (though he was too polite to bar the doors himself). The most popular English novelist of his age castigated his Russian counterpart as a moral dissolvent, only grudgingly admitting his power. Young writers such as Lawrence, according to Galsworthy, made the mistake of "gloating over Dostoevsky" and led the novel to indecent excesses of sensuality and

self-consciousness.[3] Dostoevsky was judged a monstrosity by the standards of the gentleman's code of decorum and self-possession, a code
that can be traced to Victorian notions of what is manly and acceptable.
Yet Galsworthy also wrote an anomalous essay, "Englishman and
Russian," in which he included Dostoevsky in his praise of Russian
writers, raising the provocative thesis that "the Russian and the Englishman are as it were the complementary halves of man."[4] The essay can
be read as an indirect commentary on Galsworthy's realization of his
limitations as an artist and person. While he could not abandon the
standards of his class, he admitted that Russian writers such as Dostoevsky recognized depths of human life that the English could ignore
only at their own peril.

James, as might be expected, felt no need for such an admission. His
ample figure stands in the doorway of the gentleman-writers' club
blocking the admittance of Dostoevsky. His novels, according to James,
are "fluid puddings" that lack composition and defy "economy and
architecture."[5] While the words "loose, baggy monsters" were never
actually applied to Dostoevsky's works, the phrase carries the ring of
Jamesian authority nonetheless. (He did apply the expression to
Thackeray, Dumas, and Tolstoy, and by inference it can be extended to
Dostoevsky.)[6] Unfortunately, James's barbed comments were elevated
to the status of Olympian truth, playing no small role in the English-
speaking world's reluctance to admit Dostoevsky to the rank of artist.

James's opinion, however, is more complex than it appears. It can
only be understood within the context of his idolization of Turgenev, his
disdain for Tolstoy, his friendship with Hugh Walpole, and his conservative social values as expressed in *Princess Casamassima* and various
critical essays. His struggle against Dostoevsky is primarily an aesthetic
one, but it is also the battle of an agnostic against a religious believer, a
realist against an idealist, and a conservative against one perceived as a
disruptive threat. Dostoevsky represented a social, artistic, and religious
vision that James could not recognize as legitimate without casting
doubts on the validity of his own views. Perhaps that is why the
gentleman-writer blackballed the Russian.

FORSTER'S DISCOMFORTING ADMIRATION

Like most other writers addressed in this study, Forster first read
Dostoevsky in French. His earliest comment appears in a 1910 letter to
Lady Ottoline Morrell where he confessed disappointment in his first

readings of *The Brothers Karamazov* and *Crime and Punishment,* judging the former work to be "sketchy" but by no means "insincere." Forster's letter concludes with the astounding statement that "Dostoevsky always makes one feel 'comfortable.'" The Russian writer is contrasted in this respect with Tolstoy, James, Meredith, Browning, and Swinburne, and he is acknowledged as one of the "'dears' in literature."[7] Apparently, Dostoevsky's status as a "dear" stems from the perception that he is always sincere and never ironic. The statements here suggest that Forster, like so many others of his era, thought Dostoevsky to be incapable of literary artifice. Not surprisingly, the letter expresses uncertainty about whether being a dear "has anything to do with literature."

Nine years later, Forster wrote a review of Constance Garnett's translation of *An Honest Thief and Other Stories.* His comments show that he had read Dostoevsky's major novels in the intervening years (presumably, Garnett's translations). The review gives further evidence of his misgivings about Dostoevsky, though it also explains the admiration that would be expressed more fully in *Aspects of the Novel.* Like Woolf (who published her own review of this work), Forster judged the collection of stories a failure: "it chances to contain but faint echoes of the masterpieces that have gone before. Dostoevsky seems fatigued, repeats himself, his humour becomes facetious, his pathos mawkish." The publication of works deemed inferior seems to please the reviewer: "some of the stories are so feeble that they should dispel the superstition that Dostoevsky can do no wrong. It is a dangerous superstition, because only the more intelligent people hold it."[8]

The review shows that Forster had ceased to regard Dostoevsky as "comfortable." He summarizes the plot of "An unpleasant predicament," – "one of those agitating tales that are more alive than life, and fill the reader with unbearable shame and gene" – to re-create the unsettling experience of reading Dostoevsky. This farcical story about a bureaucratic general who drops in uninvited at his clerk's wedding party, hoping to show his magnanimity but succeeding only in ruining the party and subsequently the clerk, represents a typical Dostoevskian blend of pathos and travesty. The general, Ivan Ilyich, espouses "idealistic" and "humane" views about the need for social reform. He attempts to prove his philanthropic merit by crossing class barriers to attend his clerk's party. In his arrogant and naive manner, Ivan Ilyich believes that his action will "revive nobility" among the downtrodden partygoers, and that he "will raise up the humiliated man [the clerk] morally." "I will restore him to my very self," the general muses. "They are already mine: I am their father, they are my children." The story then records the disastrous and embarrassing consequences of the general's self-deluded gesture. His arrival at the party causes consternation and fear, eventually leading to scandalous disorder when a radical student debunks his humanitarian claims. At the story's end, the clerk and his family are ruined, but the general, despite his embarrassment, remains protected by his rank and social status.

Forster recognizes the story as a success. Obviously, it struck a sympathetic chord with the writer who throughout his career was preoccupied with attempts to reach downward across class barriers, from Lilia Herriton's misguided marriage with Gino in *Where Angels Fear to Tread* to Helen Schlegel's attempt to uplift Leonard Bast in *Howards End*. Most efforts to cross class lines in Forster's fiction end in failure, and his satire is frequently aimed at the naiveté, arrogance, or insensitivity of those who initiate the attempt. Yet he never endorses class insularity. Throughout his life as a writer, and as a man, Forster attempted to reach beyond the boundaries of his own social position. He knew how difficult such crossings could be. He also knew how even good intentions could lead to disastrous consequences. Such sensitivity to class issues helps to explain why Forster empathized with Dostoevsky's "Unpleasant predicament" and regarded it as a negative moral exemplum: "The force of his [Dostoevsky's] genius has dragged you into his pages, so that instead of reading a social satire or a farcical sketch, you have a very painful and personal experience and learnt a most valuable lesson."

"The dream of the ridiculous man" is the only other work in the collection that Forster judges a success. He praises Dostoevsky's use of the dream motif ("A dream in Dostoevsky is always good – it was a form in which his genius most gladly worked") and calls to mind similarly powerful dreams in *The Idiot* and *The Brothers Karamazov*. In this fantastic monologue, the narrator, who calls himself a ridiculous man, shares many of the attributes found in the narrator of *Notes from the Underground*. At the beginning of his tale, he portrays himself as isolated, neurotically introspective, hyperconscious, and irritated by humanity, vacillating between pride and self-loathing. The ridiculous man tells of a time when he learned an important truth, a momentous event that occurred last November, on the third of the month to be precise. On that dismal evening he contemplated suicide, aware of his own absurdity and the world's indifference. But he was distracted from his objective by his own emotional outburst before a pathetic eight-year-old girl whom he encountered on street, desperately crying for her mother. After verbally abusing the girl, the man returned home, dreamt of his own suicidal death, and of his transport to paradise, an Earth-like world innocent of all sin and corruption. Though he worships the inhabitants and their blissful life, the narrator eventually proceeds to corrupt "that golden age," introducing lies, egoism, possessiveness, and other hallmarks of civilization, a progress of corruption that mirrors Rousseau's account of social evolution in his *Discourse on Inequality*. Finally, the people turn against the narrator – and he finds himself awake. Enraptured by the memory of his paradisal vision, he announces that ever since his dream he has been preaching a message of universal love and fighting against the glorification of consciousness. The destroyer of Eden will now preach its message to his reluctant contemporaries.

According to Forster's interpretation, the story is one of mystical transformation, of paradise found, lost, and regained:

The "ridiculous man" dreams, like Mitya, of something that leaves him unreasonably and ridiculously happy, of a perfect and sinless planet to which he is transported, and which he corrupts until it turns into our world of sin. There should be nothing exhilarating in such a dream. Yet the emotion makes good, and a sense of joy and peace invades the reader in the final pages.

The corruption that the narrator brings to this dream planet parallels the intellectualized corruption that threatens Forster's world, ranging from the egoistic snobbery of Cecil Vyse in *Room with a View* to the bloodless abstractions of "The machine stops," an apocalyptic fantasy portraying a future in which a machine controls all aspects of human life. In the dream of the ridiculous man, "knowledge has been enthroned above feeling, and the consciousness of life above life" – two sins that are as abominable in Forster's fictional universe as they are in Dostoevsky's. The reviewer agrees with the narrator's diagnosis of corruption, yet he also subscribes to his end-of-story belief in redemption and utopian bliss: "there shall come in the end a glory the golden age never knew, when the same man [the narrator] shall learn to suffer not for himself but for others, and to love others as if they were himself." Forster takes the narrator's conclusion at face value, and he believes that the story points to the day "when paradise will return, return at once to our earth, inoculated for ever against decay, and men will again find in daily life a foretaste of the heavenly."

Significantly, the review pays far more attention to the utopian visions at the story's beginning and end than to the vision of paradise corrupted in the story's middle, because Forster regards "The dream of the ridiculous man" as a moral and religious fable with the clear message "that we must love one another." He approaches this story as one would approach one of Tolstoy's religious stories, with the assumption that an unambiguous lesson can be easily distilled. Forster never lost his nostalgia for religious faith, though he remained critical of Christianity and disinterested in its solace. The man who wrote "The story of a panic," "The curate's friend," and the ending of *The Longest Journey* – accounts of mythic transformations that liberated the human psyche and connected it with the natural and supernatural world – found Dostoevsky to be a fellow pilgrim. But Forster was a pilgrim who never got past Vergil to Beatrice. After he identifies what he regards as the message of Dostoevsky's story, he reveals himself as an unbeliever: "However great our inability to make these particular religious jumps, we must all admit that it seemed true while we were dreaming, and that a radiance followed into life after we had closed the book." His enthusiasm for the story is tempered by his inability to believe in paradisal dreams.

Forster's great interest in Dostoevsky's transcendent moral vision prevented him from recognizing the complexities of his fiction. The story does not present an unambiguous message. On one hand, its tone is idealized, gnomic, and messianic, as Forster recognized, but on the other hand the narrator is a romantic egoist who views himself as the only apostle of truth. At all stages of the narrator's story, from his suicidal reverie at the beginning to his corruption of paradise and his subsequent regeneration, he defines himself in opposition to the rest of humanity. Even when he proclaims his message of universal love, affirming the biblical mandate to love your neighbor as yourself, he makes a corollary and suspect claim that "he is the only man to know the truth." Though he moves from indifference and despair to affirmation and love, the narrator never moves beyond his own speculation. His consciousness of salvific truth is never tested in the world. Forster, however, ignores the problematic character of the narrator, choosing to focus only on his prophetic message. In praising the narrator's dream of paradise – a dream that touched Forster's own millennial hopes for human harmony and transcendence – the English novelist became oblivious to its ambivalent context.

Ironically, the two stories that Forster praises for their message are identified by Bakhtin as exemplary of Dostoevsky's original poetics. The Russian critic views the stories as illustrative of menippean satire, with their reliance on the "creation of extraordinary situations for the provoking and testing of a philosophical idea," "scandal scenes," "moral–

psychological experimentation," "sharp contrasts and oxymoronic combinations," "elements of social utopia," and carnivalized comic elements.[9] Bakhtin argues that Dostoevsky's content can only be understood in the context of his unique artistic forms and their indebtedness to menippean satire and "other kindred genres."[10] But Forster's review ignores all such concerns for form because Forster himself could find no evidence of artistic intention. Like Lawrence, he read Dostoevsky as a writer of gospels free from ironic complexity, and he shared the younger author's inability to recognize literary shaping.

Forster's enthusiasm for the two stories cannot be counterbalanced by his fears about Dostoevsky's influence. He judges the other stories in the collection as failures that can provide an antidote to the Dostoevsky mania that afflicted England: "The great Russian – least academic of men – is too often held up like a knout before the younger generation of English novelists, with the result that they flagellate themselves with him unskillfully and mistake the weals that he has raised upon their style for literature." Though admitting that "as a stimulus" Dostoevsky "is invaluable," Forster cautions that English writers should turn away from Dostoevsky: the Russian is simply too far removed from English traditions and values.

Echoing Woolf's views, Forster offers the following measurement of the distance between Dostoevsky and the English world: "He has penetrated – more deeply, perhaps, than any English writer – into the darkness and the goodness of the human soul, but he has penetrated by a way we cannot follow. He has his own psychological method, and marvelous it is. But it is not ours." The review concludes by predicting that the collection of stories will bring down Dostoevsky "from the pedestal where the idolaters would place him." Forster reminds the English readers that the Russian "is a writer, not a god . . . a writer who, for all his greatness, is a dangerous model for those who would write in England."

Given this cautionary conclusion, it is surprising that *Aspects of the Novel* (1927), a transcription of Forster's 1927 Clark lectures at Trinity College, Cambridge, offers unmixed praise for Dostoevsky. Forster first draws attention to him when he cites "all the Dostoevsky characters" as examples of "round" characters.[11] According to his definition, a round character is "one that is capable of surprising in a convincing way . . . It has the incalculability of life about it."[12] In Forster's judgment, any novelist's primary task resides in the creation of such convincing characters; consequently, character is given precedence in the novelistic hierarchy over plot, style, and "method." Dostoevsky, by implication, must be judged a resounding success.

Later in his critical study, Forster classifies him, along with Lawrence, Melville, and Emily Brontë, as a prophetic novelist. He begins his discussion of prophecy with Bloomsbury wit:

His [the prophetic novelist's] theme is the universe, or something universal, but he is not necessarily going to "say" anything about the universe; he proposes to sing, and the strangeness of song arising in the halls of fiction is bound to give us a shock. How will the song combine with the furniture of common sense? we shall ask ourselves, and shall have to answer "not too well": the singer does not always have room for his gestures, the tables and chairs get broken, and the novel through which bardic influence has passed often has a wrecked air, like a drawing room after an earthquake or a children's party. Readers of D. H. Lawrence will understand what I mean.[13]

Despite Forster's whimsical depiction, his respect for prophetic fiction clearly emerges. In the judgment of Wilfred Stone, there can be no doubt that "prophecy is for Forster the greatest achievement. It is the breakthrough, the seeing of the visible world as the living garment of God, the miracle of natural supernaturalism."[14]

Forster analyzes the nature of prophecy by contrasting George Eliot with Dostoevsky. First, he delineates what they have in common: "They were two novelists who were both brought up in Christianity. They speculated and broke away, yet they neither left nor did they want to leave the Christian spirit which they interpreted as a loving spirit. They both held that sin is always punished, and punishment a purgation, and they saw the process . . . with tears in their eyes."[15] Then he contrasts the prison scene from *Adam Bede*, where the preacher Dinah helps the condemned Hetty confess to the murder-by-abandonment of her baby, with Dmitri Karamazov's dream of the forlorn peasant women in the burnt-out village. This dream, which takes place after his interrogation about the murder of his father, an investigation that is accumulating seemingly irrefutable evidence, fills Dmitri with an overwhelming sense of pity and an unquenchable desire for life. When he awakes to find that an unknown stranger has put a pillow on the wooden chest under his head, his "whole soul" quivers with tears and a "new light, as of joy" suffuses his face.[16]

The difference between these writers is the difference between preaching and prophecy:

George Eliot [the preacher] talks about God, but never alters her focus; God and the tables and chairs are all in the same plane, and in consequence we have not for a moment the feeling that the whole universe needs pity and love – they are only needed in Hetty's cell. In Dostoevsky [the prophet] the characters and situations always stand for more than themselves; infinity attends them; though yet they remain individuals they expand to embrace it and summon it to embrace them; one can apply to them the saying of St. Catherine of Siena that God is in the soul and the soul is in God as the sea is in the fish and the fish is in God. Every sentence he writes implies this extension.

Forster acknowledges Dostoevsky as a "great novelist in the ordinary sense – that is to say his characters have relation to ordinary life." Yet he "also has the greatness of a prophet, to which our ordinary standards are inapplicable."[17]

Dostoevsky's characters, Forster says, can only be fully understood in their symbolic context: "Mitya, taken by himself, is not adequate. He only becomes real by what he implies . . . We cannot understand him until we see that he extends." At this point, the term "round" character cannot be applied, for "the part of him [Mitya] on which Dostoevsky focused did not lie on that wooden chest or even in dreamland but in a region where it could be joined by the rest of humanity. Mitya is – all of us. So is Alyosha, so is Smerdyakov. He is the prophetic vision." Foster seems to acknowledge such characters as the highest possible achievement of novelistic creation: "The world of the Karamazovs and Myshkin and Raskolnikov . . . is not a veil, it is not an allegory. It is the ordinary world of fiction, but it reaches back . . . to be merely a person in Dostoevsky is to join up with all the other people far back."[18] Though Forster disavows the term, he views Dostoevsky as one who takes the creation of character to the edge of mysticism.

Forster's discussion of such characterization resembles St. Augustine's methods of biblical exegesis. Dostoevsky's characters are judged as convincing at the literal level, but they also achieve anagogical truth, for they point to transcendent unity and enable the reader to experience the One behind the Many. Forster uses the language of mysticism to address the effect upon the reader:

Dostoevsky's characters ask us to share something deeper than their experiences. They convey to us a sensation that is partly physical – the sensation of sinking into a translucent globe and seeing our experience floating far above us on its surface, tiny, remote, yet ours. We have not ceased to be people, we have given nothing up, but "the sea is in the fish and the fish is in the sea."

However, unlike Augustine, Forster refuses to speak about the meaning of mystical experience. Again he shows that religious nostalgia need not have anything to do with substance of faith: "There we touch the limit of our subject. We are not concerned with the prophet's message [i.e., Dostoevsky's], or rather (since matter and manner cannot be wholly separated) we are concerned with it as little as possible. What matters is the accent of his voice, his song."[19]

Forster's attempt to separate "matter and manner" masks his own discomfort with Dostoevsky and all other "prophetic" writers. While he admires the visionary fervor of Dostoevsky's novels, he apparently remains untouched by their political and psychological content, and he truncates his discussion of their religious meaning. Part of his discomfort can be traced to his interpretation of Dostoevsky, along with Melville, Lawrence, and Brontë, as a grim writer, a prophet incapable of humor. Forster resists what he regards as the joyless demands of fiction which "asks for humility and even for a suspension of the sense of humor." His discomfort can also be traced to his unwillingness to abandon rationalism, for prophetic fiction requires that "We have indeed to lay aside the single vision which we bring to most of literature and life and have been trying to use through most of our inquiry [i. e., *Aspects of the Novel*]."[20]

Earlier in his lectures, Forster addressed the novel in terms of rational control. Prophecy, and to a lesser extent fantasy, requires that the tools of rational creation be set aside: "For the first five lectures of this course we have used more or less the same set of tools. This time and last [the chapters on Prophecy and Fantasy] we have had to lay them down."[21] In portraying the prophetic novel as antithetical to other types of fiction, Forster places it beyond the bounds of rational discourse. This type of novel, according to his definition, is non-reflective, intuitive, and unfinished, characterized by a "roughness of surface . . . full of dents and grooves and lumps and spikes." By this definition, Joyce could not be judged prophetic, for he was "too workmanlike," too "tight" in his control.[22] The true subject of the prophetic novel "lies outside words" and hence outside the domain of the critic.[23]

Forster's definition of the prophetic novel points to his own ambivalence – the ambivalence of an artist who never quite made up his mind about what he wanted his own art to accomplish. He wanted his fiction to expand and open out, to "reach back" to mystic depths, yet he could not abandon his own scepticism or the conventions of realism. He criticized Henry James and Joyce for being too artistic, too much in control, yet he could never feel comfortable with prophetic writers who abandoned control. In the words of Virginia Woolf, Forster's gifts for "realism and minute observation . . . served him too well."

He has recorded too much and too literally . . . He is like a light sleeper who is always being woken by something in the room. The poet is twitched by the satirist; the comedian is tapped on the shoulder by the moralist; he never loses himself or forgets himself long in sheer delight in the beauty or the interest of things as they are. [24]

The mystic would say that Forster was too much in love with the world to transcend it.

However much Forster admired the "manner" of prophetic fiction, he could never wholly believe in its "matter," and that, I believe, helps to explain the weakness of his own attempts to write prophetically, a weakness evidenced in the endings of *The Longest Journey* and *Howards End*. Forster wanted to achieve prophetic transformations that would somehow unite the disparate elements of his fictional universe. The endings of the two novels aimed for a mystic closure that would unite the natural, human, and supernatural realms. Such transcendence, however, eluded Forster, perhaps because he never fully believed it was possible in the first place, perhaps because he hoped to achieve it without losing anything of the world that was familiar to him. He would only board the omnibus to paradise if he were assured of a return ticket, a ticket that enabled him to retain his comfortable, genteel existence.

Forster's last recorded comment on Dostoevsky further substantiates his prophetic interests. His 1941 essay "The woman and the onion" recalled his experience twenty years earlier when he formed an English Literary Society "in a small Central Indian State" where he was the only Englishman. Forster admits in good humor that his audience attended only out of politeness and that they were bored by English literature. However, he did succeed once in delighting them by retelling a story from Dostoevsky's *The Brothers Karamazov*. He told his Indian listeners about the wicked old woman who had only performed one act of kindness in her life, when she gave an onion to a woman poorer than herself. After her death, the "onion that she had once given away" was lowered to her by an angel to pull her out of the flames of hell.

She clung to it, and he began to pull her out. Another of the damned saw what was happening and clung on too. This enraged the woman, and she cried out "No, no, I won't have this. It's my onion." And as soon as she said, "It's *my* onion," the stalk of the onion broke, and she fell back into the fire.

Forster's audience understood the story immediately and recognized it as an example of *bhakti*, "a belief that we are all indivisible and bound together through love, and that personal ownership impedes." The story, according to Forster, illustrates the "natural affinity between the Indian and the Russian outlook," and marks the distance between the English and the people of those two countries.[25]

Revealingly, Forster never mentions the role that the story plays in the novel, where it is not simply a parable of universal love. Grushenka tells the story during a crisis of self-abasement. A disgraced women, kept for the last five years by the wealthy and hard-hearted Samsonov, Grushenka has recently been buffeted between the affections of Fyodor Karamazov and those of Dmitri. As she herself confesses, she had hoped to corrupt Alyosha and lead him away from his monastic ways because his virtuous innocence – he turned his eyes when she walked by – was an affront to her degradation. At this moment, she is also contemplating the possibility of a return to her officer lover, the man who left her in disgrace and poverty five years earlier, though she has no illusions of his loyalty or love. While Grushenka is drawn to the story of the onion, she identifies herself as the woman so mired in corruption that she was capable of only one act of kindness. The context of the entire scene, in sum, produces an ambivalence about the parable that is completely absent in Forster's retelling. Even more importantly, the parable reson-ates throughout this section of the novel; its artistic function is far more complex than the simple didacticism of Forster's interpretation. Each character in the novel who hears the story interprets its meaning differently; its message is never static or univocal.

Forster's comments about the woman and the onion give final proof of his inability to appreciate the open-ended and ironic nature of Dostoevsky's art. Yet Forster, in contrast to Lawrence, was at least willing to learn from Dostoevsky's prophetic message and to recognize its value for humanity. The Russian writer, near the end of his life, at a celebration honoring Pushkin's legacy, did proclaim "the universal oneness of mankind," a message implicit in *The Brothers Karamazov*, and he was indeed hailed as a prophet by the audience.[26] Forster, who would have understood the religious fervor shown by Dostoevsky's admirers, paid serious attention to the author's visions of millennial harmony and spiritual transcendence. While Forster shared Conrad's concern about Dostoevsky's impact on other writers, he shared none of the Pole's disdain for emotional excesses and religious yearnings. Though doubt-ful of Dostoevsky's artistic stature, he appreciated him as one who strove for universal truth. Such an author may not be an appropriate member of the gentleman–writers club, but Forster freely admitted his value and, at times, welcomed his disruptive presence.

GALSWORTHY AND THE LIMITS OF GENTEEL RESTRAINT

John Galsworthy made few recorded comments about Dostoevsky's work, though he, alone among the major novelists of this study, actually visited Russia as a young man. According to his biographer, Catherine Dupré, he went there for business, not for literary purposes. For the most part, the popular novelist and playwright seemed to regard the Russian author with an impatient and disdainful condescension, an attitude not unlike that of a gentleman who finds himself embarrassed in public by his servant. However, Galsworthy was enamored with other Russian writers, especially Turgenev, and his generalities about Russian fiction (including that of Dostoevsky) help to illuminate his own tragic self-division. Even at the height of his popularity, when he was celebrated as the best novelist of his generation, Galsworthy remained sceptical of his own artistic ability, and he regarded his achievement as painfully short of his potential. Yet he allowed himself to be continuously distracted from his art in pursuit of social causes and genteel philanthropy. As an artist, moralist, and social reformer, he knew the Russian writers possessed a truth that he lacked, but he could never move beyond his own native reticence to reach that truth. In effect, he sacrificed his art to Victorian notions of duty and propriety.

Russian literature provided a powerful stimulus in the early stages of Galsworthy's writing. According to his own account, he began reading Turgenev in English at the onset of his career. He credited Turgenev and Maupassant as the "first writers" who gave him "real aesthetic excitement, and an insight into the proportion of theme and economy of words."[27] Galsworthy began writing his second novel, *Villa Rubein*, immediately after reading these two master storytellers. In the opinion of Edward Garnett, "every page" of this 1902 novel "shows the disciple's devotion to the Master, Turgenev."[28] Ford Madox Ford also recognized his indebtedness to Turgenev; Galsworthy, in Ford's opinion, was strongly influenced by the Russian's depiction of tragic love relationships, as well as by his humanitarian interests in social reform.[29]

A 1902 letter to Constance Garnett, who had just completed her translation of *Anna Karenina*, shows that Galsworthy's admiration also extended to Tolstoy: "The birth and Anna's death touch the highest emotional and insightful mark of Tolstoy as far as I know him; and the interview with Karenin, Landau, and Countess Lydia the highest point of satire." Galsworthy ranks Tolstoy here even higher than Turgenev, judging him to be Shakespeare's equal. He finds Tolstoy's art "a new kind of thing altogether. It can't be compared, it's new; in fact what Edward said to me the other day is true – it touches a new and deeper self-consciousness." The letter concludes with a comment that suggests Galsworthy's own involvement in her translations: "In any case yours has been a wonderful piece of work, and I am all the more eager for *War and Peace*. I feel I should be more useful to you over sporting passages than military, but please send me anything you like."[30] Perhaps Constance sent her manuscript to him so that he could verify the accuracy or appropriateness of her translated descriptions of such gentlemen's concerns as war and sports.

Eight years later, Galsworthy showed his interest in Dostoevsky, spurred by Maurice Baring's *Landmarks in Russian Literature*. Like Arnold Bennett, Galsworthy reacted strongly to Baring's moralistic praise of Russian writers. But where Bennett used his review of Baring's work as an occasion to appeal to Heinemann for a complete translation of Dostoevsky, Galsworthy simply expressed his feelings privately in a letter to Edward Garnett: "He's piqued me up to a desire to read Dostoevsky's *The Idiot* and *The Brothers Karamazov* and *The Possessed*, but what translations are there?"[31] Interestingly, Galsworthy even draws a comparison with his beloved Turgenev: "I agree that Tolstoy and Dostoevsky reach places that Turgenev doesn't even attempt."[32]

By 1914, however, Galsworthy could offer no praise of Dostoevsky after having read *The Brothers Karamazov* twice. This time he wrote to Edward Garnett expressing a visceral dislike: "I'm bound to say that it doesn't wash. Amazing in places, of course; but my God! – what incoherence and verbiage, and what starting of monsters to make you shudder. It's a mark of these cubistic, blood-bespattered-poster times that Dostoevsky should rule the roost." Galsworthy shared the distaste of his friend Conrad for Dostoevsky's "monstrous" elements; both writers denounced his works for a lack of restraint and control, expressing embarrassment about his subject matter. Galsworthy concluded his letter by noting the superiority of the other two members of the Russian trinity: "Tolstoy is far greater, and Turgenev too."[33]

Eight days later, irritation towards Dostoevsky again surfaced. At the conclusion of a letter to Edward Garnett filled with bitter complaints about *Sons and Lovers*, Galsworthy lamented: "Confound all these young fellows: how they have gloated over Dostoevsky." By implication, Dostoevsky is aligned with Lawrence against those who write "true" novels. The Russian and the young Englishman are placed outside the tradition of the novel.

Galsworthy did not attack Lawrence's handling of the relationship between the mother and son in the novel; rather, he objected to the frank sexuality of Paul Morel's other loves, Miriam and Clara Dawes. "That kind of revelling in the shades of sex emotions," Galsworthy complains, "seems to me to be anaemic." A writer should not "spend time and ink in describing the penultimate sensations and physical movements of people getting into a state of rut." "The body's never worthwhile," Galsworthy insists, "and the sooner Lawrence recognizes this the better"; "The men we swear by, Tolstoy, Turgenev, Chekhov, Maupassant, Flaubert, France, knew that great truth; they only use the body, and that sparingly, to reveal the soul."[34] Galsworthy's lament that Lawrence had "gloated over" Dostoevsky seems at first glance far-fetched. The Russian novelist, after all, does not share Lawrence's Dionysian affirmations of the body. But Galsworthy is correct in recognizing a more profound similarity between the two writers.

Dostoevsky and Lawrence focus on the dark contradictions of the divided self. They point a glaring spotlight towards the innermost recesses of tortuously inconsistent desires. For example, characters as otherwise diverse as Paul Morel in *Sons and Lovers* and Arkady Dolgoruky in *Raw Youth* must come to terms with desires that are angelic and demonic at the same time. Arkady, the illegitimate son of Versilov, both loves and hates his father, his role model and enemy. He dreams of an ideal beauty, yet has a base longing for Akhmakova, the same woman who is tragically loved by his father. Similarly, Paul Morel is defined by contraries: the Oedipal ambivalence of his relationship for his mother; his soulful love and hate for Miriam; his elemental passion for Clara. Certainly, other novelists – including all those identified in Galsworthy's quotation – analyze the origins of desire. But few novelists can match the emotional intensity, the quicksilver mutability, or the simultaneity of contradictory desires captured by Lawrence and Dostoevsky.

Galsworthy, I believe, compared Lawrence to Dostoevsky because he found the same "sin" in both – a failure to present a vision of the human soul that is ennobling, impersonal, mysterious, dignified, and therefore comforting. In a 1910 essay about Conrad, Galsworthy identified his own artistic ideals. He noted "a certain cosmic spirit" that can be discerned behind Conrad's art. The novelist has "the power of making the reader feel the inevitable unity of all things that be; of breathing into him a solace that he himself is part of the wonderful unknown." Only few writers have such powers – Shakespeare, Turgenev, Dickens, "and Joseph Conrad not among the least." While Galsworthy retained no faith in traditional religion, he yearned for a universal truth. Such truth, he felt, could never be explained, but without it no work could achieve the venerated status of art: "Art inspired by cosmic spirit is the only document that can be trusted, the only evidence that time does not destroy . . . The just envisagement of things is then the first demand we make of art."[35]

The tragedy of Galsworthy can be found in the gap between his ideal of art and the workmanlike constructions of most of his own fiction. Even more so than Bennett, he wrote with a Midas touch. But Galsworthy could not take comfort in his fame or money, for he knew that most of his work stopped far short of greatness, and that he failed to reach deep. Catherine Dupré gives a convincing explanation for this failure:

> In his [Galsworthy's] own character, in its very virtues, were inhibitions that forbade the writing that he needed to write for his own peace of mind, for his own growth as a writer. Courage, he believed, was the highest virtue, courage – which could be called, less kindly, the "stiff upper lip" – and a courageous man does not pour his sufferings over the pages of a book, or even speak of them to another human being; he bears bravely and silently that which is hurting him.[36]

Galsworthy knew that his success came at the cost of his art. But he also knew that it could not be otherwise, given his personality and his belief in the gentleman's code. Perhaps the most eloquent testimony to Galsworthy's "essential virtues and limitations" is offered by his friend Edward Garnett: "In his love of justice, in his reserve, in his amalgam of hardness and compassion, in his fair-mindedness and his instinct for balance, in his poetical romanticism and sentimental leanings," Galsworthy "stands for the best in upper-class Englishmen of his period."[37]

The Russian literature that had provided a stimulus to the young Galsworthy served as a subtle reminder to the mature writer of all that he failed to accomplish. In 1916 Galsworthy wrote an essay "Englishman and Russian" that compared the two as the "complementary halves of man." The essay typifies its period, for there were many attempts to define national characteristics of the English and the Russians through their respective literatures. Usually, most such efforts were written in ignorance of the ethnic, racial, and religious diversity that can be found within the political boundaries of Russia. Writers mistakenly assumed Russia to be a monolithic and homogeneous culture. Galsworthy's essay, however, offers more than historical interest because it can be read as an indirect gloss on his own failure to achieve the kind of art that he valued most.

Here, Dostoevsky is joined with Gogol, Turgenev, Tolstoy, and Chekhov, all of whom are praised for "amazing direct and truthful revelations." Their works illuminate "secrets of the Russian soul" to such an extent that Galsworthy even claims "the Russians I have met seem rather clearer to me than men and women of the other foreign countries." While he still remains sceptical that the self can penetrate into the depths of the other, he believes the Russian writers have moved further in this direction than others, and he offers a testimony that calls to mind Conrad's *Heart of Darkness* and Hugh Walpole's "Russian" novel, *The Dark Forest*:

The heart of another is surely a dark forest; but the heart of a Russian seems to me a forest less dark than many, partly because the qualities and defects of a Russian impact so sharply on the perceptions of an Englishman, but partly because those great Russian novelists in whom I have delighted, possess, before all other gifts, so deep a talent for the revelation of truth.[38]

Like his friend Walpole, Galsworthy viewed Russian literature as a means of profound self-discovery. His essay serves as a tribute to the depths of self revealed there and as an indictment of English limitations.

Galsworthy contrasts the Russian "spirit of truth" with the English "passion for the forms of truth." The prototypical Englishman, he contends, mistakes pragmatic honesty ("his word is his bond – nearly always; he will not tell a lie – not often; honesty, in his policy, is the best policy") for essential truth. The Englishman approaches life as a combative struggle of self-achievement; he "seeks to win rather than to understand or to 'live.'" Galsworthy declares that this produces a habit of "self-deception" requiring the Englishman to fly "from knowledge of anything which will injure his intention to make good." From the Russian who enjoys "unbottoming the abyss of his thoughts and feelings, however gloomy," the English can learn an invaluable lesson for living. "Frank self-declaration" and "self-knowledge," Galsworthy implies, are not learned in the classrooms or playing fields of the public schools.

Russian culture offers an invigorating emotional freedom. In Russia, "time and space have no exact importance, living counts for more than dominating life, emotion is not castrated, feelings are more openly indulged in." What the English count as "good form" is "a meaningless shibboleth" in such a country. To express his vision of national differences, Galsworthy even uses a drinking metaphor: "The Russian rushes at life, drinks the cup to the dregs, then frankly admits that it has dregs, and puts up with the disillusionment. The Englishman holds the cup gingerly and sips, determined to make it last his time, not to disturb the dregs, and to die without having reached the bottom." While admitting that the Russians might profit from the English "practical common sense" and "acquired instinct for what is attainable," Galsworthy envies their "emotional abandonment" and finds the lack of that abandonment to be the "great deficiency" of his native land.

Russian writers earn his praise for bringing "a directness in the presentation of vision" and "a lack of self-consciousness" to imaginative literature: "This quality of Russian writers is evidently racial, for even in the most artful of them – Turgenev – it is as apparent as in the least sophisticated. It is part, no doubt, of their natural power of flinging themselves deep into the sea of experience and sensation; of their self-forgetfulness in a passionate search for truth." The praise is extended to twentieth-century writers such as "Kuprin, Gorky, and others" who share the Russian "quality of rendering life through – though not veiled by – the author's temperament; so that the effect is almost as if no ink were used."

Galsworthy concludes by broadly discussing the Russian influence on English literature: "Our imaginative writings, at all events, have of late been profoundly modified by the Russian literature." As Lawrence did, he uses the language of disease to discuss this influence, though the connotations here are all positive: "Some of us have become infected with the wish to see and record the truth and obliterate that competitive moralising which from time immemorial has been the characteristic bane of English art." "In other words," Galsworthy summarizes, "the Russian passion for understanding has tempered a little the English passion for winning." The English have learned to admire the "truth" and "profound and comprehending tolerance of Russian literature," and their fiction, Galsworthy suggests, has already profited. He points, in a manner not unlike Virginia Woolf, to an English literature of the future that may combine Russian "spiritual and intellectual honesty of vision" with English "assertive vigour," to the day when English writers can "sink ourselves in life and reproduce it without obtrusion of our points of view."

To be understood fully, Galsworthy's essay needs to be approached as an elaborately indirect self-confession. Simply put, he admired in Russian literature what he found lacking in himself. Spiritual truth and emotional abandonment are attributes sadly missing in his own life and literature. As a writer and a man, Galsworthy knew that he had sipped his cup gingerly. The moralist who fiercely defended the oppressed and worked tirelessly for innumerable reforms, the man who turned away no one who knocked on his door asking for help, never allowed his deepest passion – his passion for art – to guide his life. He allowed himself to be pulled in too many directions because he knew that he was constitutionally incapable of facing his own depths. What he said of his fictional characters can also be applied to his own life: "I create characters who have feelings which they cannot express."[39] As Dupré has noted, this comment reflects his "own tragedy as a creative writer."[40] Like Soames Forsyte, his most memorable creation, Galsworthy never allowed himself to talk freely about what was most important.

This sense of an unfulfilled career helps to put his last comments on Dostoevsky in context. Less than six months before his painful and ignoble death – he apparently died, according to Dupré, in despair of both his life and his art – he wrote in response to an American who had inquired about his views:

I will answer your questions in order and as best I may:
1. If I were still reading Dostoevsky I have no doubt I should find him an interesting (and in some sort irritating) writer.
2. I doubt whether he is still a universal influence for the novelist. In morals and philosophy he was a dissolvent. Against dissolution there is always reaction.
3. On the whole he is not so great a man as Tolstoy, either as an artist or as a thinker.
4. He was very unbalanced, but his insight was deep and his fecundity remarkable. I think he will live.[41]

Obviously, the English gentleman never found a taste for the "dissolvent" Dostoevsky. Still, the fact that he could acknowledge his "insight" and "fecundity," however grudgingly, shows that he possessed some of that tolerance that he so admired in Russian literature. Though Dostoevsky's literature may have been lacking in genteel virtues, Galsworthy at least recognized it as enduring, at a stage in his life when he was uncertain whether his own would endure.

JAMES AND THE SACRILEGE OF ART

James's discomfort with Dostoevsky went much further than Galsworthy's. It was untempered by any positive valuations, for Dostoevsky represented a more dangerous and disagreeable challenge to him. To understand his response, one must begin with Turgenev. Like

Galsworthy, James encountered Turgenev's fiction as a young man and became an ardent admirer. His admiration extended to the man himself, for James met and befriended Turgenev in Paris in the 1870s. The young American regarded Turgenev as a hero, an embodiment of the literary and personal virtues that he most admired. James never lost that admiration.

Leon Edel describes the first meeting as "one of the sacred moments" in James's life.[42] James himself later recalled that moment in worshipful terms: "I shall never forget the impression he made upon me at that first interview. I found him adorable; I could scarcely believe that he would prove – that any man could prove – on nearer acquaintance so delightful as that." The young writer found his elder to be a virtual saint, a man "simple," "natural," "modest," yet "interested in everything." "Not a particle of vanity" could be found in the cosmopolitan Russian who told anecdotes "at his own expense with a sweetness of hilarity": "His sense of beauty, his love of truth and right, were the foundation of his nature."[43] One can imagine how the awestruck James, surrounded by Flaubert, Zola, the Goncourts, and other literary and artistic luminaries, listened to Turgenev's pronouncements at Flaubert's legendary Sunday afternoon gatherings. The acolyte of fictional art would never forget Turgenev's devotion to the same cause: "No one could desire more than he that art should be art; always, ever, incorruptibly, art." Not incidentally, James was also impressed with the size of Turgenev's fortune: "He could write according to his own taste and mood . . . and never was in danger of becoming a hack."[44]

James's literary admiration had preceded his personal admiration. In an 1874 essay he identified Turgenev as "the first novelist of the day." He praised him as one who "belongs to the limited class of very careful writers."

His line is *narrow observation*. He has not the faculty of rapid, passionate, almost reckless improvisation – that of Walter Scott, of Dickens, of George Sand. This is an immense charm in a storyteller; on the whole, to our sense, the greatest. Turgenev lacks it; he charms us in other ways. To describe him in the fewest terms, he is *a storyteller who has taken notes*. (Emphasis mine)[45]

James describes Turgenev as one might describe the narrator in one of James's own novels. He is "a devoutly attentive observer," "remarkable for concision," with a view of the "spectacle of human life more general, more impartial, more unreservedly intelligent, than that of any novelist we know." Like a Jamesian fictional hero, Turgenev is "universally sensitive . . . to the sensuous impressions of life – to colors and odors and forms, and the myriad ineffable refinements and enticements of beauty."[46] The charm of his fiction, according to James, "resides in this impalpable union of an aristocratic temperament with a democratic intellect. To his inquisitive intellect we owe the various, abundant, human substance of his tales, and to his fastidious temperament their exquisite form."[47] In the words of Leon Edel, "what strikes us as we read the article is the extent to which Henry, in describing Turgenev, seems to be describing himself."[48]

James later discovered that even Turgenev's method of composition resembled his own. The stories of the Russian writer did not originate with a vision of human action, "an affair of plot" – "that was the last thing he thought of." Rather, the "germ of a story" began with "the figure of an individual" whom the author found "very special and interesting."[49] In his preface to *Portrait of a Lady*, James drew on Turgenev's method to defend the dominance of "character" over "story." He recounted Turgenev's descriptions of the "usual origin of the fictive picture": "It began for him almost always with the vision of some person or persons, who hovered before him, soliciting him . . . interesting him and appealing to him just as they were and by what they were."[50] Like E. M. Forster, James viewed character as the keystone of fiction; they valued fiction as the privileged rendering of human thought and feeling.

James borrowed from the language of painting and used the term "fictive picture" to describe Turgenev's achievement. He found in his work the visualized details and the convincing framework of presentation – the marks of a literary "painter" in control – that were necessary to give fiction "the air of reality."[51] Perhaps the most succinct discussion of the analogy between fiction and painting, so often used by James to elevate and explain the aesthetic status of the novel, can be found in his preface to *The Tragic Muse*. There, James contends that the writer needs to choose "an indispensable center" for his picture, a focal point towards which all elements converge. A novel without such a compositional center is like a "wheel without a hub." While James admits it is possible to achieve a "pictorial fusion" in a novel that has more than one subject as its focus – "as certain sublime Tintorettos in Venice . . . showed half a dozen actions separately taking place" – such an effort contains the fearful risk of losing composition entirely. Though the preface describes his own attempt to weave together more than one major story line in *The Tragic Muse*, he expresses his "mortal horror of two stories, two pictures in one." Without pictorial fusion, without "a common interest" between the two story lines, the battle for artistic unity would be lost: "A picture without composition slights its most precious chance for beauty."[52] Turgenev, in James's perspective, never violated the lofty standards of pictorial composition.

What happens when composition is lost? Instead of producing art, the writer produces a "loose, baggy monster." Ironically, James's response to Dostoevsky needs to be understood within the context of that phrase, though it was never applied to Dostoevsky himself. James uses the phrase to illustrate what happens when composition does not prevail, when "absolutely premeditated art" has failed to assert control. Such works, despite the absence of art, may exhibit life "incontestably . . . as 'the Newcomes' has life, as 'Les Trois Mousquetaires,' as Tolstoy's 'Peace and War,' have it, but what do such large loose baggy monsters with their queer elements of the accidental and the arbitrary artistically mean?" James chastises Thackeray, Dumas, and Tolstoy for taking the novel beyond the limits of artistic control. He refutes the argument of those who consider such expansive works "superior to art": "But we understand least of all what *that* may mean, and we look in vain for the artist, the divine explanatory genius, who will come to our aid and tell us. There is life and life, and . . . waste is only life sacrificed and thereby prevented from counting."[53] Like Arnold Bennett in his later years, the Anglicized American constructed an oversimplified dichotomy between art and life. Where Bennett took the side of life, James chose art, but both were guilty of trivializing the merits of writers perceived in the opposite camp.

James elsewhere attacked Tolstoy as the antithesis to Turgenev, "the novelists' novelist": "Tolstoy is a reflector as vast as a natural lake; a monster harnessed to his great subject – all human life! – as an elephant might be harnessed, for purposes of traction, not to a carriage, but to a coach-house." In contrast to Turgenev who is praised for "an artistic influence extraordinary," Tolstoy is feared as a disastrous model: "His own case is prodigious, but his example for others dire: disciples not elephantine he can only mislead and betray." While conceding that Tolstoy offers "a wonderful mass of life," James evaluates his work as "a splendid accident," with no evidence of the "eternal spell of method" that can be found in Turgenev.[54]

Later in his career, James used the author of *War and Peace* as a means of illustrating the deficiencies of contemporary novelists such as Wells and Bennett.

Tolstoy is the great illustrative master-hand on all this ground of the discon-
nection of method from matter . . . Of all great painters of the social picture it
was given that epic genius most to serve admirably as a rash adventurer and a
"caution," and execrably, pestilentially, as a model. In this strange union of
relations he stands alone: from no other great projector of the human image
and the human idea is so much truth to be extracted under an equal leakage of
its value.[55]

James could never make a positive comment about Tolstoy, as this
quotation indicates, without immediately following it with a more
powerful negative statement.

After spending an entire career justifying fiction as a legitimate form
of fine art, James felt that his advocacy of beauty and composition were
undermined by the influence of Tolstoy and, as shall be seen, Dostoevsky. Contrary to popular stereotypes, however, James cannot be
dismissed as a drawing-room artist who was incapable of understanding
literature different from his own. He praised the "loose and liquid"
imaginative power of George Sand, even preferring her work to that of
Flaubert. Though James recognized *Madame Bovary* as a masterpiece, he
rated the sum of Flaubert's work "as inferior to George Sand . . . [who]
has the true, the great imagination . . . She conceives more largely and
executes more nobly; she is easy and universal and – above all –
agreeable."[56] James also admired the "extraordinary vividness" of Dickens and the "moral responsibility" of George Eliot.[57] He defended
Zola's artistry and worked tirelessly to promote the work of Balzac,
admiring his "great temperament" and the "figured tapestry" of his
novels.[58] Even Thackeray and Dumas, creators of the loose baggy
monster, were praised judiciously for their merits. In the context of the
late nineteenth-century, when most of his criticism was written, James
proved himself to be an empathetic, tolerant, and sensitive reader of the
novel in all its variant expressions.

Unfortunately, he became increasingly cautious in his twentieth-
century writing about literature. His earlier writings had celebrated the
freedom of the artist to create new forms, as evidenced by his eloquent
conclusion to the "Art of fiction" (1884), where he offered an inclusive
vision of the novel that could accommodate talents as diverse as Dumas,
Austen, Dickens, and Flaubert: "There is no impression of life, no
manner of seeing it and feeling it, to which the plan of the novelist may
not offer a place."[59] Later, however, he began narrowing the parameters
of what was permissible. In his prefaces to the New York Edition (1908)
and his subsequent writings, James acted as a watchdog for the house of

fiction. He barked loudly, hoping to keep away all unworthy intruders. Sadly, the dimensions of the Jamesian house of fiction had fewer and fewer inhabitants as time progressed. The man who referred to himself as "Master" became reluctant to recognize a work as art unless it bore resemblance to his own. The writer who did as much as any other novelist in the history of the genre to elevate fiction to the status of art ended his life fighting a rear-guard battle against all those who sought freedom for new directions.

His intolerance of Dostoevsky needs to be understood in terms of that rear-guard action. James diagnosed his works as another dangerous symptom of formless decadence, and he fought vehemently against his influence. The Master, unlike most of his contemporaries, judged Dostoevsky and Tolstoy as the same type of novelist and condemned the two for failing to restrict their subject matter. James's denunciation of the monstrous twins also reflected a more personal agenda: his desperate and failed attempt to keep his own protégé Hugh Walpole from following in their footsteps.

Walpole met James in 1909. In the words of Leon Edel, "Hugh was an aspiring 'on the make' young writer . . . who ardently worshipped Henry."[60] When "Hugh had asked James how he might address him," the novelist told him that either *"très cher maître* or my dear Master" would be acceptable. Walpole complied with the request. The elder author addressed his admirer in terms of cloying affection as a sentimental master might regard a favored son or pet.[61] The disciple, however, did not share the Master's devotion to his craft; he wrote quickly, even carelessly. According to Edel, Walpole "would be two or three novels ahead of his publisher" in his mature, prolific years.[62] When he first read Constance Garnett's translation of *The Brothers Karamazov* in 1912, he was an impressionable 28-year-old. Walpole's biographer, Rupert Hart-Davis, reports that "Hugh was so overwhelmed with excitement that he dashed off a letter about it to Henry James."[63]

James's reply has become famous:

When you ask me if I don't feel Dostoevsky's "mad jumble, that flings things down in a heap," nearer truth and beauty than the picking and composing you instance in Stevenson, I reply with emphasis that I feel nothing of the sort, and that the older I grow and the more I *go* the more sacred to me do picking and composing become.

His letter identifies "strenuous selection" as the "very essence of art" and defines the novel strictly in terms of form: "Form alone *takes*, and holds and preserves substance – saves it from the welter of helpless verbiage that we swim in as in a sea of tasteless tepid pudding and that makes one ashamed of an art capable of such degradations."

Tolstoy and Dostoevsky, according to the letter to Walpole, degrade art; they are "fluid pudding." Their pudding is "not tasteless. . .because the amount of their own minds and souls in solution in the broth gives it savour and flavour, thanks to the strong, rank quality of their genius and their experience." As authors they are guilty of the heinous "vice," that original sin of novelists called "lack of composition." The two unrepentant Russian writers defy "economy and architecture." Even worse, "they are emulated and imitated" by other writers; "as subjects and models they quite give themselves away." James castigates them as proletarians of form who desecrate the temple of art. "There is nothing so deplorable as a work of art with a *leak* in its interest; and there is no such leak of interest as through commonness of form. Its opposite, the *found* (because the sought-for) form is the absolute citadel and tabernacle of interest."[64] The religious image of a tabernacle is telling, for it shows the depth of his antagonism towards two authors who represented a sacrilege of art.

James's message here is essentially consistent with his previous statements about Tolstoy. However, the tone is considerably more strident, which may be explained by James's relationship with Walpole. When the young novelist wrote enthusiastically about Dostoevsky, he was, in effect, swearing allegiance to a new master. The letter from James can be read as an effort to persuade the young writer that his newest choice of a model was seriously flawed. While the "dear Master" probably realized that his protégé possessed neither his craft nor his dedication, his letter reflects the unacknowledged pain of a great writer who needed worship at this stage of his life and who felt betrayed by the young man who had previously genuflected at the Jamesian altar.

The argument of the letter, however, goes far beyond personal concerns for it reflects James's lifelong preoccupation with the aesthetic stature of the novel and his later-life fears about its future. James worried that the new generation of writers might abandon the cause of form and composition. He feared that writers who admired what was perceived as a "mad jumble" might try to emulate that jumble and cast the novel into an abyss of formlessness. In a sense, James's letter was not only written to Walpole: it was addressed to the entire generation that he represented.

James's fear of Russian influence seems justified by Walpole's subsequent life and his imitations of Russian fiction. The young writer went to

Russia in 1914 where he worked first as a war correspondent and later as a nurse for the wounded. His letters to James give evidence that he saw his travels as a means of emotional education. For example, he explained his attraction to the "primitive" Russians: "Every Russian in the street has the softest tenderest eyes and the hard savage mouth of a barbarian. They seem to me to be three skins nearer to naked emotions than I should have believed possible."[65] In 1915 he wrote to James praising the primitive once again: "a Russian has all the human instincts at their simplest, strongest, most primitive – the instinct for beauty, for brotherhood, for dirt, for cruelty, for altruism, for selfishness, for everything – and he doesn't know what restraint is – *yet*."[66] He wrote in the same year about the increasing importance of Dostoevsky in his life: "Funny how he [Browning] and Dostoevsky have in this year abroad become the two authors who matter to me. I am, I believe, deeply religious, but led to it through my psychological interests – *not* vice versa. And that I claim is what they also are."[67]

Walpole published a "Russian" novel of his own in 1916, *The Dark Forest*.[68] The novel seems to be largely an autobiographical extension of his wartime experience. Its two main characters, Durward and Trenchard, may be viewed as two aspects of Walpole's own personality. Durward, the narrator, is a young, well-read, practical Englishman who travels to Russia to work in the Red Cross with illusions of participating in a "romantic war." Trenchard is a quixotic figure who has bookish dreams of a new spiritualized life in Russia. "He had read his Dostoevsky and Turgenev; he had looked at those books of Russian impressions that deal in nothing but snow, icons, and the sublime simplicity of the Russian peasant . . . He found them [the Russians] far different from the Karamazovs, the Raskolnikovs, of his imagination."[69] The two Englishmen work for the Red Cross and share tasks with a host of Russian doctors, nurses, and other medical people. The novel chronicles the self-discoveries of various characters as they journey towards and through the dark forest, a place where evil may be discovered and the self may be mastered, a mysterious, oppressive place analogous to the jungle in Conrad's *The Heart of Darkness*.

Two Dostoevskian characters figure prominently in the novel. One, Andrey Vassielvitch, is a nervous, self-deprecating little merchant always anxious to please. He is a friend and admirer of the self-possessed Nikitin, an aristocratic, cynical doctor who had an affair with Andrey Vassielvitch's wife. The two men are bound together in a mimetic struggle to perpetuate the memory of the woman whom they both loved. Their relationship combines resentment, imitation, rivalry, and admiration in a manner strongly reminiscent of Dostoevsky's "The eternal husband," another story of a love triangle that continues after the woman's death.

Walpole's novel exemplifies James's notion of a loose, baggy monster. Though the author shows a not inconsiderable talent, he seems to be making up the novel as he goes along, piling scene upon scene, character upon character in a sometimes inspired, sometimes pedestrian manner. His narrative style can be described as "fluid pudding"; he randomly changes tones, techniques, and even narrators in a way that blurs the distinction between experimentation and carelessness. Walpole tries stream-of-consciousness, Balzac-like descriptive catalogs, Conradian symbolism, Crane-like impressionism, and Dostoevskian dreams, but he does not create a unified whole from his disparate elements. He writes as someone who enjoys writing but not rewriting. Walpole's Russian story provides in fictional form what Maurice Baring had provided in nonfiction – a sympathetic, over-generalized account of a Russia where everyone seems to embody a large truth about the Russian people, the Russian soul. In *The Dark Forest*, James's deepest fears for the future of the novel are realized.

Walpole's other Russian novel, *The Secret City*, was published in 1919.[70] This story takes place not in the countryside but in St. Petersburg during 1916 and 1917. Its action covers the months preceding the overthrow of the Czarist government and the few months immediately following the March revolution. *The Secret City* functions as a companion-piece for *The Dark Forest*. Both novels are primarily narrated by Durward; they are also linked by a major character called Semyonov, a doctor who turns melancholy and vicious in the sequel. The first novel, with its presentation of life in the war-torn countryside, peopled with aristocrats and gentlemen in pursuit of heroism, love, and higher truths, can be seen as Walpole's imitation of Tolstoy. By contrast, *Secret City*, a more focused, interesting, and mature piece of work, owes more to Dostoevsky. Its characters are tortuously self-divided, as exemplified by Nicolai Leontievitch Markovitch. An inventor incapable of success, Nicolai loves Semyonov's niece Vera, but his love can never be requited. He fervently believes in an ideal Russia, only to have his sentimental dreams and hopes incessantly ridiculed by Semyonov, who secretly hopes to goad Nicolai into murdering him, thus ending his own tormented life. Everyone, except for two transplanted Englishmen, Durward and Henry Bohun, views Nicolai as a ridiculous figure. In a final act of desperation, he kills his tormentor in a public park and then turns the gun on himself, all while the "Marseillaise" is playing. Collectively, the characters in this novel are a mixture of the impassioned, the ridiculous, the proud, the downtrodden, and the innocent – an ensemble of Dostoevskian types. The author borrowed such narrative strategies as dreams that reflect internal discord, sudden fevers that result from psychic stress, and dramatized hallucinations. Like his Russian model, Walpole shows an interest in parasitic criminals: the crass thief and murderer known as "the Rat" hangs upon Durward just as Fedka had hung upon Stavrogin in *The Possessed*. Walpole's St. Petersburg could not exist without its Dostoevskian antecedents.

Unlike his Russian model, however, Walpole cannot adequately address ideological issues. In this respect, he reveals a similarity to James that, I believe, can be traced to the traditional limits of the English novel, which so often preclude discussion of fundamental social, political, and philosophical questions. *The Secret City* is an evocative collection of character studies, a series of vignettes about revolutionary Russia. The struggle for revolution, in Walpole's perspective, is simply a struggle between people, not ideas. In this novel Lenin exists merely as an obstacle in the melodramatic rescue of the virtuous Nina; Henry Bohun sneaks in behind the revolutionary leader, who is visiting the apartment of the villainous Boris Grogoff, to accomplish the deed. The revolutionaries in St. Petersburg are led by Grogoff, whose orders are carried out by ruffians such as "the Rat." Opposite them are the idealistic and sentimental characters who either disagree with revolution or remain indifferent to its claims. "Public" Russia, despite its dramatic interest, is simply a background for private and personal explorations, as illustrated by Semyonov's summary of the novel's theme: "there's a secret city at every man's heart. It is at that city's altars that the true prayers are offered."[71] Walpole, unlike Dostoevsky, draws a neat division between public and private lives, and he pins all his hopes on the private sector.

The social values expressed in his novels are far closer to James than to Dostoevsky. James and Walpole, despite their literary differences, shared the world view of the English gentleman. They remained indifferent to the deeper origins of social conflicts and narrowed all such conflicts to the arena of individual character. The two writers collapsed complex sociological and historical issues into more easily understood psychological ones. Human conflict, then, could only be understood in terms of personal attributes such as honor, heroism, egoism, and resentment. Though their responses to Dostoevsky were antithetical, the two friends remained essentially English in their adherence to a code of personal values.

James's resistance to ideology provides the final key to the explanation of his aversion to Dostoevsky. A study of the contrasts between *Princess Casamassima* and Dostoevsky's *Raw Youth* will serve to measure the ideological and literary chasm between the two authors.

James's preface to his story about an illegitimate youth seeking to define himself amid impoverished surroundings and secret anarchical societies begins with an admission of the author's position of social privilege. The preface celebrates his life of "freedom and ease" where doors "opened into light and warmth and cheer." James further admits that his interest in the lower-class life of "meaner conditions," with its "lower manners," "general sordid struggle," "misery," and "vice," which became the starting point of the novel, is not generated by a desire to explore social problems or contending social values. Rather, he had simply wondered what it would be like to possess the "romantic curiosity" and aesthetic sensibility of a Henry James but to be denied access to the doors of genteel existence.[72] The novel results from the curiosity of an author who was foraging for subject matter that would sustain the reader's interest. The story's genesis, then, had virtually nothing to do with the social, political, and intellectual motivations that were so important to Dostoevsky.

The preface explains that every element in *Princess Casamassima* evolved out of the need to tell an interesting and artful story. The main character, Hyacinth Robinson, was created in order to have an intelligent, imaginative, and sensitive center of interest. He would be "embroiled" in bewildering events and embark on a fascinating adventure, but the focus would remain on "a consciousness . . . subject to fine intensification and wide enlargement."[73] Though Hyacinth belonged to the lower classes, he would never fall prey to their vulgarity, for he would be the "sort of person whom we can count not to betray, to cheapen, or, as we say, give away, the value and beauty of the thing."[74] Other characters would function as the "most polished of possible mirrors" to illuminate the main character further and add interest to the story.[75] Hyacinth's involvement in the "sinister anarchic underworld" of

London and his commitment to the cause of violence are a plot device designed to give the story conflict and to heighten the *chiaroscuro* contrasts between the genteel and the sordid worlds.[76]

The movement of the plot centers around Hyacinth's agreement to perform an act of violence, presumably a political assassination, whenever he receives the orders from Hoffendahl, a mysterious revolutionary leader. The political context of the novel, however, seems to function mainly to promote romantic intrigue. Though Hyacinth has a brief moment of revolutionary fervor at a disreputable pub – which leads to his tragic promise – he soon falls prey to the beauty and sophistication of Princess Casamassima and the material splendor of her world. Rather quickly, he loses faith in the cause of revolution: he exchanges political loyalties for aesthetic and romantic pleasures, though he never renounces his promise to Hoffendahl (presumably because a gentleman does not break his word). The last part of the novel borrows from *Othello*, as Hyacinth is mistakenly led to assume that the Princess has discarded him for the friend, Paul Muniment, whom he has long admired. Tragically caught between his promise to a cause that he has abandoned and his mistaken belief in the Princess's infidelity, Hyacinth commits suicide at the novel's end.

James's revolutionaries, for the most part, are fragments torn from genteel cloth. Hyacinth may have been born in disgrace, but he has inherited the taste and sensibility of the aristocratic father who refused to acknowledge him. He speaks near-perfect French; he dreams of being a writer; he possesses discriminating reading habits; he speaks like a gentleman; and he is delicately handsome. His movement towards revolution in the first part of the novel is solely derived from his resentment about his illegitimate birth: "in his own imagination he associated bitterness with the revolutionary passion."[77] Once Hyacinth learns to appreciate the mannered habits and artistic possessions of the leisured class, he abandons the cause of revolution entirely. In the end, he reduces all revolutionary motives to class envy: "Everywhere, everywhere he saw the ulcer of envy – the greed of a party hanging together only that it might despoil another of its advantage."[78]

The Princess loves the cause for reasons stemming from resentment about how she has been treated by her family and that of her husband: "She had been married by her people, in a mercenary way, for the sake of a fortune and a great name, and it turned out as badly as her worst enemy could have wished." "Humiliated, outraged, tortured" by her fate, "she considered that she too was one of the numerous class who could be put on a tolerable footing only by revolution."[79] As Hyacinth realizes, "her behavior, after all, was more addressed to relieving herself than relieving others."[80] With a sensitive, generous temperament, the Princess clings to vague aspirations of social harmony: "The world will be beautiful enough when it becomes good enough." In her eyes, unclouded by intellect, the "degradation of the many" is an aesthetic sin producing "ugly" and "unjust distinctions."[81]

Even Paul Muniment and Poupin, genuine representatives of the working class, are respectable artisans with a sense of taste and decorum. The Poupin household is notable for "an extraordinary decency of life and a worship of proper work."[82] Paul Muniment, Hyacinth's friend-turned-rival, possesses "singular enviable" qualities, including "his fresh-coloured coolness, his easy, exact knowledge, [and] the way he kept himself clean."[83] These artisans seem natural-born aristocrats, regardless of their political agenda. None of the revolutionaries lack manners; none of them, with the possible exception of Hoffendahl, pose a serious threat to the survival of the upper classes. Though an occasional life may indeed be lost, bombs and daggers and pistols do not threaten the cultivated and secure world of Henry James.

Despite its subject matter, *Princess Casamassima* is not really about the issues of revolution or anarchy. No one ever seriously discusses revolutionary ideas in the novel because James himself never bothered to understand such ideas or their motivations. As he admitted in his preface, the novel resulted from his impressions of London back streets, not from "'authentic' information" about the London underworld.[84] One senses that ideological dialogues about political and social ideas are completely beyond the Jamesian domain. Perhaps the absence of such ideas may be partially explained by the problem of authorial control that they pose. For artistic purposes, one monologic voice governs the narration of this novel and most of James's fiction. That voice, the voice of the Jamesian narrator, is intelligent, sensitive, well-bred, and imaginative. Other voices, other points of view are either excluded or carefully subsumed within the perspective of the narrator. *Princess Casamassima* never comes close to the subject of anarchy and revolution because the chaotic, passionate, and disputatious voices of such movements are never allowed to enter the self-enclosed, finalized, univocal narration – the embodiment of what Bakhtin has identified as the monological novel. In Bakhtin's framework, this type of novel unites all narrative elements in "a single objective world, illuminated by a single authorial consciousness."[85]

By contrast, Dostoevsky's *Raw Youth* can be understood as a novel that creates its subject from all that James excludes. Outwardly, the novel bears an interesting resemblance to *Princess Casamassima*. Its hero, Arkady Dolgurky, is an illegitimate son of a genteel father. He shares Hyacinth's deep resentment about his birth, and he is also attracted, though only temporarily, to the revolutionary underworld. Both novels chronicle the hero's pursuit of beauty; the main characters can be understood in terms of the development of their aesthetic sensibilities. But there the resemblance ends. The social hierarchies that James keeps intact are exploded by Dostoevsky, a dissolution which becomes the principal means of creating interest.

Unlike Hyacinth, Arkady pursues his father, confronts him, emulates him, and embarrasses him. The equivocal relationship between Arkady and Versilov becomes the dominating center of the novel. To avenge himself against a world that has cast him aside, Arkady, the narrator–hero, first sets out to gain power by accumulating the wealth of a Rothschild. At the invitation of his father, Versilov, whom he only glimpsed as a child, Arkady goes to St. Petersburg. Once he comes in contact with the father who abandoned him, his resentment is mixed with adoration, a painful compound of love and hate. Versilov, the novel's most compelling character, is a many-faceted reflection of Russia's intellectual culture. A philosophic visionary, he pursues an ideal of nobility that embraces all of humanity, nurturing a dream of a golden age. Yet his own life is marked by disorder and secret carnality. The father of two illegitimate children, as well as two legitimate ones, Versilov lives with Arkady's mother, whose legal husband, the holy pilgrim Makar, still visits her. Though Versilov tenderly loves his virtual wife, the angelic Sofya Andreyevna, he is tormented by his desire for Akhmakova, the wife of a general, who also becomes the object of Arkady's dark yearnings. Divided passions thus define both son and father. Perhaps this self-division is best illustrated when Versilov, who insisted on the paramount importance of Christ and a belief in God, breaks an icon in impulsive sacrilegious defiance.

Raw Youth is charged with polyphonic explorations of ideology, for in Dostoevsky's world characters can only be understood in terms of the ideas they engage. Arkady can only hope to discover his true identity through dialogue with the contending voices of capitalism, genteel utopianism, revolution, romantic egoism, and spiritual asceticism. As the novel progresses, Arkady experiments with various responses to the dilemmas of modern life, becoming an entrepreneur, a dandy, a gambler, and a romantic dreamer; he flirts with blackmail, revolution, adultery, and other symptoms of a society that has lost its moral imperatives. His sentimental education necessitates coming to terms with the contradictions that define his epoch. Such contradictions are embodied not only in the characters that Arkady encounters but also within the vacillations of his consciousness. One hears in his character many voices, not one. Indeed, *Raw Youth* may be the most polyphonic of all of Dostoevsky's major novels, for its narration is inseparable from the contrapuntal dissonance of those voices – the sounds of ideologies, ideals, and passions colliding within the soul of Arkady and his entire generation.

Dostoevsky's novel, like the other novels of his maturity, depicts a world in passionate tumult, and every narrative element purposefully reflects that chaos. The story, in typical Dostoevsky fashion, includes a whirlwind of subplots, of mysteries to be untangled and paradoxes to be resolved. It progresses by a dizzying series of conflicts, scandals, and self-proclamations that often hide as much as they reveal. Naturally, the style of the novel bears virtually no resemblance to a Jamesian creation. Its radically heterogeneous material resists stylistic and tonal unity. This novel, which Dostoevsky entitled *Disorder* in his working drafts, is the most frenzied and chaotic of his major works. For that reason, most critics consider it less successful than the acknowledged masterpieces: the work simply cannot hold all of its swirling elements together. While Dostoevsky admired the classical restraint, balance, and harmony that he found in Raphael's paintings and Pushkin's writings, he knew that his own centrifugal epoch defied description by such techniques. Classical serenity cannot describe a vortex.

Every stability that James takes for granted is subject to dispute in Dostoevsky's fictional world. Values and ideas of all kinds are argued openly and insistently because all important questions – religious, social, political, familial, and artistic – are still unresolved. The characters broach subjects that are never addressed in a Jamesian novel. They reveal their most private longings and consistently embarrass themselves in public, breaking all rules of decorum. The self-censorship that Anglo-American breeding inculcates is not to be found here, perhaps because no norms of behavior, no traditions of collective values, are strong enough to control the characters' desperate need to search noisily and unrestrainedly for meaning. A sense of impending emergency pervades the novel, suspending all usual inhibitions.

James castigated Dostoevsky for that lack of restraint. According to James, he took the novel beyond the boundaries of art, and abandoned all hope for authorial control. James's antagonism towards Dostoevsky, along with Tolstoy, goes deeper than matters of novelistic inclusiveness, for he showed that he was able to appreciate other writers of "monstrous" inclusiveness, such as Dickens and Thackeray. His inability to appreciate the two Russians can be traced to their use of fiction to explore metaphysical issues and the foundations of the social order. Their works raised questions that James believed were irrelevant to art and potentially destructive, questions that would only distract an artist from the task of pictorial and psychological representation. James apparently believed that a stable society with a fixed, unquestioned hierarchical order offered the best support for artistic endeavor; that stability was threatened by the ultimate questions posed by Tolstoy and Dostoevsky.[86] He could not forgive the two writers for speaking in public about issues that no English gentleman would address. The mark of a gentleman, after all, is knowing what not to say.

Because Dostoevsky violated that maxim, he earned mixed praise from Forster, denunciation from Galsworthy, and scorn from James. The three gentleman–writers, like the other authors discussed in this study, mistakenly regarded Dostoevsky as an interloper in the house of fiction, one whose monstrous subject and visionary fervor disallowed the possibility of artistry.

Conclusion

As we have seen, Dostoevsky proved to be a lively and disputatious guest in the English house of fiction. Prophet, sage, sadist, monster – none of the writers were quite certain how to name him. He didn't seem a novelist in the usual sense, yet the power of his works could not be blunted, even by his enemies. People speculated about Dostoevsky's lineage, to the point of finding demonic or angelic origins, as if he were a literary foundling badly in need of an explanation. Few bothered to look in the most obvious places for his literary pedigree; Hugo, Balzac, Dickens and other practitioners seemed too far removed from one so exotically Russian.

Perhaps Forster's designation of prophet best encapsulates the English response to Dostoevsky. The prophetic novelist, by Forster's standard, lived beyond the boundaries of rationality. Writers such as Brontë, Melville, Dostoevsky, and Lawrence put aside the usual tools of literary creation to communicate a mystic insight. The "novel through which bardic influence has passed," Forster drolly points out, "often has a wrecked air, like a drawing room after an earthquake or a children's party."[1] Forster and his novelist-compatriots all detected a "wrecked air" in Dostoevsky's works. Like Heathcliff at Thrushcross Grange or Queequeg at the Spouter-Inn, the Russian writer bore the marks of an alien; his works were generally regarded as the spume of a tortured soul, not consciously created artifacts of the literary imagination. In key respects, expectations defined artlessness: looking for dross, readers found dross – Truth, prophetic truth, inartistically rendered.

Prophets, from Jeremiah to Cassandra to Luther, seldom elicit leisured conversation. In the presence of a prophet's taunts, the audience quickly becomes polarized; the mantic word slashes and discomforts. To Lawrence, Dostoevsky was the last and greatest prophetic voice of Christianity, a tradition that denied the body and maimed the self. Of course, Lawrence felt compelled to struggle to the death with such a man. Conrad, too, engaged in a mighty fight; like Jacob, he wrestled throughout the night with an enemy who could not be named. Dostoevsky posed a profound threat to the creative identity of these two authors; in their chafing, we can find evidence of a rivalry crucial to the development of their own art. Could Lawrence have become the Lawrence we know without the spur of Dostoevsky? We cannot be certain, but we have our suspicions. Lawrence needed anger to fuel his artistic vision; the Russian novelist provided an endlessly renewable resource. With Conrad the evidence is more direct: it is virtually impossible to conceive of *Under Western Eyes* without its Dostoevskian antecedents. Without the hated Russian, Conrad's achievement would have been diminished. Ironically, Conrad's confrontation with his rival may have also contributed to the decline of his art. So costly was the battle that Conrad never again ventured into the darkest depths.

It seems less likely that Dostoevsky influenced the course of Woolf's art. At a crucial time in her development, he did serve as a prop to support her rebellion against her Edwardian elders. By coming to terms with Dostoevsky, Woolf moved further in her efforts to liberate the modern novel from all fetters. The acidic strength of his works helped to weaken the chains of English convention, the inhibitions that kept the real Mrs. Brown hidden and unknown. In a sense, Woolf exploited Dostoevsky; she capitalized on the interest in all things Russian to justify and defend the nascent modernists. When she no longer needed him, she put him aside. Stimulated, no doubt she was, but never haunted or infuriated. Without Dostoevsky, one suspects, her train would have reached the same destination.

Henry James, we may imagine, would always be Henry James. Inevitably, James had to disdain Dostoevsky; the enemy of Turgenev could be no friend of his. More importantly, James owed his artistic development to French and English literary traditions. Dostoevsky and all the Russians (*sans* the international Turgenev, of course) were simply too far removed from the cultural traditions that nourished his own creativity to merit serious attention. The Master's fusillades against the Russian novelists mark an unfortunate episode in the history of the novel; James spoke with such authority to later generations that his attacks carried an Olympian imprint, blinding many to the aesthetic merits of Tolstoy and Dostoevsky. For that, we can probably blame Hugh Walpole, the Jamesian infidel – that, and old age.

Woolf, Lawrence, Conrad, and James all reached great heights, in part because they were steadfast in the struggle to define themselves as modern artists. Even when audiences were unappreciative, they held on to their vision; their innovations proved costly, but in the end earned them each a prominent place in the roll-call of modernity. By clarifying their responses to Dostoevsky, we enrich our understanding of their divergent artistic quests. Naturally, their readings of his works are notable for their misapprehension – what Harold Bloom calls *misprision,* a word with rich criminal connotations. Perhaps strong writers must always refract light from competing sources. In the act of forging a unique creative voice, other voices, other visions, must not be given dominance. Great artificers stand alone, or so they must tell themselves.

By comparison, Forster, Bennett, and Galsworthy scaled less ambitious heights, perhaps because each writer vacillated in his response to modernity. Forster wanted prophetic transfigurations, without the necessary fervor, a mystic art without self-denial. What he once said about Dostoevsky might better be applied to his own life and art: he was one of the "dears" – a quintessential nice man who only sometimes allowed himself to gaze unflinchingly into the abyss of modern life. Even in the dismal days of the Second World War, Forster preached a mild civility, as if good manners might overcome the Third Reich. Not surprisingly, he was never quite certain how to judge Dostoevsky; the creator of Rogozhin and Raskolnikov would probably never fit in with the enlightened Cambridge crowd.

Arnold Bennett stands as one who made his home too well in the modern world. Though in his ascendancy he was a good European dedicated to the cause of art, a champion of the neglected Dostoevsky, he never wholly abandoned himself to his cause. Ever mindful of his audience, lured by its rewards, Bennett eventually became rote in his artistic discipline. An engine for the production of copy, he veered towards standards of mass production; like Henry Mynor, the owner of the pottery works in *Anna of the Five Towns,* he became spellbound by ceaseless utility, too much in love with the productions of time. Bennett's lifelong defense of Dostoevsky no doubt deserves approbation, but the English writer simplified modernity to his own detriment. He defended a caricature of Dostoevsky to resist the influence of modernist writers who were rude to him in public. If he had been willing to sacrifice remuneration and had been more self-critical about his methods, he might have achieved more.

Galsworthy likewise felt ostracized by the younger generation. More guilt-ridden than his fellow Edwardian, the author of *The Forsyte Saga* found his own art lacking and felt discomfort in his own social status.

Always sensitive to injustice, Galsworthy proved himself modern in the inclusiveness of his subjects: divorce, vivisection, adultery, prison reform, the rights of coal miners, and so on. In his hands, however, the boundaries between art and social tract became blurred, a symptom of the modern writer too devoted to Asclepius, so earnest in his effort to heal the rifts of his era that he sacrificed his own art to their cataloging. Galsworthy came to admit a depth in Dostoevsky and the Russians that he himself could not achieve, a recognition too late to alter the compromises of his craft.

In an important sense, Dostoevsky serves as interlocutor for each of our English novelists. In their responses to his works, we can overhear self-revealing dialogues. Like the conversation between Ivan and the gentleman–devil, or those between Porfiry and Raskolnikov, such occasions give us privileged insight. We listen with ears pressed, like Svidrigailov in *Crime and Punishment,* patiently biding time in a secret room adjoining Sonya's, waiting to hear self-incriminating revelations. Or, perhaps, we listen like Alyosha by the feet of his spiritual master, Zossima, hoping to garner a wisdom that comprehends the chaos of modernity. What we hear is never exactly what we expect, but it is provocative nonetheless. Dostoevsky, as Bakhtin reminds us, would appreciate the value of such dialogues, for he "could hear dialogic relationships everywhere, in all manifestations of conscious and intelligent life." Indeed, "where consciousness began, there dialogue began for him as well."[2] Following Bakhtin, we might say that the last word is never spoken, though ours is.

Notes

I INTRODUCTION

1 W. H. Jansen, *History of Art* (Englewood Cliffs: Prentice-Hall, 1962), p. 520.
2 Malcolm Bradbury, *The Social Context of Modern English Literature* (New York: Shocken, 1969), p. 74.
3 Carl Jung, "The spiritual problem of modern man," *The Portable Jung*, ed. Joseph Campbell, trans. R. F. C. Hull (New York: Viking-Penguin, 1971), p. 456.
4 Quentin Bell, *Virginia Woolf: A Biography*, 2 vols. (London: Hogarth, 1973), vol. II, p. 7.
5 P. N. Furbank, *E. M. Forster: A Life*, 2 vols. (New York: Harcourt Brace Jovanovich, 1978), p. 214.
6 Margery M. Morgan, "John Galsworthy," *British Writers*, 8 vols. (New York: Scribners, 1983), vol. IV, p. 270.
7 Harry T. Moore, *Henry James and His World* (London: Thames, 1974), p. 107.
8 Randolph Bourne, "The immanence of Dostoevsky," *Dial* 63 (28 June 1917), 24–25.
9 René Girard, *Violence and the Sacred*, trans. Patrick Gregory (Baltimore: Johns Hopkins University Press, 1977), p. 160.
10 D. H. Lawrence, "Letter to Lady Ottoline Morrell," 1 February 1916, *Letters of D. H. Lawrence*, ed. James T. Boulton *et al.*, 8 vols. (Cambridge University Press, 1979–), vol. II, p. 521.
11 Virginia Woolf, "More Dostoevsky," *Books and Portraits*, ed. Mary Lyon (New York: Harcourt Brace Jovanovich, 1978), p. 116; first published in *Times Literary Supplement*, 22 February 1917.
12 Bloom's descriptive model of poetic misreading applies with remarkable accuracy to the responses of Conrad and Lawrence, if one substitutes *novelist* for *poet:* "Poetic Influence – when it involves two strong authentic poets – always proceeds by a misreading of the prior poet, an act of creative correction, that is actually and necessarily a misinterpretation. The history of fruitful poetic influence . . . is a history of anxiety and self-serving caricature, of distortion, of perverse, willful revisionism without which modern poetry as such could not exist" (Harold Bloom, *The Anxiety of Influence: A Theory of Poetry* [New York: Oxford University Press, 1973], p. 30).

13 Richard Ellmann, *James Joyce* (New York: Oxford University Press, 1982), p. 499.

14 This definition is supplied by Wlad Godzick in his introduction to Hans Robert Jauss, *Aesthetic Experience and Literary Hermeneutics* (Minneapolis: University of Minnesota Press, 1982), p. xii.

15 Leenhardt's fascinating studies of collective responses to literary texts offer a corrective to post-modernist tendencies to forget sociological and historical dynamics of readings: "By establishing national patterns of literary perception, our research points to the predominant unifying schemes whose efficiency is felt even in the most general attitudes of readers toward the text." Jacques Leenhardt, "Toward a Sociology of Reading," *The Reader in the Text: Essays on Audience Interpretation*, ed. Susan R. Suleiman and Inge Crossman (Princeton University Press, 1980), p. 223.

16 See Helen Muchnic, *Dostoevsky's English Reputation (1881–1936)*, Smith College Studies in Modern Languages, vol. 20, nos. 3–4 (Northampton: Smith College, 1939). Her work, by virtue of its bibliographic comprehensiveness, remains indispensable today.

17 For a discussion of these obituaries, see ibid., p. 8.

18 F. W. J. Hemmings does an excellent job of placing *Le roman russe* within the context of French literary culture in *The Russian Novel in France, 1884–1914* (London: Oxford University Press, 1950). Hemmings reports that "the significance of Vogüé's masterpiece cannot be grasped unless it is seen as an attempt at utter demolishment of the naturalist aesthetic theory: it can be viewed, for instance, as a counterblast to Zola's *Roman Experimental*, which had come out only a few years previously" (p. 30). Hemmings argues that the influence of Vogüé regarding Tolstoy and Dostoevsky cannot be underestimated: "At as late a date as 1880 their very names were unknown to anyone in France but the merest handful of specialists. By the end of the decade, however . . . their names had become household words, everyone had read, or pretended to have read, their chief works, young novelists were imitating them, older ones reading them for inspiration" (p. 2).

19 E. M. de Vogüé, *The Russian Novel*, trans. H. A. Sawyer (New York: Knopf, 1916), p. 204.

20 Ibid., pp. 260–61. The French critic, despite his enormous influence, cannot be cited as one who appreciated the literary merit of Dostoevsky. He dismissed *The Brothers Karamazov* as "no more than a dialogue between two tub-thumpers or 'brain pickers' who with the craftiness of a Red Indian try to get at each other's secrets." Few Russians, he reports, "have had the courage to read this interminable story to the end." See pp. 250, 259.

21 Gilbert Phelps, *The Russian Novel in English Fiction* (London: Anchor, 1950), p. 35.

22 This was the figure claimed by Zola's English publisher, Henry Vizetelly. Appropriately, Vizetelly was also the man who published Whishaw's translations of Dostoevsky in the 1880s. The publisher was jailed in 1889 for his publication of Zola's novels, which were judged to be in violation of

England's censorship laws. See Samuel Hynes, *The Edwardian Turn of Mind* (Princeton University Press, 1968), p. 310.

23 The term "moral disease" was used in a review of *The Idiot* which appeared in the *Athenaeum* 2 (1887), 534; quoted by Muchnic, *Dostoevsky's English Reputation*, p. 21.

24 Muchnic, *Dostoevsky's English Reputation*, p. 21, quoting William Sharp in the *Academy* 31 (1887), 270.

25 Muchnic, *Dostoevsky's English Reputation*, p. 19, quoting the *Scottish Review* 10 (1887), 199.

26 Donald Davie, introduction, *Russian Literature and Modern English Fiction*, ed. Donald Davie (University of Chicago Press, 1965), p. 3.

27 Quoted by Muchnic, *Dostoevsky's English Reputation*, p. 17. Muchnic also recognizes the surface similarities between *Crime and Punishment* and "Markheim," but she argues that "the differences are more profound; they display a thorough incompatibility of taste and of artistic intent" (ibid., p. 173).

28 Ibid., p. 31.

29 Ibid., p. 49.

30 Phelps, *Russian Novel in English Fiction*, p. 160.

31 Muchnic, *Dostoevsky's English Reputation*, p. 32.

32 Hynes, *Edwardian Turn of Mind*, p. 308.

33 For a discussion of the effort to establish university programs in Russian and other Slavic languages, see Dorothy Brewster, *East–West Passage: A Study in Literary Relationships* (London: George Allen and Unwin, 1954), p. 149.

34 Turner's unique role as cultural liaison is addressed by Brewster, ibid., pp. 142–43.

35 It should also be noted that travel to Russia became increasingly popular in the early years of the twentieth century. Brewster reports that "the troubled events between 1905 and 1917 had more English and American observers in Russia than at any preceding period" (ibid., p. 156). Both John Galsworthy and Hugh Walpole visited Russia during these years.

36 D. S. Merezhkovsky, "Dostoievsky and Tolstoy," in Davie, *Russian Literature and Modern English Fiction*, p. 77; originally published in *Tolstoi as Man and Artist* (London: Constable, 1902).

37 P. A. Kropotkin, *Ideals and Realities in Russian Literature* (New York: Knopf, 1915; originally published in London, 1905), pp. 168–70.

38 D. S. Mirsky, *A History of Russian Literature: From the Earliest Times to the Death of Dostoyevsky* (New York: Knopf, 1927), p. 346.

39 Ibid., p. 358.

40 D. S. Mirsky, The *Intelligentsia of Great Britain*, trans. Alec Brown (New York: Covice, Friede 1935), p. 107.

41 George Jefferson, *Edward Garnett: A Life in Literature* (London: Jonathan Cape, 1982), p. 32.

42 Virginia Woolf, "Phases of fiction," *Collected Essays*, 4 vols. (London: Hogarth, 1966), vol. IV, p. 74.

43 Edward Garnett, "A literary causerie: Dostoevsky," *Academy* 71 (1906), 202–3.

44 Maurice Baring, *Landmarks in Russian Literature* (London: Methuen, 1910), p. 261.

45 Maurice Baring, *An Outline of Russian Literature* (New York: Henry Holt, 1915), p. 222. Baring's subsequent works provided popular and simple-minded descriptions of Russian culture, history, government, and literature.

46 Jacob Tonson [Arnold Bennett], "Books and persons," *New Age* 6 (31 March 1910), 518–19.

47 Ibid., 518–19.

48 Muchnic, *Dostoevsky's English Reputation*, p. 165.

49 Friedrich Nietzsche, *Twilight of the Gods*, trans. Anthony Ludovici (n.p., 1911), p. 104.

50 John Burt Foster, Jr., *Heirs to Dionysus: A Nietzschean Current in Literary Modernism* (Princeton University Press, 1981), p. 7.

51 Hynes, *Edwardian Turn of Mind*, p. 164. Freud contributed substantially to the English discussion of Dostoevsky through his article, "Dostoevsky and parricide," which was translated in the *Realist* 1 (1929), 18–33. Freud analyzed Dostoevsky's epilepsy as psychologically induced, the result of a suppressed wish for parricide and subsequent guilt about his father's alleged murder by his peasants. See Joseph Frank's refutation of Freud's position in "Freud's case-history of Dostoevsky," the appendix to *Dostoevsky: The Seeds of Revolt, 1821–1849* (Princeton University Press, 1976), pp. 379–91.

52 "Great Dostoevsky nights" was a phrase used by Gordon Campbell to describe the intellectual debates that took place at the Lawrence household. See Anthony Alpers, *The Life of Katherine Mansfield* (New York: Viking, 1980), p. 169. J. Middleton Murry described himself, in relation to his Dostoevsky work, as "the victim of the strange sensation of being hardly more than the amanuensis of a book that wrote itself." See Murry's autobiographical *Between Two Worlds* (London: Jonathan Cape, 1935), pp. 368–69.

53 Katherine Mansfield, "Some aspects of Dostoevsky," *Athenaeum*, 4674 (28 November 1919), 1256.

54 Gosse's comment appears in a 1926 letter to André Gide, quoted by Muchnic, *Dostoevsky's English Reputation*, p. 139.

55 Quoted by Brewster, *East–West Passage*, p. 165.

56 Ibid., p. 166, quoting Somerset Maugham's novel, *Ashendon, or the British Agent*.

57 Hynes, *Edwardian Turn of Mind*, p. 336.

58 Quoted by Brewster, *East–West Passage*, p. 172.

59 Ibid., p. 186, quoting a 1914 review by England's first biographer of Dostoevsky, J. A. T. Lloyd. His biography, *A Great Russian Realist: Feodor Dostoieffsky* (London: Stanley Paul, 1912), contributed nothing of substance to an understanding of the author or his works, though it did exemplify the psychological interests of the age. Lloyd praised Dostoevsky for his pity, his

understanding of humiliation, his abstention from middle-class subjects, and his freedom from "our Anglo-Saxon religion of the front pews, of our policeman morality, of our insurance-policy piety" (p. 174).

60 Donald Davie makes the same point about the general influence of Russian literature: "the truest way of regarding the history of Russian fiction in English translation, and the history of how English-speaking readers have reacted to Russian fiction, is as the story of a challenge presented to Anglo-American literary culture, and of the response made to that challenge" (Davie, *Russian Literature and Modern English Fiction*, p. 9).

61 Woolf, "Mr. Bennett and Mrs. Brown," *Collected Essays*, vol. I, p. 321.

62 Hynes, *Edwardian Turn of Mind*, p. 326.

63 Hans Robert Jauss, *Toward an Aesthetic of Reception*, trans. Timothy Bahti, intro. Paul de Man (Minneapolis: University of Minnesota Press, 1982), pp. 25, 30.

64 E. D. Hirsch, Jr., *Validity in Interpretation* (New Haven: Yale University Press, 1967), p. 74.

65 E. D. Hirsch, Jr., *The Aims of Interpretation* (University of Chicago Press, 1976), pp. 32, 34.

66 Hirsch, *Validity*, pp. 80–81.

67 Ibid., p. 5.

68 Ibid., p. 8.

69 Wolfgang Iser, *The Act of Reading* (Baltimore: Johns Hopkins University Press, 1978), p. 172.

70 Mirsky, *Russian Literature*, pp. 353–55. René Wellek provides a useful description of the European and American response to Dostoevsky in his introduction to *Dostoevsky: A Collection of Critical Essays*, (Englewood Cliffs: Prentice-Hall, 1962), pp. 1–15.

71 Robert Belknap offers an admirably concise and comprehensive summary of Dostoevsky's reading practices in "Dostoevsky's reading," in his *The Genesis of* The Brothers Karamazov: *The Aesthetics, Ideology, and Psychology of Making a Text* (Evanston: Northwestern University Press, 1990). A penetrating analysis of Dostoevsky's statements about his aesthetic views and their relation to his own art is provided by Robert Louis Jackson, *Dostoevsky's Quest for Form – A Study of His Philosophy of Art* (New Haven: Yale University Press, 1966). Jackson has found Dostoevsky to be diffident in the artistic assessment of his own creations: "We note throughout Dostoevsky's creative life a persistent, nagging tendency to underrate himself as an artist–craftsman, a creator of form" (Jackson, *Dostoevsky's Quest for Form*, p. 2).

Robin Feuer Miller discusses one particularly striking example of Dostoevsky's concern for art. He abandoned a whole year's work on the manuscript of *The Possessed*, because, in his words, "there was a major insufficiency in the whole thing." Though he badly needed money at the time, he changed directions for the sake of a new artistic plan. Miller cites this instance as an example of the author's patience with his fiction: "Instead of the vision of an author pressured by time into writing rapidly and spoiling his ideas, we see in Dostoevsky a man who could wait for years, even indefinitely, before he would seek to transform an idea into a novel." See Robin Feuer Miller, *Dostoevsky and* The Idiot*: Author, Narrator, and Reader* (Cambridge: Harvard University Press, 1981), p. 35.

The following quotation from Dostoevsky shows how different his values were from the popular English misconceptions: "How does one recognize the high artistic quality in a work of art? By the fact that we see the fullest harmony between the artistic idea and the form in which it is embodied" (quoted by Miller, ibid., p. 39).

72 Mikhail Bakhtin, *Problems of Dostoevsky's Poetics*, ed. and trans. Caryl Emerson (Minneapolis: University of Minnesota Press, 1984), p. 5.

73 Ibid., p. 43.

74 Frank, *Seeds of Revolt*, p. 6.

75 Ibid., p. xii.

76 Virginia Woolf, "The Russian Point of View," *The Common Reader* (New York: Harcourt, Brace and World), p. 182.

77 "Letter to Edward Garnett," 27 May 1912, *Letters from Conrad, 1895–1924*, ed. Edward Garnett (London: Nonesuch Press, 1928), pp. 260–61.

78 Henry James, "Letter to Hugh Walpole," 19 May 1912, *Letters*, ed. Leon Edel, 4 vols. (Cambridge: Belknap-Harvard University Press, 1984), vol. IV, pp. 618–19.

79 John Galsworthy, "Letter to Edward Garnett," 5 April 1914, *Letters from Galsworthy* (London: Jonathan Cape, 1934), p. 217.

80 Quoted by Bakhtin, *Dostoevsky's Poetics*, pp. 14–15. Another comment of Grossman's also seems relevant:

The distinguishing feature of *The Brothers Karamazov* is maximum tension in composition and in drawing. Everything here is taken to the limit, to the extremity, with the utmost acuity of expression, "in fever and synthesis" to use the author's own words.

As in *Raw Youth*, Dostoevsky makes no attempt at unity of construction or strict economy in means of presentation, but once again strives to express in the very form of his narrative his own horrified vision of the complete disintegration, disruption and decomposition of the great whole that he so piously revered. Into this new myth about a leprous but curable Russia he puts the entire fierce struggle of the political trends of the day, and presents a revealing picture of the convulsive divisiveness and pathological disharmony of all the everyday components of that struggle. Dostoevsky required precisely this kind of complex deformation of the whole, the destratification and distortion of traditional beauty, the unnatural intersection of planes, and the disorienting contrasts of the elements, in order to contrast the chaos of the present to his dream of a Golden Age of universal happiness. Leonid Grossman, *Dostoevsky: A Biography*, trans. Mary Mackler (Indianapolis: Bobbs-Merrill, 1965), pp. 591–92.

81 Bakhtin, *Dostoevsky's Poetics*, p. 6.

82 Ibid., p. 27.

83 Ibid., p. 6.

84 Victor Terras, "The young Dostoevsky: an assessment in light of recent scholarship," *New Essays on Dostoevsky*, ed. Malcolm V. Jones and Garth M.

Terry (Cambridge University Press, 1983), pp. 21–37. Also see Joseph Frank, *Dostoevsky: The Stir of Liberation, 1860–1865* (Princeton University Press, 1986), p. 346; René Wellek, "Bakhtin's view of Dostoevsky: 'polyphony' and 'carnivalesque,'" *Dostoevsky Studies* 1 (1980), 31–39.

85 Jackson, *Dostoevsky's Quest for Form*, p. 47.
86 Ibid., p. 58.

2 PROPHETIC RAGE AND RIVALRY: D. H. LAWRENCE

1 "Letter to S. S. Koteliansky," ?8 April 1915, *The Quest for Rananim: D. H. Lawrence's Letters to S. S. Koteliansky*, ed. George Zytaruk (Montreal: McGill-Queen's University Press, 1970), p. 37.

2 "Letter to Blanche Jennings," 8 May 1909, *Letters of Lawrence*, vol. 1, p. 126.

3 This information comes from Jessie Chambers's account of Lawrence's early years, *D. H. Lawrence: A Personal Record* (London: Jonathan Cape, 1935), p. 114.

4 Lawrence's letter to May Holbrook, Jessie's sister, praises Tolstoy, along with Ibsen and Balzac, as a "great man." See *Letters of Lawrence*, vol. 1, p. 96.

5 See George Zytaruk's documentation of Lawrence's response to Tolstoy in his *D. H. Lawrence's Response to Russian Literature* (The Hague: Mouton, 1971).

6 Chambers, *Lawrence*, p. 123.

7 Ibid., p. 218.

8 Garnett's essay is discussed in chapter 1.

9 Garnett's relationship to Conrad is addressed in chapter 5.

10 While Lawrence was writing *Sons and Lovers*, he read Garnett's favorable review of J. A. T. Lloyd's *A Great Russian Realist: Fyodor Dostoieffsky*, which appeared in the *Daily News*, 3 April 1912. See "Letter to Edward Garnett," 3 April 1912, *Letters of Lawrence*, vol. 1, p. 380. Later, Lawrence wrote from Europe to inquire about his friend's progress on a life of Dostoevsky. As it turned out, Garnett was working on a life of Tolstoy, not Dostoevsky, but Lawrence's mistaken assumption shows that he recognized his mentor's interest in Dostoevsky. Garnett's *Tolstoy: His Life and Letters* was published in 1914.

11 Lawrence recognized Constance's work habits as the mark of a true writer. In an interview he recalled seeing her "turning out reams of her marvelous translations . . . she would finish a page and throw it off on a pile on the floor without looking up, and start a new page. The pile would be this high – really almost to her knees, and all magical" (Carolyn Heilbrun, *The Garnett Family* [New York: Macmillan, 1961], p. 164).

12 Lawrence and Frieda also became close friends of the Garnetts' only child, David. In his autobiography, David tells of his own involvement with Russian literature: "In the large picture of the interior of the dining room with Vanessa [Bell] and me sitting at the table which Duncan [Grant] was painting at that time, I was engaged in translating 'The Dream of The Ridiculous Man' by Dostoevsky, who proved an author too difficult for me

... I gave my attempt at translating to Constance." See David Garnett, *The Flowers of the Forest* (London: Chatto and Windus, 1955), p. 169.

13 Lawrence's relationship to Koteliansky is described in George Zytaruk's introduction to *Quest for Rananim* and Harry T. Moore's Lawrence biography *The Priest of Love: A Life of D. H. Lawrence* (New York: Farrar, Straus, and Giroux, 1974).

14 See Zytaruk, "D. H. Lawrence's reading of Russian literature," *Lawrence's Response*, pp. 13–37.

15 The research of Zytaruk and the evidence of Lawrence's letters reveal that the English novelist also read at least the following works of Dostoevsky: *Crime and Punishment, The Brothers Karamazov, The Idiot, The Possessed, The House of the Dead,* and *Letters from the Underworld.* Two of Koteliansky's translations, *Pages from the Journal of an Author* (1916) and Dostoevsky's *Letters and Reminiscences* (1923) list Middleton Murry as a co-translator. Another, *Stavrogin's Confession and the Plan of the Life of a Great Sinner,* lists Virginia Woolf.

16 Leonard Woolf, "Kot," *New Statesman and Nation* 49, 1248 (5 February 1955), 170–72.

17 Moore, *Priest of Love,* p. 347. Zytaruk's *Quest for Rananim* contains a letter from Lawrence to Koteliansky that confirms this: "I don't want my names printed as a translator. It won't do for me to appear to dabble in too many things. If you don't want to appear alone – but why shouldn't you? – put me a *nom de plume* like Richard Haw or Thomas Ball" ("Letter to S. S. Koteliansky," 10 August 1919 *Quest for Rananim*).

18 The publisher, Secker, reported that the entire manuscript was rewritten in Lawrence's own hand due to his extensive revision of Koteliansky's manuscript. See G. M. Hyde, *D. H. Lawrence and the Art of Translation* (Totowa: Barnes and Noble, 1981), p. 2.

19 Zytaruk could find no confirming evidence for Rota's report of Lawrence's involvement in the translation. See Zytaruk, *Lawrence's Response,* pp. 59–60.

20 "Letter to S. S. Koteliansky," ?8 April 1915, *Quest for Rananim,* p. 37.

21 The only other clear admission of his attraction to Dostoevsky that I have found appears in Lawrence's "Letter to Catherine Carswell," 2 December 1916: "Oh, I don't think I would belittle the Russians. They have meant an enormous amount to me, Turgenev, Tolstoy, Dostoevsky – mattered almost more than anything, and I thought them the greatest writers of all time" (*Letters of Lawrence,* vol. III, p. 45).

22 "Letter to S. S. Koteliansky," 4 September 1916, *Letters of Lawrence,* vol. II, p. 649.

23 "Two Realists: Russian and English," *Athenaeum,* 4414 (1 June 1912), 613–14.

24 This information comes from the introduction to the second volume of *Letters of Lawrence,* pp. 1–4.

25 Katherine Mansfield, it should be noted, was also an ardent admirer of Dostoevsky, as her journal and letters reveal. Helen Muchnic quotes the following statement: "Why do I feel like this about Dostoevsky – my

Dostoevsky – no one else's – a being who loved, in spite of everything, adored life even when he knew the dark, dark places" (Muchnic, *Dostoevsky's English Reputation*, p. 107).

26 "Letter to Cynthia Asquith," *Letters of Lawrence*, vol. II, p. 386. Lawrence included Katherine Mansfield in the plans; she was to "do her little satirical sketches."

27 Katherine Mansfield, Frieda, and various guests were often included in such discussions. See Alpers, *Life of Katherine Mansfield*, p. 169.

28 John Carswell, *Lives and Letters: A. R. Orage, Beatrice Hastings, Middleton Murry, S. S. Koteliansky* (New York: New Directions, 1978), p. 116.

29 John Middleton Murry, *Reminiscences of D. H. Lawrence* (London: Jonathan Cape, 1933), p. 84.

30 Murry, *Between Two Worlds*, pp. 368–69.

31 John Middleton Murry, *Fyodor Dostoevsky: A Critical Study* (New York: Russell, 1924; originally published in London, 1916), p. 33.

32 Murry, *Dostoevsky*, p. 52.

33 Murry explicitly discusses Dostoevsky in terms of Nietzsche in an essay, "The Dream of a Queer Fellow," published in 1916. He regards that Dostoevsky short story as a meditation on "the Descartes-like question: 'What if we are only queer fellows dreaming?'" "The queer fellow," according to Murry, "went but one day's journey along the eternal recurrence which threatens human minds and human destinies. Friedrich Nietzsche dreamed this very dream in the mountains of Engadine. When he returned, he, too, was queer." This essay is included in Murry's *The Evolution of an Intellectual* (Freeport: Books for Libraries, 1926).

34 Murry, *Dostoevsky*, p. 55.

35 Ibid., pp. 46–47.

36 Ibid., p. 44.

37 Ibid., p. 111.

38 Ibid., p. 118.

39 Ibid., pp. 115, 118.

40 Ibid., p. 124.

41 Ibid., p. 190.

42 Ibid., p. 258.

43 George Zytaruk in *Lawrence's Response* also draws attention to the Murry–Lawrence dispute over Dostoevsky, but he does not explore the grounds of their disagreement in great detail. Zytaruk, I think, misses crucial aspects of Lawrence's response to Dostoevsky. He ignores Lawrence's acute sense of rivalry, as well as the common ground between his works and those of the Russian author. As a result, he glosses over the depth of Lawrence's antagonism. However, I am indebted to Zytaruk for his fine bibliographic detection work.

44 "Letter to John Middleton Murry and Katherine Mansfield," 17 February 1916, *Letters of Lawrence*, vol. II, p. 646.

45 Murry, *Reminiscences of Lawrence*, pp. 82–83.

46 "Letter to John Middleton Murry," 28 August 1916, *Letters of Lawrence*, vol. II, p. 646.

47 "Letter to S. S. Koteliansky," 15 December 1916, *Letters of Lawrence*, vol. III, p. 53. There is another letter to Kot that deserves mention. Kot was a witness to the famous incident in the Café Royal in which Katherine Mansfield snatched a copy of *Amores* from some unnamed individuals who were ridiculing Lawrence's poems in the volume. Lawrence refers to the incident, which he reworked for a similarly famous scene in *Women in Love*, as Kot's "Dostoevsky evening" (letter to S. S. Koteliansky, 4 September 1916, *Letters of Lawrence*, vol. II, p. 649).

48 Bakhtin, *Dostoevsky's Poetics*, p. 12.

49 See Lawrence's "Psychoanalysis and the unconscious," *Fantasia of the Unconscious* (London: Heinemann, n.d.), p. 207.

50 Ibid., p. 171.

51 Ibid., p. 208.

52 Ibid., p. 211.

53 Jackson, *Dostoevsky's Quest for Form*, p. 277.

54 D. H. Lawrence, "The Crown," *Reflections on the Death of a Porcupine and Other Essays* (Philadelphia: Centaur, 1925), pp. 55–56.

55 Ibid., pp. 11–12.

56 D. H. Lawrence, "Hawthorne I," *Symbolic Meaning: The Uncollected Versions of Studies in Classic American Literature* (New York: Viking, 1964), p. 129. Part of this essay was first published in the *English Review*, (May 1919), but for reasons of space the editor substantially cut Lawrence's work, leaving out the comparisons to Dostoevsky.

57 Ibid., p. 140.

58 D. H. Lawrence, *Studies in Classic American Literature* (New York: Thomas Selzer, 1923), p. 2. Lawrence notes in his foreword that "Two bodies of modern literature seem to me to have come to a real verge: the Russian and the American" (i. e., Hawthorne, Cooper, Poe, Melville, and Whitman). Both explore the extremes of consciousness and open new territories for literary exploration: "The furthest frenzies of French modernism or futurism have not yet reached the pitch of extreme consciousness" achieved by the nineteenth-century Americans and Russians.

59 D. H. Lawrence, "Preface to Max Havelaar," *Phoenix: The Posthumous Papers of D. H. Lawrence*, ed. Edward D. McDonald (London: Heinemann, 1936), pp. 237–38. This preface was originally published with the novel in 1927.

60 Lawrence, "Review of *Solitaria*," *Phoenix*, pp. 367–68. This review first appeared in *Calendar of Modern Letters* (July 1927). When Lawrence received a copy of Rozanov's work from Koteliansky, he could not resist taking another shot at Middleton Murry: "I was very pleased to have Rozanov – I'm really tired of Chekov and Dostoevsky people: they're so Murryish." Lawrence, "Letter to S. S. Koteliansky," 27 April 1927, *Quest for Rananim*, p. 310.

61 Lawrence, "Preface to *Mastro-don Gesualdo*," *Phoenix*, pp. 217–18. This ver-

sion of the essay was never published with the novel for reasons that remain unexplained. It first appeared in the *Phoenix* collection.

62 Lawrence, "Introduction to *Mastro-don Gesualdo,*" *Phoenix II*, ed. Warren Roberts and Harry T. Moore (London: Heinemann, 1968), pp. 283–88. This version was published with Lawrence's translation of the novel (London: Jonathan Cape, 1928).

63 George Panichas, "F. M. Dostoevskii and D. H. Lawrence: their vision of evil," *Dostoevskii and Britain*, ed. W. J. Leatherbarrow (Oxford: Berg, 1995); originally published in *Renaissance and Modern Studies*, 5 (1961).

64 Ibid., pp. 255–56.

65 Quoted by Panichas, ibid., p. 254.

66 Ibid., p. 250.

67 Quoted by Panichas, ibid., p. 258.

68 *Letters of Lawrence*, vol. II, p. 311.

69 René Girard, *Deceit, Desire, and the Novel: Self and Other in Literary Structure*, trans. Yvonne Freccero (Baltimore: Johns Hopkins University Press, 1965).

70 "Letter to Lady Ottoline Morrell," 1 February 1916, *Letters of Lawrence*, vol. II, p. 251.

71 Grossman's statement is quoted by Bakhtin, *Dostoevsky's Poetics*, p. 14; this pivotal statement is also discussed in chapter 1.

72 Feodor Dostoevsky, *The Grand Inquisitor*, trans. S. S. Koteliansky, intro. D. H. Lawrence (London: Elkin, Mathews, and Marrot, 1930), p. 283. The publication of this work apart from *The Brothers Karamazov* typifies a central problem of Dostoevsky's reception in England. To assume that the part can be detached from the whole and published separately without a loss of meaning reflects a larger assumption that the novel itself lacks literary integrity. Perhaps the best analysis of the artistic structure of the novel can be found in Robert L. Belknap, *The Structure of* The Brothers Karamazov (The Hague: Mouton, 1967).

73 Lawrence, *"Grand Inquisitor,"* *Phoenix*, p. 287.

74 Ibid., pp. 284–85.

75 Ibid., p. 290. Lawrence's preference for aristocratic leadership is voiced elsewhere: "The secret is, to commit into the hands of the sacred few the responsibility which now lies like torture on the mass. Let the few, the leaders, be increasingly responsible for the whole. And let the mass be free: free, save for the choice of leaders. Leaders – this is what mankind is craving for" (*Fantasia*, p. 81).

76 Lawrence, *"Grand Inquisitor,"* *Phoenix*, p. 287.

77 Freud provided a similar psychological interpretation of Dostoevsky's epilepsy in "Dostoevsky and parricide." Where Freud attributes the epilepsy to unacknowledged patricidal urges and subsequent guilt about the alleged murder of Dostoevsky's father, Lawrence explains the Russian author's diseased personality in terms of mental consciousness. See Joseph Frank's analysis of the shortcomings of Freud's analysis, "Freud's case-history of Dostoevsky," *Dostoevsky: Seeds of Revolt*, pp. 379–91.

78 Lawrence, *"Grand Inquisitor," Phoenix*, p. 287.
79 Ibid., p. 285.
80 Lawrence, *Classic American Literature*, p. 2.
81 Malcolm V. Jones, *Dostoyevsky: The Novel of Discord* (London: Elek, 1976), p. 184.
82 Robert L. Belknap, "The rhetoric of an ideological novel," *Literature and Society in Imperial Russia, 1800–1914*, ed. William Mills Todd, III (Stanford University Press, 1978), p. 194. Belknap convincingly refutes the argument that Dostoevsky identified so thoroughly with Ivan and his legend that he never succeeded in undermining the Inquisitor's sceptical and despairing vision. According to Belknap, the "task of the novel is to confute Ivan's argument: to justify the ways of God to man" (p. 183). To show how the novel succeeds in its task and how other characters and events undermine the logic and integrity of both Ivan and his legend, Belknap analyzes a crucial Dostoevsky letter, literary sources for the legend, and the social events and contemporary personalities that are echoed within it.
83 D. H. Lawrence, *Kangaroo* (London: Heinemann, 1923), p. 107.
84 Ibid., p. 110.
85 Fyodor Dostoevsky, *The Brothers Karamazov*, trans. Constance Garnett (1912; New York: Modern Library, n.d.), p. 62.
86 Lawrence, *"Grand Inquisitor," Phoenix*, p. 290.
87 Ibid., p. 284.
88 Lawrence, *Kangaroo*, p. 290.
89 Ibid., p. 136. John Burt Foster, Jr., "Dostoevsky versus Nietzsche in modernist fiction: Lawrence's *Kangaroo* and Malraux's *La Condition Humaine*," *Stanford Literature Review* 2 (Spring 1985), 47–83, also discusses this novel as a response to Dostoevsky. His analysis focuses on Kangaroo's restatement of "reverence for life" as "living life," a phrase that Foster traces to *Notes from the Underground*. He argues that Kangaroo represents a Dostoevskian imperative of love that is associated with authoritarian politics, while Somers represents a Nietzschean imperative of power associated with independence of spirit. Yet Somers, according to Foster, evolves away from Nietzschean values, which are rejected for being too transcendent and spiritual, towards the Dostoevskian reverence for the mystery of the earth. In other words, Somers in his rejection of the mass politics of love sides politically with Nietzsche; religiously, he sides with Dostoevsky's embrace of the earth.
90 Lawrence, *"Grand Inquisitor," Phoenix*, p. 286.
91 Ibid., p. 289.
92 D. H. Lawrence, *The Man Who Died* (London: Martin Secker, 1931), p. 43. The novella was published as *The Escaped Cock* in two parts in 1928. After Lawrence's death, it was released as a single volume and given a new, non-sexual title, *The Man Who Died*. In deference to Lawrence's choice of title, I refer to this work as *The Escaped Cock* in my text, though my references are drawn from the edition entitled *The Man Who Died*.
93 Ibid., p. 53.

94 Ibid., p. 60.
95 Ibid., pp. 144–45.
96 Ibid., p. 157.
97 Lawrence, "The crown," *Death of a Porcupine*, p. 99.
98 Lawrence, "Why the novel matters," *Phoenix*, p. 535.
99 Lawrence, "Morality and the novel," *Phoenix*, p. 532.

3 A MODERNIST AMBIVALENCE: VIRGINIA WOOLF

1 The information about Woolf's sexually disappointing honeymoon comes from Bell, *Woolf.*
2 Virginia Woolf, "The Russian Point of View," *Common Reader*, p. 184.
3 *The Diary of Virginia Woolf*, Anne Olivier Bell (ed.), 5 vols. (New York: Harcourt Brace Jovanovich, 1977–84), vol. IV, pp. 172–73.
4 Virginia Woolf, "Letter to Lytton Strachey," 1 September 1912, in Nigel Nicolson and Joanne Trautman (eds.), *The Letters of Virginia Woolf*, 6 vols. (London: Hogarth, 1975–80), vol. I, p. 5.
5 Virginia Woolf, "Letter to Lytton Strachey," *Virginia Woolf and Lytton Strachey: Letters*, ed. Leonard Woolf and James Strachey (London: Hogarth, n.d.), p. 47.
6 Lytton Strachey, "Dostoievsky," *Spectatorial Essays*, ed. James Strachey (London: Chatto and Windus, 1964, pp. 174–79); first published in the *Spectator*, 28 September 1912. According to his biographer, Michael Holroyd, Strachey had been introduced to Dostoevsky's works through his friends, the painters Henry Lamb and Augustus John, both early and enthusiastic admirers of the Russian author. Though Strachey only wrote two short essays about Dostoevsky, he was a fine judge of his literary merit; in my view, the best of his generation. Strachey's essays are noteworthy for their appreciation of literary craft and their perception of Dostoevsky's resemblance to other literary artists (Cervantes, Molière, Shakespeare, and other Elizabethan dramatists). Strachey also stood apart from his contemporaries in his ability to recognize the irony and humor that pervades nearly all of Dostoevsky's works. His second essay, a review of *The Possessed*, was aptly titled "A Russian humorist." The essay can be found in *The Shorter Strachey*, ed. Michael Holrord and Paul Levy (New York: Oxford University Press, 1980), pp. 183–87; it was first published in the *Spectator*, 11 April 1914.
7 V. Woolf, "Letter to Lytton Strachey," 22 October 1915, in Nicolson and Trautman, *Letters of Woolf*, vol. II, p. 67.
8 Diary entry, 22 October 1915, *Woolf Diary*, vol. II, pp. 22–23.
9 V. Woolf, "The Russian point of view," *Common Reader*, pp. 180–81, 185–86.
10 Virginia Woolf, "The novels of Turgenev," *Collected Essays*, vol. II, p. 250; also in *The Captain's Death Bed and Other Essays* (London: Hogarth, 1950). Through her friendship with S. S. Koteliansky and her work with Hogarth Press, Woolf undoubtedly became familiar with other Russian writers, but

no other Russian besides Tolstoy, Dostoevsky, Turgenev, and Chekhov
seemed as capable of engaging her imagination. The Woolfs' libraries only
included the works of the four. See *Catalog of Books from the Library of Leonard
and Virginia Woolf* (Brighton, Holleyman and Treacher, 1975).

11 Richard Pevear, Introduction, *The Brothers Karamazov*, Richard Pevear and
Larissa Volokhonsky (trans.) (New York: Vintage-Random, 1991), p. xvi.

12 Virginia Woolf, "More Dostoevsky," *Books and Portraits*, ed. Mary Lyon
(New York: Harcourt Brace Jovanovich, 1978), p. 116; first published in
Times Literary Supplement, 22 February 1917.

13 Ibid., pp. 118–19.

14 Virginia Woolf, *To the Lighthouse* (1927; New York: Harvest-Harcourt, Brace
and World, 1955), p. 294.

15 V. Woolf, "On re-reading Meredith," *Collected Essays*, vol. ii, pp. 233–34;
first published in *Times Literary Supplement*, 25 July 1918.

16 V. Woolf, "Dostoevsky in Cranford," *Books and Portraits*, pp. 121–22; first
published in *Times Literary Supplement*, 23 October 1919. It should be noted
that Woolf never wrote a review of a major Dostoevsky novel. That, in part,
may be attributed to her reluctance to reread his novels. It also may be a
sign of her deference to Lytton Strachey, who reviewed *The Brothers
Karamazov* for the *Spectator* (28 September 1912) and discussed both *The Idiot*
and *The Possessed* in his essay, "A Russian humorist."

17 V. Woolf, "English prose," *Books and Portraits*, pp. 16–17; first published in
the *Athenaeum*, 30 January 1920.

18 According to Victor Luftig, Woolf began learning Russian in January of
1921; after nearly six months of lessons, a summer illness "presumably put
an end" to her lessons. Luftig places Woolf's efforts to learn Russian within
the context of her friendship with S. S. Koteliansky, her assistance in his
translations, and the Hogarth Press publications of Russian translations
(Victor Luftig, "The wonderful eye: Virginia Woolf's translations of Tolstoi," unpublished paper, Stanford University, 1985).

Woolf herself became involved in translating in a minor way. Like
Lawrence, and her husband Leonard, she assisted S. S. Koteliansky in his
translating efforts, presumably editing his English. The Woolfs' Hogarth
Press published seven Koteliansky translations, three of which listed Vir-
ginia as a co-translator: Dostoevsky's *Stavrogin's Confession and the Plan of the
Life of a Great Sinner* (previously unpublished material from *The Possessed* and
notes for Dostoevsky's unwritten novel; 1922); *Talks with Tolstoi* by the
Russian musician, A. B. Goldenveizer (selections from his diary; 1923); and
Tolstoi's Love Letters, With a Study on the Autobiographical Elements in Tolstoi's Work
by Paul Birykov (1923).

19 Virginia Woolf, "Mr. Bennett and Mrs. Brown," *Nation and Athenaeum* 34 (1
December 1923), 342–43.

20 Diary entry, 19 June 1923, *Woolf Diary*, vol. ii, pp. 248–49. An earlier diary
entry also seems relevant here. Woolf recorded a conversation with T. S.
Eliot on 26 September 1922: "So we got on to S. Sitwell who merely

explores his sensibility – one of the deadly crimes as Tom [Eliot] thinks: to Dostoevsky – the ruin of English literature, we agreed" (Ibid., vol. II, p. 203). Judging from the juxtaposition of Dostoevsky and Sitwell, "ruin" apparently has a positive connotation here, for Woolf implies that the Russian novelist forces the English to move in new directions.

It should also be noted that Woolf reviewed a distorted and unrevealing biography of Dostoevsky written by his daughter Aimée. Woolf correctly sensed that the daughter failed to render the complexity and interest of her father's life: "One feels rather as if one had been admitted to the kitchen where the cook is smashing the china or to the drawing room where the relations are gossiping in corners, while Dostoevsky sits upstairs alone in his study" (Virginia Woolf, "Dostoevsky the father," rev. of *Fyodor Dostoevsky: A Study*, by Aimée Dostoevsky, *Times Literary Supplement*, 12 January 1922; reprinted in *Books and Portraits*, pp. 112–14).

21 V. Woolf, "Modern fiction," *Common Reader*, p. 151. The literary dispute between Woolf and Bennett is thoroughly documented in Samuel Hynes, "The whole contention between Mr. Bennett and Mrs. Woolf," *Novel* 1, 1 (Fall 1967) 34–44. The first attack came from an unsigned essay by Woolf, "Modern novels," that appeared in *TLS* in April of 1919 (that essay was later substantially revised and retitled as "Modern fiction"). In 1923 Bennett responded with "Is the novel decaying," an essay that faulted Woolf for her failure to create convincing characters. From then on there were numerous reviews, essays, lectures, and even a joint appearance in a symposium (in the summer of 1924), all of which served to fuel the debate between them until Bennett's death in 1931. For further discussion, also see Hyne's introduction, *The Author's Craft and Other Critical Writings of Arnold Bennett*, ed. Samuel Hynes (Lincoln: University of Nebraska Press, 1968).

22 V. Woolf, "Modern Fiction," *Common Reader*, pp. 153–54.

23 Ibid., p. 155.

24 Wilfred Stone views Woolf's dichotomy as evidence of a "lapsed Nonconformist's need" to maintain a "separation between body and mind." In other words, she provides a secularized extension of a religiously motivated dualism (Wilfred Stone, letter to the author, 15 June 1987). While Woolf obviously relied on such dualism to argue against her Edwardian counterparts, I do not believe that she fully endorsed it. On one hand, her choice of terms can be judged as a rhetorical stratagem used to present her argument in a context that would be familiar to her audience. As N. G. Annan has pointed out, the English intelligentsia of her era was dominated by lapsed Nonconformists. See "The Intellectual Aristocracy," *Studies in Social History: A Tribute to G. M. Trevelyan* (London: Green, 1955), pp. 241–87. On the other hand, Woolf argued herself into a corner, for her emphasis on the spiritual and the mental led her readers to assume that her own fiction rests on such a mind–body dichotomy. Woolf, as a result, became known as an explorer of private consciousness who was unconcerned with issues beyond the mind.

25 V. Woolf, "Modern Fiction," *Common Reader*, pp. 156–58.
26 According to Robert Lord, Woolf's fascination with the Russian soul is derived from a mistranslation. While Lord admits that the Russian word *dasha* can be translated as "soul," he argues that the English word "heart" is very often "a better and more accurate translation." In his judgment, if Constance Garnett had used "heart" instead of "soul," the English readers would not have regarded Dostoevsky and other Russian writers as so far removed from English traditions, "for it cannot be said that 'heart' is foreign to the English sensibility." See Robert Lord, "An English point of view," *Dostoevsky: Essays and Perspectives* (London: Chatto and Windus, 1970), p. 1.
27 V. Woolf, "The Russian point of view," *Common Reader*, pp. 182–84.
28 Woolf, "Phases of fiction," *Collected Essays*, vol. II, pp. 85–86.
29 Kirpotin makes the interesting point that "Dostoevsky thought in psychologically wrought images, but he thought socially . . . His psychologism is a special artistic method for penetrating the objective essence of the contradictory human collective, for penetrating into the very heart of the social relationships that so agitated him, and a special artistic method for reproducing them in the art of the word" (quoted by Bakhtin, *Dostoevsky's Poetics*, pp. 36–37).
30 Ibid., p. 252. Bakhtin provides valuable insight into the dialogical nature of Dostoevsky's art, especially in his emphasis on the connections between dialogue and consciousness. "Dostoevsky could hear dialogical relationships everywhere, in all manifestations of conscious and intelligent life; where consciousness began, there dialogue began for him as well" (p. 40).
31 Ibid., p. 30.
32 Ibid., p. 211.
33 Joseph Frank, *Dostoevsky: The Miraculous Years, 1865–1871* (Princeton University Press, 1995), p. 497.
34 V. Woolf, "Phases of fiction," *Collected Essays*, vol. II, pp. 86–87.
35 Alex Zwerdling, *Virginia Woolf and the Real World* (Berkeley: University of California Press, 1986), p. 253.
36 Thomas C. Caramagno, "Manic-depressive psychosis and critical approaches to Virginia Woolf's life and work," *PMLA* 103.1 (1988), 10–23, competently explains Woolf's bouts of madness as evidence of manic-depressive psychosis, drawing upon current medical literature, her own descriptions (both personal and literary), and those of witnesses. Her psychotic phases, according to Caramagno, were characterized by "sudden outbreaks of hostility, particularly toward Leonard," "heightened perception," "hallucinations," "racing thoughts," and other symptoms of a self beyond control. Woolf found these same symptoms expressed in Dostoevsky's fiction, which mirrored the extreme emotions, psychic anguish, and mood swings that marked her own most anguished and unproductive periods. Her inability to recognize Dostoevsky as an artist in control may be partially explained by the fact that he came too close to her own experiences

of disintegration. While attracted to the flame of his genius, she also felt compelled to draw away from it: coming too close might spell the death of the artist.

37 V. Woolf, "Phases of fiction," *Collected Essays*, vol. ɪɪ, pp. 87–89.

38 Ibid., p. 100.

39 Bakhtin, *Dostoevsky's Poetics*, p. 6.

40 Like Woolf, Bell complains about the constraints of "realism" in art, and he severely criticizes those who insist that the visual arts must accurately represent material from life: "Creating a work of art is so tremendous a business that it leaves no leisure for catching a likeness or displaying address. Every sacrifice made to representation is something stolen from art." See Clive Bell, *Art* (New York: Capricorn Books, 1958), p. 38; Bell's work was originally published in 1913. Like Woolf's "Mr. Bennett and Mrs. Brown" essay, it has the quality of a carefully reasoned manifesto designed to protect the interests and values of the moderns.

41 Zwerdling quotes one of Woolf's diary entries – "Why admit anything to literature that is not poetry" – as evidence of her preoccupation with the poetic (Zwerdling, *Woolf and Real World*, pp. 10–11). His study, however, proceeds to show that Woolf did not abandon an interest in the external world, and that her work seeks to "expand the theory and practice of realism" by merging the "life of solitude" with the "life of society" (p. 24).

Lucio P. Ruotolo, *The Interrupted Moment: A View of Virginia Woolf's Novels* (Stanford University Press, 1986), argues that Woolf's novels "abound with anarchist notions." Her

recurring impulse to break derived sequences of art and politics reveals a growing critique of something more fundamental than either patriarchal hierarchy or the "bourgeois Victorianism" that so inspired Bloomsbury irreverence. Along with the most prominent anarchist theoreticians, she comes to question the validity of social structure itself, which is to say, those hierarchical assumptions that underlie most Western theories of governance. (p. 220)

42 Stephen Spender describes Woolf's writing in terms of "an imagistic poetic method." He analyzes the dispute between Woolf and Bennett as a quarrel between the "poetic method' and the "prose method." In his perspective, Woolf is aligned with the "modern I" of Rimbaud, Joyce, Proust, and Eliot's *Prufrock* against the "contemporary I" of Shaw, Wells, Bennett, and others. According to Spender, "the poetic method sees the centre of consciousness as the point where all that is significant in the surrounding world becomes aware and transformed; the prose method requires a description of that world in order to explain the characteristics of the people in it. The hero of the poetic method is Rimbaud; of the prose method, Balzac" (Stephen Spender, *The Struggle of the Modern* [Berkeley: University of California Press, 1963], p. 118).

43 Bakhtin, *Dostoevsky's Poetics*, p. 124.

44 Ibid., p. 176.

45 Diary entry, 16 August 1933, *Woolf Diary*, vol. ɪv, pp. 172–73.

46 "Letter to S. S. Koteliansky," 21 August 1933, in Nicolson and Trautman, *Letters of Woolf*, vol. v, pp. 216–17.

47 Woolf noted in her diary: "Ideas that struck me. That the more complex a vision the less it lends itself to satire: the more it understands the less it is able to sum up and make linear. For example: Shre and Dostoevsky neither of them satirise" (diary entry, 6 May 1934, *Woolf Diary*, vol. iv, p. 309).

48 "The young can describe passing things – a bridge seen from the train. No. One doesn't remember them. We read Tolstoy. I kept Dos[toevs]ky to myself in a selfish way" (diary entry, 20 April 1940, ibid., vol. v, p. 280).

49 Virginia Woolf, *Mrs. Dalloway* (1925; New York: Harvest-Harcourt, Brace and World, 1953), p. 244.

50 V. Woolf, *Lighthouse*, p. 42.

51 Zwerdling notes that "Clarissa's party is strictly class-demarcated. No Septimus, no Rezia, no Doris Kliman could conceivably set foot in it . . . Clarissa defends her parties as an expression of her ideal of unity . . . But the London neighborhoods she mentions are upper-middle-class preserves, the residential areas where the members of the Dalloway set are likely to live" (Zwerdling, *Woolf and Real World*, p. 127).

52 Though Zwerdling discusses Woolf as a social satirist whose targets are much broader and more inclusive than is often realized, he admits the social limits of her perspective: "The middle class Woolf knew intimately and could criticize from within. The aristocracy she had observed closely with a mixture of envy and intellectual condescension . . . Her fiction is characterized by a refusal or inability to describe anyone below the rank of middle class in persuasive detail. The apparent exceptions (Charles Tansley, Septimus Smith) are really aspirants to middle-class status" (ibid., p. 96).

53 Virginia Woolf, *The Years* (1937; San Diego: Harvest/Harcourt Brace Jovanovich, 1965), p. 398.

54 Ibid., p. 404.

55 Ibid., p. 430.

56 Ruotolo aptly describes her as heroic: "Open to the unpargeted diversity of modern life, free of restrictive discriminations involving age, gender, or race, Eleanor embraces a reality impervious to syntheses of the past" (Ruotolo, *Interrupted Moment*, p. 202).

57 Fyodor Dostoevsky, *The Possessed*, trans. Constance Garnett (1914; New York: Modern Library, 1936), p. 476.

58 Frank, *The Miraculous Years*, p. 308. The letter is quoted (and translated) by Frank.

59 The narrative issues in *The Idiot* are analyzed with great depth and insight in Miller's *Dostoevsky and* The Idiot. For Miller's discussion of Nastasya's name-day party, see pp. 106–08 and 175–87.

60 Dostoevsky contrasted his efforts to achieve a "new word" to the works of Tolstoy and Turgenev: "all that is landowner's literature. It has said all there is to say (beautifully in the case of Tolstoy). But that, the apogee of the landowner's word, was the very last. The new word that is to replace that of

the landowners has not yet been heard" (Fyodor Dostoevsky, "Letter to N. N. Strakhov," 18/30 May, *Selected Letters of Fyodor Dostoevsky*, ed. Joseph Frank and David I. Goldstein, trans. Andrew R. MacAndrew [New Brunswick: Rutgers University Press, 1987], p. 361).

Joseph Frank notes that Dostoevsky defined Tolstoy's work "as being that of a 'historian,' not a novelist. For, in his view, Tolstoy depicted the life 'which existed in the tranquil and stable, long-established landowners' family of the middle-upper stratum.'" Tolstoy's fiction, as a result, could not do justice to the "confusion and moral chaos" of the present age (Frank, *Seeds of Revolt*, p. 6).

4 SYMPATHY, TRUTH, AND ARTLESSNESS: ARNOLD BENNETT

1 The figure of "Mr. Nixon" in Pound's poem has long been accepted as a caricature of Bennett:

> In the cream gilded cabin of his steam yacht
> Mr. Nixon advised me kindly, to advance with fewer
> Dangers of delay. "Consider
> "Carefully the reviewer.
>
> "I was as poor as you are;
> "When I began I got, of course,
> "Advance on royalties, fifty at first," said Mr. Nixon,
> "Follow me, and take a column,
> "Even if you have to work free.
>
> "Butter reviewers. From fifty to three hundred
> "I rose in eighteen months;
> "The hardest nut I had to crack
> "Was Dr. Dundas.
>
> "I never mentioned a man but with the view
> "Of selling my own works.
> "The tip's a good one, as for literature
> "It gives no man a sinecure.
>
> "And no one knows, at sight, a masterpiece.
> "And give up verse, my boy,
> "There's nothing in it."

From Ezra Pound, "Hugh Selwyn Mauberly," *Selected Poems of Ezra Pound* (New York: New Directions, 1957), pp. 67–68.

2 Arnold Bennett, *The Author's Craft and Other Critical Writings of Arnold Bennett*, ed. Samuel Hynes (Lincoln: University of Nebraska Press, 1968), p. ix, draws a distinction between the two sides of Arnold Bennett: Mr. Nixon and the Conscious Artist. The target of Pound's poem represented only the former side: "This was the Bennett who managed his writing like a one-man factory; who watched production and measured it against costs; who

set his fees by the word and by the hour, and gave exactly ten shillings worth of work for ten shillings pay; and who read the small print of his contracts and badgered his agent for better terms." Hynes quotes a 27 April 1904 letter of Bennett's in which he describes himself as "an engine for the production of fiction"; according to Hynes, "he was so copious a writer that he had to vary his work so as not to flood the market" (p. xii).

3 Samuel Hynes discusses Woolf's class snobbery and the dispute between her and Bennett in "The Whole Contention Between Mr. Bennett and Mrs. Woolf" *Novel* 1.1. (Fall 1967), 34–44. Hynes quotes Woolf's reaction to news of Bennett's death, as recorded by her diary in March of 1931:

Arnold Bennett died last night, which leaves me sadder than I would have supposed. A lovable, genuine man; impeded, somehow a little awkward in life; well meaning; ponderous; kindly; coarse; knowing he was coarse; dimly floundering and feeling for something else; glutted with success; avid; thick lipped; prosaic intolerably; rather dignified; set upon writing; yet always taken in; deluded by splendour and success; but naive; an old bore; an egotist; much at the mercy of life for all his competence; a shopkeeper's view of literature." (Quoted on p. 43 in Hynes's essay)

4 Bennett's question comes from a letter of 13 April 1913, quoted by Hynes in his introduction to *Author's Craft*, p. xii. The information on Bennett's life and literary impact comes from three sources: Hyne's introduction to *Author's Craft*; Margaret Drabble's *Arnold Bennett: A Biography* (New York: Knopf, 1974); and Dudley Barker's *Writer by Trade: A Portrait of Arnold Bennett* (New York: Atheneum, 1966).

5 Hynes, introduction, *Author's Craft*, pp. xi–xii; xvii–xviii.

6 Arnold Bennett, "Ivan Turgenev," *Author's Craft*, pp. 107–08; originally published in *Academy*, 1435 (4 November 1899), 514–17.

7 Ibid., p. 101.

8 Bennett, "The novel reading public," *Author's Craft*, p. 78; originally published in *New Age* 5 (4, 11, 18 February 1909), 304, 325, 347.

9 Arnold Bennett, "Books and persons," *New Age* 6 (24 March 1910), 494.

10 Arnold Bennett, "Books and persons," *New Age* 6 (31 March 1910), 518–19. Bennett wrote his *New Age* columns under the pseudonym of Jacob Tonson; judging from the letters to the editor, however, it seemed well known that the articles were penned by Bennett.

11 Arnold Bennett, *The Journal of Arnold Bennett* (Garden City: Garden City Publishing, 1932), p. 382.

12 Arnold Bennett, *The Old Wives' Tale* (1908; Middlesex: Penguin, 1983), p. 613.

13 Ibid., p. 423.

14 Ibid., p. 249.

15 Arnold Bennett, "Books and persons in London and Paris," *New Age* 8 (9 February 1911), 349–50. Apparently, Bennett's preoccupation with French literature and his lengthy stays in Paris had prompted him to retitle his "Books and persons" column, starting on 12 January 1911. His influence through his *New Age* columns would be hard to overestimate. In the words of Margaret Drabble: "He was now regarded as one of England's few contacts

with Continental taste. He taught the English to admire the Russian ballet . . . and the Russian novel . . . He introduced his own favorite French writers, such as Romain Rolland, Gide, Valéry, and Claudel. As a result of Bennett's enthusiasm for Chekhov the *New Age* began to publish his short stories" (Drabble, *Arnold Bennett* , p. 165).

16 Arnold Bennett, "Marguerite Audoux," *Books and Persons* (New York: George H. Doran, 1917). This book is a collection of some of Bennett's *New Age* columns.

17 Arnold Bennett, "Books and persons in London and Paris," *New Age* 8 (23 March 1911), 492. As in his Turgenev essay, Bennett shows here his knowledge of French criticism: "Two books on him are soon to appear in Paris, one by André Gide and the other by Suares."

18 Bennett, *Author's Craft*, p. 9. This essay was originally published as "The storyteller's craft" in *English Review* 14 (April, June, and July 1913), 17–29, 349–60, 556–68, and 15 (October 1913), 331–42.

19 Bennett, *Author's Craft*, p. 13. Woolf's charge against Bennett strikes a similar tone and makes a similar point: "Mr. Bennett has never once looked at Mrs. Brown in her corner." She goes on to include all of the Edwardians in her charge, those writers who "have looked very powerfully . . . but never at her, never at life, never at human nature" (Virginia Woolf, "Mr. Bennett and Mrs. Brown," *Collected Essays*, vol. 1, p. 330). In key respects, Woolf's essay can be read as a parody of Bennett's essay.

20 Bennett, *Author's Craft*, p. 11.

21 Arnold Bennett, *Hilda Lessways* (London: Metheun, 1911), p. 6.

22 Arnold Bennett, *Anna of the Five Towns* (1902; Middlesex: Penguin, 1978), pp. 117–23.

23 Bennett, *Author's Craft*, p. 12.

24 Ibid., pp. 21–22.

25 Ibid., pp. 18–19.

26 Bennett, "Some adventures among Russian fiction," *Author's Craft*, pp. 116–19; first published in an anthology of essays edited by Winifred Stephens, *The Soul of Russia* (London: Macmillan, 1916), pp. 84–88.

27 In his later years, he often separated the novel from art altogether. His 1928 article for the *Realist* defined the novel as social criticism, in contrast to his earlier views: "The chief mark of the serious novelist, after fundamental creative power, is that he have a definite critical attitude towards life." In a review of *A Room of One's Own*, he made an unfortunate distinction between his own work and that of Woolf's: "She is the queen of the high-brows; and I am a low-brow. But it takes all sorts of brows to make a world, and without a large admixture of low-brows even Bloomsbury would be uninhabitable." Woolf accepted Bennett's dichotomy between art and life as characteristic of the difference between her and Bennett. While working on *The Years* in May of 1933, she noted that her problem was "how [to] give ordinary waking Arnold Bennett life the form of art" (Hynes, "Contention between Bennett and Woolf," pp. 42–44).

28 Bennett, *Journal*, p. 382.
29 "Letter to Frank Swinnerton," 28 September 1919, *Letters of Arnold Bennett*, ed. James Hepburn, 4 vols., vol. III (London: Oxford University Press, 1970), p. III.
30 "Letter to André Gide," 10 September 1920, ibid., p. 131. According to the editor of his letters, James Hepburn, Bennett first met Gide while living in Paris in 1911.
31 André Gide, *Dostoevsky*, intro. Arnold Bennett (London: J. M. Dent, 1925), p. 103.
32 Ibid., p. 150.
33 "Letter to André Gide," 15 August 1923, *Letters of Bennett*, vol. III, pp. 196–97.
34 Arnold Bennett, introduction to Gide, *Dostoevsky*, p. vi.
35 Ibid., pp. vi–viii.
36 Gide, *Dostoevsky*, pp. 71–72.
37 Bennett, introduction, ibid., p. xviii.
38 Arnold Bennett, "The 'cowardice' of Thackeray," *The Evening Standard Years: "Books and Persons," 1926–1931*, ed. Andrew Mylett (London: Chatto and Windus, 1974), pp. 30–32.
39 Bennett, "The twelve finest novels," *Evening Standard Years*, pp. 32–34. Ironically, the attributes that Bennett temporarily ascribes to Tolstoy – "commonplace, banal, vulgar, material" – were also characteristic of Woolf's reproaches of Bennett's own work. Bennett rounded out his list of twelve with four Turgenev novels – *Torrents of Spring*, *Virgin Soil*, *On the Eve*, and *Fathers and Children* – and Gogol's *Dead Souls*.
40 In July of 1927, Bennett penned another list of favorite novels, this time a list with a decidedly Gallic flavor, in an article entitled "Holiday reading – and some famous names." This one includes translations of Balzac's *Cousin Bette* and *Curé of Tours*, Zola's *Nana*, Maupassant's *Pierre and Jean*, and Charles Louis Philippe's *Bubu de Montparnasse*, as well as *The Brothers Karamazov*. This column is noteworthy for its impatience with all English novels: "As for English novels in general even the masterpieces are rendered insular for me by our racial sentimentality and prudery, and few of them would I read again except for a cash payment" (Bennett, *Evening Standard Years*, pp. 66–67).
41 Bennett, "Books that make one see," *Evening Standard Years*, p. 338.
42 Hemmings, *Russian Novel in France*, p. 30.
43 Bennett, "The progress of the novel," *Author's Craft*, pp. 92–96; originally published in *Realist* 1 (April 1929), 3–11.
44 Bennett, "Another criticism of the New School," *Evening Standard Years*, pp. 4–5.
45 Robin Feuer Miller has done an admirable job of explaining the importance of *indirection* in the relationship between Dostoevsky's personal values and his literary works: "Dostoevsky understood narration as a strategy, as a subtle means for persuasion rather than as a simple vehicle for direct expression of his thoughts. In fact, Dostoevsky believed that he must always avoid direct expression of his thoughts" (Miller, *Dostoevsky and* The Idiot, p. 12).

5 KEEPING THE MONSTER AT BAY: JOSEPH CONRAD

1 Quotations are from Joseph Conrad's "A glance at two books," *Last Essays* (London: Dent, 1926), p. 197; and his preface to *The Nigger of the "Narcissus": A Tale of the Sea* in *Conrad's Prefaces to His Works*, ed. Edward Garnett (London: Dent, 1937).

2 Conrad, "Glance at two books," *Last Essays*, p. 7.

3 Robert Gathorne-Hardy (ed.), *Ottoline: The Early Memoirs of Lady Ottoline Morrell* (London: Faber and Faber, 1963), pp. 241–42. Consider Bertrand Russell's account of his first meeting with Conrad: "We looked into each other's eyes, half appalled and half intoxicated to find ourselves in such a region. The emotion was as intense as passionate love, and at the same time all-embracing. I came away bewildered, and hardly able to find my way among ordinary affairs." Though their encounters were few, Russell was so captivated by Conrad that he named his first son John Conrad in his honor (Bertrand Russell, *The Autobiography of Bertrand Russell*, 2 vols. [London: George Allen and Unwin, 1967–8], vol. i, pp. 207–9).

4 Conrad's claim that he knew practically nothing about the Russians was made in a letter to Edward Garnett's sister Olive, published in *Letters from Conrad*, pp. 250–51.

5 "Letter to Edward Garnett," 27 May 1912, ibid., pp. 260–61.

6 See Irving Howe's chapters on Dostoevsky and Conrad in *Politics and the Novel* (New York: Meridian, 1957). Howe metaphorically describes Conrad's repressive struggle as a conflict between Dostoevsky and James: "the Jamesian Conrad directs, the Dostoevskian Conrad erupts" (p. 80).

7 "Letter to Edward Garnett," 2 May 1917, *Letters from Conrad*, p. 268.

8 "Letter to Edward Garnett," 7 December 1897, *Letters from Conrad*, pp. 108–9.

9 "Letter to Edward Garnett," 2 May 1917, *Letters from Conrad*, p. 268.

10 The pivotal role played by the Garnetts in helping to introduce Turgenev's works to the English is discussed by Edward's biographer, George Jefferson: "If most contemporary authors came to read Turgenev through his wife's translations, it was Edward's systematic and comprehensive analysis in the prefaces that pioneered a full appreciation of Turgenev as a novelist." See Jefferson's *Edward Garnett*, p. 161.

11 Constance Garnett, "Letter to Joseph Conrad," 30 December 1897, *Letters from Conrad*, p. 111.

12 Zdzislaw Najder quotes from a letter of Conrad's to Hugh Clifford in which the novelist justifies his attention to style:

words, groups of words, words standing alone, are symbols of life, have the power in their sound or their aspect to present the very thing you wish to hold up before the mental vision of your readers. The things "as they are" exist in words; therefore words should be handled with care lest the picture, the image of truth abiding in facts, should become distorted – or blurred.

See Najder's *Joseph Conrad: A Chronicle* (New Brunswick: Rutgers University Press, 1983), p. 116.

13 All of the quotations here are from Conrad's preface to *The Nigger of the "Narcissus"* in his *Prefaces*, pp. 49–52.

14 "Letter to Edward Garnett," 27 May 1912, *Letters from Conrad*, pp. 260–61.

15 Ivan Turgenev, *A Desperate Character Etc.*, trans. Constance Garnett, intro. Edward Garnett (London: Heinemann, 1920; originally pub. 1899).

16 "Letter to Edward Garnett," 26 October 1899, *Letters from Conrad*, p. 154.

17 Conrad, "Glance at two books," *Last Essays*, p. 197.

18 Ibid., pp. 198–99.

19 Ibid., pp. 203–4.

20 See Karl's *Joseph Conrad: The Three Lives* (New York: Farrar, Straus, and Giroux, 1979), p. 91. According to Bernard Meyer, Conrad's "father had been a student at the University of St. Petersburg" and knew the Russian language well. See Meyer's *Joseph Conrad: A Psychoanalytic Biography* (Princeton University Press, 1967), p. 214. I have not yet found any other source that substantiates this.

21 "Letter to Edward Garnett," 2 May 1917, *Letters from Conrad*, pp. 268–70.

22 Joseph Conrad, introduction to Edward Garnett, *Turgenev: A Study*, in *Notes on Life and Letters* (London: Dent, 1921), pp. 62–65.

23 The letter to Blackwood is quoted in Morton Dauwen Zabel's introduction to an anthology of Conrad short stories, *Tales of Heroes and History* (Garden City: Anchor-Doubleday, 1960), p. viii.

24 "Letter to Edward Garnett," 28 August 1908, *Letters from Conrad*, pp. 225–26.

25 Morton Dauwen Zabel, introduction to Joseph Conrad, *Under Western Eyes* (Garden City: Anchor-Doubleday, 1963), p. liii. Zabel's introduction provides an admirable discussion of Conrad's debt to both Turgenev and Dostoevsky.

26 Jefferson, *Edward Garnett*, p. 19.

27 Ibid., p. 32; also see David Garnett's account of his mother's political activities and friendships in *The Golden Echo* (New York: Harcourt Brace, 1954).

28 Jefferson, *Edward Garnett*, pp. 19–20. Andrej Busza reports that Edward first came to know Russian political exiles in the 1890s through his friendship with the Rossettis. The exiles were "mostly revolutionaries, who had belonged to the Populist Chaykovsky Circle, and included in addition to N. V. Chaykovsky himself, F. Volkhovsky, P. A. Kropotkin, A. A. Cherkesov, and S. M. Kravchinsky [Stepniak]." See Andrej Busza, "Rhetoric and ideology in Conrad's *Under Western Eyes*," *Joseph Conrad: A Commemoration*, Papers from the 1974 International Conference on Conrad, ed. Norman Sherry (New York: Barnes and Noble, 1977), p. 116n.

29 This version is reported as truth by George Jefferson in *Edward Garnett*, p. 21. It is presumably based on the similarly worded account provided by David Garnett in *Golden Echo*, pp. 12–13. However, Thomas C. Moser shows that the historical evidence surrounding Stepniak's crime is far more complex than either Jefferson or David Garnett realized. See his article, "An English context for Conrad's Russian characters: Sergey Stepniak and the diary of

Olive Garnett," *Journal of Modern Literature* 11.1 (March 1984), 3–44

30 Besides dealing with literary influences, Moser's "English context for Conrad's Russian characters" provides an admirably researched account of Stepniak's life and its unsolved mysteries.

31 David Garnett, *Golden Echo*, pp. 19–20.

32 Jefferson, *Edward Garnett*, p. 23. David Garnett (*Golden Echo*, p. 11) provides a more detailed description of his mother's cloak-and-dagger mission to Russia. Since David was only six months old when his mother left for Russia, his account may be tainted by family mythology or by his own imagination.

33 See David Garnett, *Golden Echo*, pp. 116–20. One wonders if the Russian bureaucracy grew suspicious of women named Vera.

34 Jefferson wrongly reports that this phrase refers to the Cearne (*Edward Garnett*, p. 173). Richard Garnett, David's son, informs me otherwise (Richard Garnett, letter to the author, 31 July 1989).

35 Thomas C. Moser, "Ford Madox Hueffer and *Under Western Eyes*," *Conradiana* 15.3 (1983), 163–80.

36 Edward Garnett, "Mr. Joseph Conrad," *Academy* 1380 (15 October 1898), 82–83.

37 [Edward Garnett], "Mr. Conrad's new books," *Academy and Literature* 63 (6 December 1902), 606. This is a review of Conrad's "Youth," "Heart of darkness," and "The end of the tether" published in a single volume.

38 [Edward Garnett], "The novel of the week," *Nation* 1 (28 September 1907), 1096. Nearly a year later, Edward published a review of Conrad's *A Set of Six*. Once again, he praised his friend's Slavic orientation:

Mr. Conrad's rare gifts may, indeed, have been fertilised by his cosmopolitan life, and have fructified through their transplantation into English soil, but anything less English than his ironic, tender, and sombre vision of life it would be hard to find . . . [The humor in his stories] is essentially Slav in its ironic acceptance of the pathetic futility of human nature, and quite un-English in its refinement of tender, critical malice . . . What is of especial interest to the critic is that he has been a liberating force to our English insularity . . . [Conrad's stories] are Continental in their literary affinities, Slav in their psychological insight, and Polish in their haunting and melancholy cadence.

See Edward Garnett, "The genius of Mr. Conrad," *Nation* 3.21 (22 August 1908), 746–47.

Frederick R. Karl has offered an interesting perspective on this review: "Within the context of his comments, Garnett is basically correct, and his wording is delicate and praiseworthy; yet Conrad, the author of 'Amy Foster,' was aware of how forcefully he beat against the door of England and how carefully he tried to shape the language so as to be understood by Englishmen" (Karl, *Conrad: Three Lives*, p. 650).

39 Edward Garnett, "Mr. Conrad's new novel," *Nation* 10 (21 October 1911), 141–42.

40 "Letter to Edward Garnett," 20 October 1911, *Letters from Conrad*, pp. 248–50.

41 "Letter to Olive Garnett," 20 October 1911, *Letters from Conrad,* pp. 250–51.
42 Joseph Conrad, "Autocracy and war," *Notes on Life and Letters,* pp. 115–16.
43 Ibid., p. 119.
44 Ibid., p. 123.
45 Ibid., p. 132.
46 See Najder, *Joseph Conrad,* p. 309.
47 Conrad, "Autocracy and war," *Notes on Life and Letters,* p. 134.
48 Ibid., p. 125.
49 Fyodor Dostoevsky, "Letter to A. N. Maikov," 18 January 1856, *Selected Letters,* p. 83.
50 Conrad, "Autocracy and war," *Notes on Life and Letters,* pp. 133–34.
51 See Zabel, introduction, *Tales of Heroes,* p. xxxiv; also see Albert J. Guerard, *Conrad the Novelist* (Cambridge: Harvard University Press, 1958).
52 Richard Curle, *The Last Twelve Years of Joseph Conrad* (London: Sampson Low, Marston, 1928), p. 16.
53 Ibid., pp. 28–29.
54 Russell, *Autobiography,* p. 72. Unlike Curle, Russell cannot be accused of any bias in favor of Russian subjects. About his visit to post-revolutionary Russia, he reported:

> Bolshevism is a close tyrannical bureaucracy, with a spy system more elaborate and terrible than the Tsar's . . . No vestige of liberty remains, in thought or speech or action. I was stifled and oppressed by the weight of the machine as by a cope of lead. Yet I think it the right government for Russia at this moment. If you ask yourself how Dostoevsky's characters should be governed, you will understand. (p. 77)

55 E. M. Forster, "Joseph Conrad: a note," *Abinger Harvest* (New York: Harvest/Harcourt Brace Jovanovich, 1936), p. 136.
56 "Letter to Edward Garnett," 27 May 1912, *Letters from Conrad,* pp. 260–61.
57 I have not yet been able to identify the French translations of Dostoevsky that Conrad read. Ralph E. Matlaw argues that "it is inconceivable that Conrad, who was in close touch with French letters, was unaware" of Dostoevsky's enormous influence in the France of the late nineteenth and early twentieth centuries. Matlaw points out that virtually all major French novelists of that time were reacting strongly to Dostoevsky, that his works were "frequently discussed in all leading periodicals," and that numerous French translations were available ("Dostoevskij and Conrad's political novels, *American Contributions to the Fifth International Congress of Slavists* [The Hague: Mouton, 1963], p. 215).
58 Joseph Conrad, *The Sisters,* intro. Ford Madox Ford (New York: Crosby Gaige, 1928), p. 22.
59 Ibid., pp. 19–20.
60 Ibid., p. 51.
61 Ford Madox Ford, intro. to Conrad, *Sisters,* pp. 7–8. Ford confuses the identity of the two sisters, mistaking the elder for the younger. Though Ford was often wrong about details, I believe that his account of Conrad's intentions is quite plausible.

62 Eloise Knapp Hay, *The Political Novels of Conrad* (University of Chicago Press, 1963), pp. 298–99.

63 Leo Tolstoy, *Anna Karenina* trans. Louise Maude, Aylmer Maude, and George Gibian (New York: Norton, 1995), p. 698.

64 Avrom Fleishman, *Conrad's Politics* (Baltimore: Johns Hopkins University Press, 1967), p. 15.

65 Hay, *Political Novels of Conrad*, p. 298.

66 Fleishman, *Conrad's Politics*, p. 15.

67 Ford, preface to Conrad, *Sisters,* pp. 2–3. Ford elsewhere voiced his complaint about Dostoevsky's lack of artistry, comparing him unfavorably to Turgenev: "And against Turgenev, Young England erects the banner of Dostoevsky, as if the fame of that portentous writer of enormous detective stories, that sad man with the native Slav genius for telling immensely long and formless tales, must destroy the art, the poetry, and the exquisiteness that are in the works of 'the beautiful genius' [i.e., Turgenev]" (Ford Madox Ford, *Henry James: A Critical Study* [New York: Albert and Charles Boni, 1915; originally printed in England in 1914], p. 11).

Ford later felt compelled to respond to complaints that were made about his condemnation of Dostoevsky and offered the following Conrad-like definition of novelistic form: "You may put it that every word in a novel should help the story towards . . . your final effect." He went on to explain that he could find no such purpose or direction in the "elaborate passages, the magnificently strong scenes, in the monastery of the Karamazov book" (Ford Madox Ford, "Literary portraits – xx: Mr. Gilbert Canaan and 'Old Mole,'" *Outlook* [London] 33 [24 January 1914], 110–11).

Less than a month later, he reviewed *The Idiot*, attacking the Russian novelist once more for his perceived lack of artistry and faulting him for his failure to adhere to the standards of realism:

Whatever Dostoevsky may be, he certainly isn't a Realist. His characters are extraordinarily vivid; but they are too vivid for the Realist school. They are too much always in one note; they develop little; they are static. His strong scenes are strong to the point of frenzy, but they are too full dress: everybody has to be in them at once . . . the author very frequently doesn't trouble himself to prepare them. Ford Madox Hueffer [Ford], "Literary portraits – xxiii: Fyodor Dostoievsky and 'The Idiot,'" *Outlook* (London) 33 (14 February 1914), 206–7.

68 Ford, preface, *Sisters,* p. 5.

69 Ibid., p. 16.

70 Guerard, *Conrad the Novelist,* p. 32.

71 Martin Seymour-Smith, introduction, *Nostromo: A Tale of the Seaboard*, by Joseph Conrad (Middlesex: Penguin, 1983), p. 12. Conrad's friendship with Cunninghame Graham deserves closer scrutiny. Though numerous critics have noted Graham's socialist positions, and the difference between his views and Conrad's, Graham is usually depicted as a thoughtful and well-meaning gradualist in the Fabian mold. Critics have not done justice to his radicalism, as suggested by David Garnett's account: "Looking like Charles I, with his aristocratic features and Vandyke beard, and exquisitely

dressed he [Graham] held up a thin, carefully manicured hand and began
his speech with the words: 'I am not one of those who tremble at the word –
ASSASSINATION!'" (David Garnett, *Golden Echo*, p. 119).

I suspect that Graham may have functioned as a double in Conrad's
personal life, representing an aristocratic endorsement of violence and
revolution that Conrad repudiated yet found enthralling. Perhaps Graham
can be seen as part Victor Haldin, part Leggott.

72 See Moser's physical description of Stepniak in his "English context for
Conrad's Russian characters," p. 8.

73 Joseph Conrad, *The Secret Agent: A Simple Tale* (1907; New York: Anchor-
Doubleday, 1953), p. 179.

74 Howe, *Politics and the Novel*, p. 86. Howe's comments here are applied to both
The Secret Agent and *Under Western Eyes*.

75 Interestingly, Conrad describes his writing in the third person, showing his
need to distance himself from his Russian subject matter even when corresponding to a friend and ally. "He [Conrad] is writing a story the title of
which is *Razumov*. Isn't it expressive. I think that I am trying to capture the
very soul of things Russian – *Cosas de Russia*. It is not an easy work but it may
be rather good when it's done." See G. Jean Aubrey (ed.), *Joseph Conrad: Life
and Letters*, 2 vols. (New York: Doubleday, page, 1927), vol. II, p. 64.

76 Edward Garnett, introduction to Conrad, *Conrad's Prefaces*, p. 26.

77 Conrad, author's note in *Under Western Eyes* (London: Methuen, 1911),
p. lx.

78 Jessie Conrad, *Joseph Conrad As I Knew Him* (London: Heinemann, 1926),
p. 56.

79 Curle, *Last Twelve Years*, p. 120.

80 Jocelyn Baines, *Joseph Conrad: A Critical Biography*, (London: Weidenfeld and
Nicolson, 1960), pp. 360–61.

81 Conrad, author's note, *Western Eyes*, p. lxi.

82 Howe, *Politics and the Novel*, p. 86.

83 Matlaw, "Conrad's political novels," p. 218.

84 Quoted by Hay, *Political Novels of Conrad*, p. 280.

85 Karl, *Conrad: Three Lives*, p. 679. Albert Guerard also notes the similarity
between the analysis of Razumov's guilt and of Raskolnikov's:
> The novel's anatomy of guilt is Dostoevskian, which means that it is true; the
> difference is that Conrad's method is infinitely more selective. His dramatization of
> the phantom, for instance, and its slow attenuation from sharp hallucination to
> symbolic force and allusion, is remarkably tactful and convincing. The original
> vision on the snow (coinciding with the decision to give Haldin up) is reported in a
> cool, matter-of-fact prose. Guerard, *Conrad the Novelist*, p. 236.

86 Baines, *Joseph Conrad*, p. 370. Though the comparison between texts is
illuminating, it also shows the weakness of Baines's scholarship. His analysis
is anachronistically based on the 1914 Garnett translation of Dostoevsky,
and no mention is made of the likelihood that Conrad relied on French
translations for his knowledge of the Russian novelist. Still, the verbal

echoes cannot be explained by mere coincidence, and I believe that
Baines is essentially correct.

87 Hay, *Political Novels of Conrad,* p. 282.
88 Ibid., p. 292.
89 Conrad, author's note, *Western Eyes,* p. lxi.
90 Conrad, *Western Eyes,* p. 16.
91 Guerard, *Conrad the Novelist,* p. 246.
92 See Baines, *Joseph Conrad,* pp. 369–70.
93 Howe, *Politics and the Novel,* pp. 86–87.
94 Karl, *Conrad: Three Lives,* pp. 678–79.
95 Howe, *Politics and the Novel,* p. 89.
96 Jackson, *Dostoevsky's Quest for Form,* p. 58.
97 Ibid., p. 112.
98 Joseph Frank, "The World of Raskolnikov," *Encounter* (June 1966), 30.
99 Jackson, *Dostoevsky's Quest for Form,* p. 110.
100 Conrad's letter quoted by Hay, *Political Novels of Conrad,* p. 310. Conrad
    explained his distaste for Christianity in a letter to Edward Garnett:
    the base from which he [Tolstoy] starts – Christianity – is distasteful to me. I am
    not blind to its services but the absurd oriental fable from which it starts irritates
    me. Great, improving, softening, compassionate it may be but it has lent itself with
    amazing facility to cruel distortion and is the only religion which, with its impossi-
    ble standards, has brought an infinity of anguish to innumerable souls – on this
    earth. "Letter to Edward Garnett," 23 February 1914, *Letters from Conrad,* p. 265.
101 Jackson, *Dostoevsky's Quest for Form,* p. 58.
102 Dostoevsky, "Letter to N. D. Fonvizina," 15 February–2 March 1854,
    Dostoevsky Letters, ed. Frank and Goldstein, p. 68.
103 Frank, *Dostoevsky: The Years of Ordeal, 1850–1859* (Princeton University Press,
    1983), p. 162.
104 Quoted by Frank, ibid., p. 122.
105 Ibid., p. 124.
106 Quoted by Ian Watt, *Conrad in the Nineteenth Century* (Berkeley: University of
    California Press, 1979), pp. 32–33.
107 Jeffrey Berman, *Joseph Conrad: Writing as Rescue* (New York: Astra Books,
    1977), pp. 146–47. Berman provides an interesting analysis of Conrad's
    behavior after completing *Under Western Eyes:* "Astonishingly, the identical
    qualities that Conrad had detested in Dostoevsky . . . appeared to domi-
    nate his own behavior after completing the Russian novel." Conrad
    apparently railed "against his family and friends with the paranoia of a
    man suspecting betrayal from everywhere."
108 Karl, *Conrad: Three Lives,* p. 70.

6 DOSTOEVSKY AND THE GENTLEMAN–WRITERS:
E. M. FORSTER, JOHN GALSWORTHY, AND HENRY JAMES

1 Quoted by Furbank, *Forster,* vol. II, p. 163.

2 Catherine Dupré, *John Galsworthy: A Biography* (New York: Coward, McGann & Geoghegan, 1976), p. 284.

3 "Letter to Edward Garnett," 13 April 1914, *Letters from John Galsworthy*, ed. Edward Garnett (London: Jonathan Cape, 1934), p. 219.

4 John Galsworthy, "Englishman and Russian," *Another Sheaf* (London: William Heinemann, 1919), p. 64.

5 Henry James, "Letter to Hugh Walpole," 19 May 1912, *Letters*, vol. IV, pp. 618–19.

6 The "loose, baggy monsters" expression can be found in James's preface to *The Tragic Muse*. See Henry James, *Literary Criticism*, ed. Leon Edel, 2 vols. (New York: Library of America, 1984), vol. I, pp. 1107–8.

7 "Letter to Ottoline Morrell," 2 April 1910, *Selected Letters of E. M. Forster*, ed. Mary Lago and P. N. Furbank, 2 vols. (London: Collins, 1983), vol. I, pp. 105–6.

8 E. M. Forster, "The end of the samovar," rev. of *An Honest Thief and Other Stories*, by Feodor Dostoevsky, trans. Constance Garnett, *Daily News* (London), 11 November 1919. All subsequent quotations in the discussion of these stories are taken from the review. Forster quotes liberally from Garnett's translation throughout the review.

9 Bakhtin, *Dostoevsky's Poetics*, pp. 114–19. Bakhtin lists fourteen major characteristics of menippean satire, all of which can be found in Dostoevsky's work. He discusses "The dream of the ridiculous man" on pages 149–54. "An unpleasant predicament" is discussed (under the title "A nasty story") on page 155.

10 Ibid., p. 156.

11 E. M. Forster, *Aspects of the Novel* (London: Harcourt, Brace, and World, 1927), pp. 68–69.

12 Ibid., p. 78.

13 Ibid., p. 25.

14 Wilfred Stone, *The Cave and the Mountain: A Study of E. M. Forster* (Stanford University Press, 1966), p. 47.

15 Forster, *Aspects*, p. 127. Forster's assumption that Dostoevsky "broke away" from Christianity was a commonplace one of his era. The readers of the Garnett translations often identified the views of Dostoevsky's unbelievers as his own. However, as the work of Joseph Frank has shown, there is a consistency to Dostoevsky's religious beliefs that can be traced throughout his life.

16 Ibid., p. 132.

17 Ibid., pp. 132–33.

18 Ibid., pp. 133–34.

19 Ibid., p. 135. Forster uses mystical language elsewhere to describe the effects of art. In "Anonymity: an enquiry" (1925) he maintains that artistic creation comes from the "obscure recesses of our being," where "we near the gates of the Divine." This "deeper personality" of the artist has "something in common with all deeper personalities." Forster's conception of deeper

personality bears a striking resemblance to Jung's theory of the collective unconscious. The essay is in Forster's *Two Cheers for Democracy* (New York: Harvest-Harcourt Brace Jovanovich, 1951).

In "Raison d'être of criticism in the arts" (1947) Forster compares aesthetic comprehension to "the nature of a mystic union": "A work of art . . . has the power of transforming the person who encounters it towards the condition of the person who created it . . . We – we the beholders or listeners or whatever we are – undergo a change analogous to creation. We are rapt into a region near to where the artist worked and like him when we return we feel surprised" (Forster, *Two Cheers*, pp. 117–18).

20 Forster, *Aspects*, p. 146.

21 Ibid., p. 147.

22 Ibid., p. 137.

23 Forster points out that the "prophetic song" of *Moby Dick* "lies outside words" (ibid., p. 138). His use of musical analogies to address the power of prophecy emphasizes the privileged position of prophetic fiction within his hierarchy of values, for Forster shared Pater's belief that music represented the most perfect and transcendent expression of art. On one hand, he freely admitted the inability of criticism, with its earth-bound dependency on language, to capture the mystic depths of art: "The critical state has many merits, and employs some of the highest and subtlest faculties of man. But it is grotesquely remote from the [creative] state responsible for the works it affects to expound (Forster, "Raison d'être of criticism in the arts," *Two Cheers*, p. 116). On the other hand, however, the entire enterprise of *Aspects of the Novel* can be seen as an attempt to develop a vocabulary and conceptual framework that could address fictional art in terms of rational control. However much Forster yearned for mystic, prophetic vision, I believe that he could never escape the Cambridge and English rationalism of his upbringing and that, furthermore, he never wholly desired such escape.

24 Woolf's comments are quoted by Furbank, *Forster*, vol. II, p. 145.

25 E. M. Forster, "The woman and the onion," *Listener*, 26.672, 27 November 1941, 720.

26 Fyodor Dostoevsky, "Letter to A. G. Dostoyevskaya," 8 June 1880, *Dostoevsky Letters*, ed. Frank and Goldstein, p. 504.

27 Quoted from Galsworthy's *The Triad* (1924) by H. V. Marrot, *The Life and Letters of John Galsworthy* (London: William Heinemann, 1935), p. 136.

28 Edward Garnett, introduction, *Letters from Galsworthy*, p. 8.

29 See Ford's "John Galsworthy," *Mightier Than the Sword* (London: George Allen and Unwin, 1938). Ford satirizes the typical Galsworthy plot:

His one "effect" as a novelist was to present a group of conventionally virtuous, kindly people sitting about and saying the nicest things about all sorts of persons . . . A divorced woman is thrown over their garden hedge and breaks her collar bone, and all the kindly people run away and do not so much as offer a cup of tea. (p. 184)

30 "Letter to Constance Garnett," 10 May 1902, *Letters from Galsworthy*, pp. 36–37.

31 It is quite possible that Galsworthy had already read *Crime and Punishment* in a French translation, like so many other English writers of the age.

32 "Letter to Edward Garnett," 24 April 1910, *Letters from Galsworthy*, p. 177.

33 "Letter to Edward Garnett," 5 April 1914, *Letters from Galsworthy*, p. 217.

34 "Letter to Edward Garnett," 13 April 1914, *Letters from Galsworthy*, p. 219.

35 John Galsworthy, "Disquisition on Joseph Conrad," quoted by Dupré, *John Galsworthy*, p. 126.

36 Dupré, *John Galsworthy*, p. 133.

37 Edward Garnett, introduction, *Letters from Galsworthy*, p. 6.

38 Galsworthy, "Englishman and Russian," *Another Sheaf*, pp. 64–68.

39 Quoted by Dupré, *John Galsworthy*, p. 277.

40 Ibid., p. 277.

41 Marrot, *Life and Letters of Galsworthy*, p. 804.

42 Leon Edel, *Henry James*, vol. II: *The Conquest of London* (Philadelphia: Lippincott, 1962), p. 203.

43 "Ivan Turgenieff," in James, *Literary Criticism*, vol. II, p. 1009. This essay originally appeared in *Atlantic Monthly* (January 1884).

44 Ibid., pp. 1014–19.

45 "Ivan Turgenev," *Henry James: Representative Selections*, Lyon N. Richardson (ed.) (New York: American Book, 1941), pp. 910. This essay was first published in *North American Review* (April 1874).

46 Ibid., pp. 13–15.

47 Ibid., p. 34.

48 Edel, *Henry James*, vol. II, p. 167.

49 "Ivan Turgenieff," in James, *Literary Criticism*, vol. II, p. 1021.

50 Preface, *The Portrait of a Lady*, New York edition (1908), in James, *Literary Criticism*, vol. II, p. 1072.

51 "I may venture to say that the air of reality (solidity of specification) seems to me to be the supreme virtue of a novel" ("The art of fiction," in James, *Selections*, p. 85).

52 All of the quotations here are from the preface to *The Tragic Muse*, New York edition (1908), in James, *Literary Criticism*, vol. II, p. 1107.

53 Ibid., pp. 1107–8.

54 "Ivan Turgenev (1818–1883)," in James, *Literary Criticism*, vol. II, pp. 1027–30.

55 "The new novel," in James, *Literary Criticism*, vol. I, p. 134. This essay was published in James's *Notes on Novelists* (London: J. M. Dent, 1914).

56 James, *Literary Criticism*, vol. II, p. 183. Despite James's praise, Sand's "loose, liquid, and iridescent" compositions and her "imaginative expansiveness" did not make her an adequate model for "students of the novel." James preferred Flaubert as a safer literary model for writers. See his introduction to *Madame Bovary* (1902), ibid., pp. 333–34.

57 See James's comments on Dickens's method of characterization in "Honoré de Balzac" (1875), in James, *Literary Criticism*, vol. II, pp. 52–53. Also see "The life of George Eliot," in James, *Selections*, p. 101.

58 See "Honoré de Balzac" in James, *Literary Criticism*, vol. II, p. 47, and "The lesson of Balzac" (1905) in James, *Literary Criticism*, vol. II, p. 138. Also see the other essays on Balzac and Zola in that collection.

59 The quote continues, "you have only to remember that talents as dissimilar as those of Alexandre Dumas and Jane Austen, Charles Dickens and Gustave Flaubert have worked in this field with equal glory. Do not think too much about optimism and pessimism; try and catch the color of life itself" ("The art of fiction," in James, *Selections,* p. 96).

60 Edel, *Henry James,* vol. V, p. 399.

61 Ibid., p. 401. According to Edel, Walpole's relationship with James had homosexual overtones: "In his later years Hugh told the young Stephen Spender that he had offered himself to the Master and that James had said, 'I can't, I can't'" (p. 477).

62 Ibid., p. 399.

63 Rupert Hart-Davis, *Hugh Walpole: A Biography* (London: Macmillan, 1952), pp. 90–91.

64 "Letter to Hugh Walpole," 19 May 1912, *Letters,* vol. IV, pp. 618–19.

65 Quoted by Hart-Davis, *Hugh Walpole,* p. 126.

66 Quoted by Hart-Davis, ibid., p. 131.

67 Quoted by Hart-Davis, ibid., p. 141.

68 Hugh Walpole, *The Dark Forest* (New York: George H. Doran, 1916).

69 Ibid., pp. 60–61.

70 Hugh Walpole, *The Secret City* (New York: George H. Doran, 1919).

71 Ibid., p. 347.

72 Henry James, preface, *The Princess Casamassima* (New York: Perennial Harper, 1968), pp. 8–9. The novel was originally published in *Atlantic Monthly* in 1885 and 1886. Dostoevsky's *Raw Youth* was published in 1875.

73 James, preface, *Princess Casamassima,* p. 12.

74 Ibid., p. 13.

75 Ibid., p. 15.

76 Ibid., p. 19.

77 Ibid., p. 102.

78 Ibid., p. 342.

79 Ibid., p. 202.

80 Ibid., p. 405.

81 Ibid., p. 349.

82 Ibid., p. 88.

83 Ibid., p. 329.

84 Ibid., p. 19.

85 Bakhtin's comments about monological approaches to Dostoevsky can serve as a postscript to James's inability to recognize artistic intent: "From the viewpoint of a consistently monological visualization and understanding of the represented world, from the viewpoint of some monological canon for the proper construction of novels, Dostoevsky's world may seem a chaos, and the construction of his novels some sort of conglomerate of

disparate materials and incompatible principles for shaping them" (Bakhtin, *Dostoevsky's Poetics*, pp. 6–8).

I do not mean to oversimplify the complexity of James's fiction or ignore the modernist ambivalences within his work, which have been ably addressed by Margery Sabin in *Dialect of the Tribe: Speech and Community in Modern Fiction* (New York: Oxford University Press, 1987). However, I believe that the ambivalence in James resides primarily in his moral vision and his assessment of character – not in his aesthetic criteria for narration or in his conservative social values.

86 James's comments about Balzac's world identify his nostalgia for a premodern world:

Nothing is happier for us than that he [Balzac] should have enjoyed his outlook before the first half of the century closed. He could then still treat his subject as comparatively homogeneous . . . He was free therefore to arrange the background of the comedy in the manner that seemed to him best to suit anything so great . . . The church, the throne, the noblesse, the bourgeoisie, the people, the peasantry, all in their order and each solidly kept in it, these were precious things. ("Honoré de Balzac" [1902], in James, *Literary Criticism*, vol. II, p. 109)

CONCLUSION

1 Forster, *Aspects*, p. 125.
2 Bakhtin, *Dostoevsky's Poetics*, p. 40.

Selected bibliography

DOSTOEVSKY AND RELATED WORKS

Bakhtin, Mikhail, *Problems of Dostoevsky's Poetics*, ed. Caryl Emerson, Minneapolis: University of Minnesota Press, 1984.

Baring, Maurice, *Landmarks in Russian Literature*, London: Methuen, 1910.

The Mainsprings of Russia, London: Thomas Nelson, 1914.

An Outline of Russian Literature, New York: Henry Holt, 1915.

The Russian People, London: Methuen, 1911.

Belknap, Robert L., *The Genesis of The Brothers Karamazov: The Aesthetics, Ideology, and Psychology of Making a Text*, Evanston: Northwestern University Press, 1990.

"The rhetoric of an ideological novel," *Literature and Society in Imperial Russia, 1800–1914*, ed. William Mills Todd, III, Stanford University Press, 1978.

The Structure of The Brothers Karamazov, The Hague: Mouton, 1967.

Berdyaev, Nicholas, *Dostoievsky*, trans. Donald Attwater, New York: Sheed, 1934.

Bourne, Randolph, "The immanence of Dostoevsky," *Dial* 63 (28 June 1917), 24–25.

Brandes, George, *Friedrich Nietzsche*, trans. A. G. Chater, London: Heinemann, 1914.

Brewster, Dorothy. *East–West Passage: A Study in Literary Relationships*, London: George Allen and Unwin, 1954.

Bruckner, A., *A Literary History of Russia*, trans. H. Havelock, London: T. Fisher Unwin, 1908.

Curle, Richard, *Characters of Dostoevsky: Studies from Four Novels*, London: Heinemann, 1950.

Davie, Donald (ed.), *Russian Literature and Modern English Fiction*, University of Chicago Press, 1965.

Dostoevsky, Aimée, *Fyodor Dostoevsky: A Study*, New York: Haskell House, 1972.

Dostoevsky, Anna, *Dostoevsky: Reminiscences*, trans. Beatrice Stillman, New York: Liveright, 1977.

Dostoevsky, Fyodor, *The Brothers Karamazov*, trans. Constance Garnett, London: Heinemann, 1912.

Crime and Punishment, trans. Constance Garnett, London: Heinemann, 1914.
Dostoevsky: Letters and Reminiscences trans. S. S. Koteliansky and J. M. Murry, London: n.p., 1923.
The Eternal Husband and Other Stories, trans. Constance Garnett, London: Heinemann, 1977.
The Friend of the Family; or, Stepanchikovo and Its Inhabitants, and Another Story, trans. Constance Garnett, London: Heinemann, 1920.
The Gambler and Other Stories, trans. Constance Garnett, London: Heinemann, 1917.
The Grand Inquisitor, trans. S. S. Koteliansky, intro. D. H. Lawrence, London: Elkin, Mathew, and Marrot, 1930.
An Honest Thief and Other Stories, trans. Constance Garnett, London: Heinemann, 1919.
The House of the Dead, trans. Constance Garnett, London: Heinemann, 1915.
The Idiot, trans. Constance Garnett, London: Heinemann, 1913.
The Insulted and Injured, trans. Constance Garnett, London: Heinemann, 1915.
The Letters of Dostoyevsky to His Wife trans. Elizabeth Hill and Doris Mudie, intro. D. S. Mirsky, New York: Smith, 1930.
Letters of Fyodor Michailovitch Dostoevsky to His Family and Friends, trans. E. C. Mayne, London: n.p., 1914.
The Possessed, trans. Constance Garnett, London: Heinemann, 1914.
A Raw Youth, trans. Constance Garnett, London: Heinemann, 1916.
Selected Letters of Fyodor Dostoevsky, ed. Joseph Frank and David I. Goldstein, trans. Andrew R. MacAndrew, New Brunswick: Rutgers University Press, 1987.
Stavrogin's Confession and the Plan of the Life of a Great Sinner, trans. S. S. Koteliansky and Virginia Woolf, Richmond: Hogarth, 1922.
White Nights and Other Stories, trans. Constance Garnett, London: Heinemann, 1918.
Fanger, Donald, *Dostoevsky and Romantic Realism*, University of Chicago Press, 1965.
"Dostoevsky today: some recent critical studies," *Survey* 36 (1961), 13–19.
Foster, John Burt, Jr., *Heirs to Dionysus: A Nietzschean Current in Literary Modernism*, Princeton University Press, 1981.
Frank, Joseph, *Dostoevsky: The Miraculous Years, 1865–1871*, Princeton University Press, 1995.
Dostoevsky: The Seeds of Revolt, 1821–1849, Princeton University Press, 1976.
Dostoevsky: The Stir of Liberation, 1860–1865, Princeton University Press, 1986.
Dostoevsky: The Years of Ordeal, 1850–1859, Princeton University Press, 1983.
Freeborn, Richard, *Turgenev: The Novelists' Novelist*, London: Oxford University Press, 1963.
Garnett, Edward, 'A literary causerie: Dostoevsky," *Academy* 71 (1906), 202–3.
Turgenev: A Study, London: Collins, 1917.
Garnett, Richard, *Constance Garnett, A Heroic Life*, London: Sinclair-Stevenson, 1991.

Gide, André, *Dostoevsky*, intro. Arnold Bennett, London: J. M. Dent, 1925.
Grossman, Leonid, *Dostoevsky: A Biography*, trans. Mary Mackler, Indianapolis: Bobbs-Merrill, 1965.
Hemmings, F. W. J., *The Russian Novel in France, 1884–1914*, London: Oxford University Press, 1950.
Holquist, Michael, *Dostoevsky and the Novel*, Princeton University Press, 1977.
Jackson, Robert Louis, *The Art of Dostoevsky*, Princeton University Press, 1981.
   Dostoevsky's Quest for Form – A Study of His Philosophy of Art, New Haven: Yale University Press, 1966.
Jackson, Robert Louis (ed.), *Dostoevsky: New Perspectives*, Englewood-Cliffs: Prentice-Hall, 1984.
Jones, Malcolm V., *Dostoyevsky: The Novel of Discord*, London: Elek, 1976.
Jones, Malcolm V. and Terry, Garth M. (eds.), *New Essays on Dostoevsky*, Cambridge University Press, 1983.
Kropotkin, P. A., *Ideals and Realities in Russian Literature*, New York: Knopf, 1915.
Lavrin, Jancko, *Dostoevsky and His Creation: A Psycho-Critical Study*, London: Collins, 1920.
Leatherbarrow, W. J. (ed.), *Dostoevskii and Britain*, Oxford: Berg, 1995.
Lloyd, J. A. T., *A Great Russian Realist: Feodor Dostoieffsky*, London: Stanley Paul, 1912.
Lord, Robert, *Dostoevsky: Essays and Perspectives*, London: Chatto and Windus, 1970.
Mackail, J. W., *Russia's Gift to the World*, London: Hodder and Stoughton, 1915.
Mansfield, Katherine, "Some aspects of Dostoevsky," *Athenaeum* 4674 (28 November 1919), 1256.
Masaryk, Tomás Garrigue, *The Spirit of Russia: Studies in History, Literature, and Philosophy*, trans. Eden Paul and Cedar Paul, London: George Allen and Unwin, 1919.
Merezhovsky, D. S., *Tolstoi as Man and Artist*, London: Constable, 1902.
Miller, Robin Feuer, *Dostoevsky and* The Idiot*: Author, Narrator, and Reader*, Cambridge: Harvard University Press, 1981.
Mirsky, D. S., *A History of Russian Literature: From the Earliest Times to the Death of Dostoyevsky*, New York: Knopf, 1927.
   The Intelligentsia of Great Britain trans. Alec Brown, New York: Covice, Friede, 1935.
Mochulsky, Konstantin, *Dostoevsky: His Life and Work*, trans. Michael A. Minihan, Princeton University Press, 1967.
Morson, Gary Saul and Emerson, Caryl, *Michael Bakhtin: Creation of a Prosaics*, Stanford University Press, 1990.
Muchnic, Helen, *Dostoevsky's English Reputation (1881–1936)*, Smith College Studies in Modern Languages 20, 3–4, Northampton: Smith College, 1939.
Murry, John Middleton, *Fyodor Dostoevsky: A Critical Study*, New York: Russell, 1924.
Neuhäuser, Rudolf, "Recent Dostoevskii studies and trends in Dostoevskii research," *Journal of European Studies* 2 (1972), 355–73.

Pevear, Richard, Introduction, *The Brothers Karamazov*, by Fyodor Dostoevsky, trans. Richard Pevear and Larissa Volokhonsky, New York: Vintage-Random, 1991.
Phelps, Gilbert, *The Russian Novel in English Fiction*, London: Anchor, 1955.
Riasanovsky, Nicholas, *A History of Russia*, 2nd edn, New York: Oxford University Press, 1969.
Shestov, Lev, *All Things Are Possible*, trans. S. S. Koteliansky, Foreword by D. H. Lawrence, London: Martin Secker, 1920.
Steiner, George, *Tolstoy or Dostoevsky: An Essay in the Old Criticism*, New York: Knopf, 1959.
Strachey, Lytton, "Dostoievsky,"*Spectatorial Essays*, ed. James Strachey, London: Chatto and Windus, 1964, 174–79.
"A Russian humorist," *The Shorter Strachey*, ed. Michael Holroyd and Paul Levy, New York: Oxford University Press, 1980, 183–87.
Terras, Victor, *A Karamazov Companion: Commentary on the Genesis, Language, and Style of Dostoevsky's Novel*, Madison: University of Wisconsin Press, 1981.
Young Dostoevsky, 1846–1849: A Critical Study, The Hague: Mouton, 1969.
Turgenev, Ivan, *A Desperate Character Etc.*, trans. Constance Garnett, intro. Edward Garnett, London: Heinemann, 1920.
Turner, Charles Edward, *Studies in Russian Literature*, London: Sampson, Marston, Searle, and Rivington, 1882.
Vogüé, E. M. de, *Le roman russe*, Paris: Plon, Nourrit et Cie, 1886.
The Russian Novel, trans. H. A. Sawyer, New York: Knopf, 1916.
Wasiolek, Edward, *Dostoevsky: The Major Fiction*, Cambridge: MIT Press, 1964.
Wellek, René, "Bakhtin's view of Dostoevsky: 'polyphony' and 'carnivalesque,'" *Dostoevsky Studies* 1 (1980), 31–39.
Introduction, *Dostoevsky: A Collection of Critical Essays*, Englewood Cliffs: Prentice-Hall, 1962, 1–15.
Yarmolinsky, Avrahm, *Dostoevsky: A Life*, New York: Harcourt, Brace, 1934.
Zernov, Nicolas, *Three Russian Prophets*, London: S. C. M. Press, 1944.

ENGLAND'S LITERARY AND CULTURAL SCENE, 1900–1930

Alpers, Anthony, *The Life of Katherine Mansfield*, New York: Viking, 1980.
Annan, N. G., "The intellectual aristocracy," *Studies in Social History: A Tribute to G. M. Trevelyan*, ed. J. H. Plumb, London: Green, 1955, 241–87.
Bates, H. E., *Edward Garnett*, London: Max Parrish, 1950.
Bell, Clive, *Art*, New York: Capricorn Books, 1958.
Bradbury, Malcolm, *The Social Context of Modern English Literature*, New York: Shocken, 1969.
Carswell, John, *Lives and Letters: A. R. Orage, Beatrice Hastings, Middleton Murry, S. S. Koteliansky*, New York: New Directions, 1978.
Dangerfield, George, *The Strange Death of Liberal England*, New York: Smith, 1935.
Ellmann, Richard, *James Joyce*, New York: Oxford University Press, 1982.

Ellman, Richard, (ed.), *The Modern Tradition*, New York: Oxford University Press, 1965.

Ford, Ford Madox, *Critical Writings of Ford Madox Ford*, Lincoln: University of Nebraska Press, 1964.

Henry James: A Critical Study, New York: Albert and Charles Boni, 1915.

"Literary portraits – xx: Mr. Gilbert Canaan and 'Old Mole,'" *Outlook* (London) 33 (24 January 1914), 110–11.

"Literary portraits – xxiii: Fyodor Dostoievsky and 'The Idiot,'" *Outlook* (London) 33 (14 February 1914), 206–7.

Mightier Than the Sword, London: George Allen and Unwin, 1938.

Return to Yesterday, New York: Horace Liveright, 1932.

Freud, Sigmund, "Dostoevsky and parricide," *Realist* 1 (1929), 18–33.

Garnett, David, *The Flowers of the Forest*, London: Chatto and Windus, 1955.

The Golden Echo, New York: Harcourt Brace, 1954.

Garnett, Edward, *Friday Nights: Literary Criticisms and Appreciations*, New York: Knopf, 1922.

Gathorne-Hardy, Robert (ed.), *Ottoline: The Early Memoirs of Lady Ottoline Morrell*, London: Faber and Faber, 1963.

Gosse, Edmund, "Melchior de Vogüé," *Contemporary Review* 97 (1910), 568–79.

Hart-Davis, Rupert, *Hugh Walpole: A Biography*, London: Macmillan, 1952.

Heilbrun, Carolyn, *The Garnett Family*, New York: Macmillan, 1961.

Holroyd, Michael, *Lytton Strachey: A Critical Biography*, 2 vols. New York: Holt, Rinehart, and Winston, 1968.

Hunter, Jefferson, *Edwardian Fiction*, Cambridge: Harvard University Press, 1982.

Hynes, Samuel, *The Auden Generation*, London: Bodley Head, 1976.

Edwardian Occasions, London: Routledge and Kegan Paul, 1972.

The Edwardian Turn of Mind, Princeton University Press, 1968.

Jefferson, George, *Edward Garnett: A Life in Literature*, London: Jonathan Cape, 1982.

Journal of Katherine Mansfield, ed. John Middleton Murry, London: Constable, 1954.

Mair, G. H., *English Literature: Modern and New*, New York: Henry Holt, 1911.

Moser, Thomas C., *The Life in the Fiction of Ford Madox Ford*, Princeton University Press, 1980.

Murry, John Middleton, *Between Two Worlds*, London: Jonathan Cape, 1935.

The Evolution of an Intellectual, Freeport: Books for Libraries, 1926.

Pound, Ezra, "Hugh Selwyn Mauberly," *Selected Poems of Ezra Pound*, New York: New Directions, 1957.

Russell Bertrand, *The Autobiography of Bertrand Russell*, 2 vols., London: George Allen and Unwin, 1967–68.

Spender, Stephen, *The Struggle of the Modern*, Berkeley: University of California Press, 1963.

Swinnerton, Frank, *The Georgian Literary Scene*, New York: Farrar and Rinehart, 1948.

Walpole, Hugh, *The Dark Forest*, New York: George H. Doran, 1916.
  The English Novel: Some Notes on Its Evolution, Cambridge University Press, 1925.
  The Secret City, New York: George H. Doran, 1919.
Waugh, Arthur, *Tradition and Change: Studies in Contemporary Literature*, London: Chapman and Hall, 1919.
Wellek, René, *English Criticism, 1900–1950*, vol. v of *A History of Modern Criticism, 1750–1950*, 5 vols., New Haven: Yale University Press, 1988.
Wells, H. G., *Experiment in Autobiography*, Toronto: Macmillan, 1934.
  Tono-Bungay, Lincoln: University of Nebraska Press, 1966.
Woolf, Leonard, "Kot," *New Statesman and Nation* 49.1248 (5 February 1955), 170–72.

GENERAL CRITICISM, CRITICAL THEORY, AND MODERN THOUGHT

Albright, Daniel, *Personality and Impersonality*, University of Chicago Press, 1978.
Auerbach, Erich, *Mimesis: The Representation of Reality in Western Literature*, trans. Willard R. Trask, Princeton University Press, 1955.
Bakhtin, Mikhail, *The Dialogic Imagination*, ed. Michael Holquist, trans. Caryl Emerson and Michael Holquist, Austin: University of Texas Press, 1981.
Barthes, Roland, *S/Z*, trans. Richard Miller, New York: Farrar, Straus, and Giroux, 1974.
Beach, Joseph Warren, *The Twentieth Century Novel: Studies in Technique*, New York: Century, 1932.
Benjamin, Walter, *Illuminations*, ed. Hannah Arendt, New York: Schocken, 1969.
Bloom, Harold, *The Anxiety of Influence: A Theory of Poetry*, New York: Oxford University Press, 1973.
Booth, Wayne C., *The Rhetoric of Fiction*, University of Chicago Press, 1961.
Burke, Kenneth, *A Grammar of Motives*, Berkeley: University of California Press, 1969.
Derrida, Jacques, *Of Grammatology*, trans. Gayatri Chakravorty Spivak, Baltimore: Johns Hopkins University Press, 1976.
Freud, Sigmund, *Civilization and Its Discontents*, trans. James Strachey, New York: Norton, 1961.
  Group Psychology and the Analysis of the Ego, trans. James Strachey, New York: Norton, 1959.
Frye, Northrup, *Anatomy of Criticism*, New York: Atheneum, 1968.
Girard, René, *Deceit, Desire, and the Novel: Self and Other in Literary Structure*, trans. Yvonne Freccero, Baltimore: Johns Hopkins University Press, 1965.
  Violence and the Sacred, trans. Patrick Gregory, Baltimore: Johns Hopkins University Press, 1977.
Gombrich, E. H., *Art and Illusion*, Princeton University Press, 1960.
Hirsch, E. D., Jr., *The Aims of Interpretation*, University of Chicago Press, 1976.
  Validity in Interpretation, New Haven: Yale University Press, 1967.
Husserl, Edmund, *Phenomenology and the Crisis of Philosophy*, trans. Quentin Lauer, New York: Harper Torchbooks-Harper, 1965.

Iser, Wolfgang, *The Act of Reading*, Baltimore: Johns Hopkins University Press, 1978.
    Prospecting: From Reader Response to Literary Anthropology, Baltimore: Johns Hopkins University Press, 1989.
Jauss, Hans Robert, *Aesthetic Experience and Literary Hermeneutics*, Minneapolis: University of Minnesota Press, 1982.
    Toward an Aesthetic of Reception, trans. Timothy Bahti, Minneapolis: University of Minnesota Press, 1982.
Krieger, Murry and Dembo, L. S. (eds.), *Directions for Criticism: Structuralism and Its Alternatives*, Madison: University of Wisconsin Press, 1977.
Lévi-Strauss, Claude, *Structural Anthropology*, trans. Claire Jacobson and Brooke Grundfest Schoepf, New York: Basic Books, 1963.
Lukács, Georg, *The Theory of the Novel*, Cambridge: MIT Press, 1971.
Nietzsche, Friedrich, *The Birth of Tragedy* and *The Genealogy of Morals*, trans. Francis Golfing, New York: Anchor-Doubleday, 1956.
Ortega y Gassett, José, *The Dehumanization of Art and Other Writings on Art and Culture*, Garden City: Doubleday, n.d.
Saussure, Ferdinand, *Course in General Linguistics*, New York: McGraw Hill, 1959.
Searle, John, *Speech Acts: An Essay in Philosophy of Language*, Cambridge University Press, 1970.
Sennett, Richard (ed.), *Classic Essays on the Culture of Cities*, Englewood Cliffs: Prentice-Hall, 1969.
Suleiman, Susan R. and Crossman, Inge (eds.), *The Reader in the Text: Essays on Audience Interpretation*, Princeton University Press, 1980.
Trilling, Lionel, *Sincerity and Authenticity*, Cambridge: Harvard University Press, 1971.
Wilson, Edmund, *Axel's Castle*, New York: Charles Scribner's Sons, 1931.

D. H. LAWRENCE

[Chambers, Jessie], *D. H. Lawrence: A Personal Record*, London: Jonathan Cape, 1935.
Foster, John Burt, Jr., "Dostoevsky versus Nietzsche in modernist fiction: Lawrence's *Kangaroo* and Malraux's *La Condition Humaine*," *Stanford Literature Review* 2 (Spring 1985), 47–83.
Hyde, G. M., *D. H. Lawrence and the Art of Translation*, Totowa: Barnes and Noble, 1981.
Kermode, Frank, *D. H. Lawrence*, New York: Viking, 1973.
Lawrence, D. H., *Aaron's Rod*, London: Martin Secker, 1922.
    Amores: Poems, London: Duckworth, 1916.
    Apocalypse, New York: Viking, 1932.
    Collected Letters of D. H. Lawrence, ed. Harry T. Moore, 2 vols., New York: Viking, 1962.
    Fantasia of the Unconscious, London: Heinemann, n.d.

Introduction, *The Grand Inquisitor*, by Feodor Dostoevsky, trans. S. S. Koteliansky, London: Elkin Mathews and Marrot, 1930.
John Thomas and Lady Jane, New York: Viking, 1972.
Kangaroo, London: Heinemann, 1923.
Lady Chatterley's Lover, London: Heinemann, 1936.
The Letters of D. H. Lawrence, ed. Aldous Huxley, London: Heinemann, 1932.
Letters of D. H. Lawrence, ed. James T. Bolton *et al.*, 8 vols., Cambridge University Press, 1979–.
The Man Who Died, London: Martin Secker, 1931.
Phoenix: The Posthumous Papers of D. H. Lawrence, ed. Edward D. McDonald, London: Heinemann, 1936.
Phoenix II, ed. Warren Roberts and Harry T. Moore, London: Heinemann, 1968.
The Plumed Serpent, London: Martin Secker, 1926.
Psychoanalysis and the Unconscious, New York: Thomas Seltzer, 1921.
The Quest for Rananim: D. H. Lawrence's Letters to S. S. Koteliansky, ed. George Zytaruk, Montreal: McGill-Queens University Press, 1970.
The Rainbow, London: Methuen, 1915.
Reflections on the Death of a Porcupine and Other Essays, Philadelphia: Centaur, 1925.
Sons and Lovers, London: Duckworth, 1913.
Studies in Classic American Literature, New York: Thomas Seltzer, 1923.
Symbolic Meaning: The Uncollected Versions of Studies in Classic American Literature, New York: Viking, 1964.
Twilight in Italy, London: Heinemann, 1956.
Women in Love, London: Martin Secker, 1921.
Lawrence, Frieda, *"Not I, But the Wind . . .,"* New York: Viking, 1934.
Leavis, Frank Raymond, *D. H. Lawrence, Novelist*, London: Chatto and Windus, 1955.
Moore, Harry T., *The Intelligent Heart*, New York: Grove, 1962.
The Priest of Love: A Life of D. H. Lawrence, New York: Farrar, Straus, and Giroux, 1974.
Murry, John Middleton, *Reminiscences of D. H. Lawrence*, London: Jonathan Cape, 1933.
Nehls, Edward (ed.), *D. H. Lawrence: A Composite Biography*, 3 vols., Madison: University of Wisconsin Press, 1957–59.
"Two realists: Russian and English," *Athenaeum* 4414 (1 June 1912), 613–14.
Zytaruk, George, *D. H. Lawrence's Response to Russian Literature*, The Hague: Mouton, 1971.

VIRGINIA WOOLF

Ames, Christopher, "The life of the party: festive vision in modern fiction," Ph.D. thesis, Stanford University, 1984.
Bell, Quentin, *Virginia Woolf: A Biography*, 2 vols., London: Hogarth, 1973.

Caramagno, Thomas C., "Manic-depressive psychosis and critical approaches to Virginia's Woolf's life and work,' *PMLA* 103.1 (1988), 10–23.

Catalog of Books from the Library of Leonard and Virginia Woolf, Brighton: Holleyman and Treacher, 1975.

Daiches, David, *Virginia Woolf*, Norfolk: New Directions, 1942.

Edel, Leon, *Bloomsbury: A House of Lions*, New York: Avon, 1979.

Foster, E. M., *Virginia Woolf*, Cambridge University Press, 1942.

Gordon, Lydall, *Virginia Woolf: A Writer's Life*, New York: Norton, 1985.

Johnstone, J. K., *The Bloomsbury Group: A Study in E. M. Forster, Lytton Strachey, Virginia Woolf, and Their Circle*, London: Secker and Warburg, 1954.

Kirkpatrick, Brownlee Jean, *A Bibliography of Virginia Woolf*, London: Hart-Davis, 1967.

Luftig, Victor, "The wonderful eye: Virginia Woolf's translations of Tolstoi," unpublished paper, Stanford University, 1985.

Majumader, Robin and McLaurin, Allen (eds.), *Virginia Woolf: The Critical Heritage*, London: Methuen, 1975.

Marcus, Jane, *Virginia Woolf and the Languages of Patriarchy*, Bloomington: Indiana University Press, 1987.

Marcus, Jane (ed.), *New Feminist Essays on Virginia Woolf*, Lincoln: University of Nebraska Press, 1981.

Nicolson, Nigel, and Joanne Trautman (eds.), *The Letters of Virginia Woolf*, 6 vols., London: Hogarth, 1975–80.

Pater, Walter, *The Renaissance*, 4th edn., Berkeley: University of California Press, 1980.

Rubinstein, Roberta, "Virginia Woolf's response to Russian literature," Ph.D. thesis, University of London, 1969.

Ruotolo, Lucio P., *The Interrupted Moment: A View of Virginia Woolf's Novels*, Stanford University Press, 1986.

Silver, Brenda R., *Virginia Woolf's Reading Notebooks*, Princeton University Press, 1983.

Spater, George and Parsons, Ian, *A Marriage of True Minds: An Intimate Portrait of Leonard and Virginia Woolf*, New York: Harcourt Brace Jovanovich, 1977.

Virginia Woolf and Lytton Strachey: Letters, ed. Leonard Woolf and James Strachey, London: Hogarth, n.d.

Woolf, Leonard, *Beginning Again: An Autobiography of the Years 1911–1918*, London: Hogarth, 1964.

Downhill All the Way: An Autobiography of the Years 1919–1939, London: Hogarth, 1967.

Woolf, Virginia, *Between the Acts*, New York: Harcourt, Brace, 1941.

Books and Portraits, ed. Mary Lyon, New York: Harcourt, Brace and Jovanovich, 1978.

The Captain's Death Bed and Other Essays, London: Hogarth, 1950.

Collected Essays, 4 vols., London: Hogarth, 1966.

The Common Reader, New York: Harcourt, Brace and World, 1925.

The Death of the Moth and Other Essays, New York: Harcourt, Brace, 1942.

The Diary of Virginia Woolf, ed. Anne Olivier Bell, 5 vols., New York: Harcourt Brace Jovanovich, 1977–84.

Jacob's Room, New York: Harcourt Brace Jovanovich, 1922.

"Modern novels," *Times Literary Supplement*, 10 April 1919, 90.

Monday or Tuesday, London: Hogarth, 1921.

"Mr. Bennett and Mrs. Brown," *Nation and Athenaeum* 34 (1 December 1923), 342–43.

Mrs. Dalloway, London: Harcourt, Brace, 1925.

Orlando: A Biography, London: Hogarth, 1928.

A Room of One's Own, New York: Harcourt, Brace, 1929.

Second Common Reader, New York: Harcourt, Brace, 1932.

Three Guineas, New York: Harcourt, Brace, 1938.

To The Lighthouse, New York: Harcourt, Brace and World, 1927.

The Waves, New York: Harcourt Brace Jovanovich, 1931.

The Years, New York: Harcourt Brace Jovanovich, 1937.

Zwerdling, Alex, *Virginia Woolf and the Real World*, Berkeley: University of California Press, 1986.

ARNOLD BENNETT

Barker, Dudley, *Writer By Trade: A Portrait of Arnold Bennett*, New York: Atheneum, 1966.

Bennett, Arnold, *Anna of the Five Towns*, Salem: Ayer, 1978, rpt. of 1902 edn.

The Author's Craft and Other Critical Writings of Arnold Bennett, ed. Samuel Hynes, Lincoln: University of Nebraska Press, 1968.

Books and Persons, New York: George H. Doran, 1917.

"Books and persons," *New Age* 6 (24 March 1910), 494.

"Books and persons," *New Age* 6 (31 March 1910), 518–19.

"Books and persons in London and Paris," *New Age* 8 (9 February 1911), 349–50.

"Books and persons in London and Paris," *New Age* 8 (23 March 1911), 492.

Clayhanger, London: Methuen, 1910.

The Evening Standard Years: "Books and Persons," 1926–1931, ed. Andrew Mylett, London: Chatto and Windus, 1974.

Fame and Fiction: An Inquiry into Certain Popularities, London: G. Richards, 1901.

Hilda Lessways, London: Methuen 1911.

How to Become an Author: A Practical Guide, London: C. A. Pearson, 1903.

The Journal of Arnold Bennett, Garden City: Garden City Publishing, 1932.

Letters of Arnold Bennett, ed. James Hepburn, 4 vols., London: Oxford University Press, 1966–86.

Lord Raingo, London: Cassell, 1926.

The Old Wives' Tale, London: Chapman and Hall, 1908.

Riceyman Steps, London: Cassell, 1923.

Drabble, Margaret, *Arnold Bennett: A Biography*, New York: Knopf, 1974.

Hynes, Samuel, "The Whole Contention Between Mr. Bennett and Mrs.

Woolf," *Novel* 1.1 (Fall 1967), 34–44.

Kreutz, Irving, "Mr. Bennett and Mrs. Woolf," *Modern Fiction Studies* 8.2 (Summer 1962), 103–15.

Simons, J. B., *Arnold Bennett and His Novels: A Critical Study*, Oxford: Blackwell, 1936.

JOSEPH CONRAD

Aubrey, G. Jean (ed.), *Joseph Conrad: Life and Letters*, 2 vols., New York: Double-day, Page, 1927.

Baines, Jocelyn, *Joseph Conrad: A Critical Biography*, London: Weidenfeld and Nicolson, 1960.

Berman, Jeffrey, *Joseph Conrad: Writing as Rescue*, New York: Astra Books, 1977.

Busza, Andrzej, "Rhetoric and ideology in Conrad's *Under Western Eyes*," *Joseph Conrad: A Commemoration*, papers from the 1974 International Conference on Conrad, ed. Norman Sherry, New York: Barnes and Noble, 1977.

Conrad, Jessie, *Joseph Conrad and His Circle*, London: Jarrolds, 1935.

Joseph Conrad As I Knew Him, London: Heinemann, 1926.

Conrad, Joseph, *Conrad's Prefaces to His Works*, ed. Edward Garnett, London: Dent, 1937.

Last Essays, London: Dent, 1926.

Letters from Conrad, 1895–1924, ed. Edward Garnett, London: Nonesuch Press, 1928.

Lord Jim: A Tale, Edinburgh: Blackwood, 1900.

The Nigger of the "Narcissus": A Tale of the Sea, London: Heinemann, 1898.

Nostromo: A Tale of the Seaboard. New York: Harper, 1904.

Notes on Life and Letters, London: Dent, 1921.

A Personal Record, London: Dent, 1919.

The Secret Agent: A Simple Tale, London: Methuen, 1907.

The Shadow Line: A Confession, Garden City: Doubleday, Page, 1917.

The Sisters, intro. Ford Madox Ford, New York: Crosby Gaige, 1928.

Typhoon, and Other Stories, London: William Heinemann, 1903.

Under Western Eyes, London: Methuen, 1911.

Youth, and Two Other Stories, New York: McClure, Phillips, 1903.

Crankshaw, Edward, "Conrad and Russia," *Joseph Conrad: A Commemoration*, papers from the 1974 International Conference on Conrad, ed. Norman Sherry, New York: Barnes and Noble, 1977.

Curle, Richard, *Joseph Conrad: A Study*, London: Kegan Paul, Trench, Trubner, 1914.

The Last Twelve Years of Joseph Conrad, London: Sampson Low, Marston, 1928.

Fleishman, Avrom, *Conrad's Politics*, Baltimore: Johns Hopkins University Press, 1967.

Ford, Ford Madox, *Joseph Conrad: A Personal Remembrance*, London: Duckworth, 1924.

[Garnett, Edward], "Mr. Conrad's new books," rev. of *Youth: A Narrative, and Two Other Stories*, *Academy and Literature* 63 (6 December 1902), 606.

Garnett, Edward, "Mr. Conrad's new novel," rev. of *Under Western Eyes*, *Nation* 10 (21 October 1911), 141–42.

"The genius of Mr. Conrad," rev. of *A Set of Six*, *Nation* 3.21 (August 1908), 746–47.

"Mr. Joseph Conrad," *Academy* 1380 (15 October 1898), 82–83.

[Garnett, Edward], "The novel of the week," rev. of *The Secret Agent*, by Joseph Conrad, *Nation* 1 (28 September 1907), 1096.

Guerard, Albert J., *Conrad the Novelist*, Cambridge: Harvard University Press, 1958.

Hay, Eloise Knapp, *The Political Novels of Conrad*, University of Chicago Press, 1963.

Howe, Irving, *Politics and the Novel*, New York: Meridian Books, 1957.

Karl, Frederick R., *Joseph Conrad: The Three Lives*, New York: Farrar, Straus, and Giroux, 1979.

Matlaw, Ralph E., "Dostoevskij and Conrad's political novels," *American Contributions to the Fifth International Congress of Slavists*, The Hague: Mouton, 1963.

Meyer, Bernard, *Joseph Conrad: A Psychoanalytic Biography*, Princeton University Press, 1967.

Morf, Gustav, *The Polish Heritage of Joseph Conrad*, London: Sampson Low, Marston, 1930.

Moser, Thomas C., "An English context for Conrad's Russian characters: Sergey Stepniak and the diary of Olive Garnett," *Journal of Modern Literature* 11.1 (March 1984), 3–44.

"Ford Madox Hueffer and *Under Western Eyes*," *Conradiana* 15.3 (1983), 163–80.

Joseph Conrad: Achievement and Decline, Cambridge: Harvard University Press, 1957.

Najder, Zdzislaw, *Joseph Conrad: A Chronicle*, New Brunswick: Rutgers University Press, 1983.

Said, Edward W., *Joseph Conrad and the Fiction of Autobiography*, Cambridge: Harvard University Press, 1966.

Sherry, Norman, *Conrad's Western World*, Cambridge University Press, 1971.

Watt, Ian, *Conrad in the Nineteenth Century*, Berkeley: University of California Press, 1979.

Zabel, Morton Dauwen, introduction, *Tales of Heroes and History*, by Joseph Conrad, Garden City: Anchor-Doubleday, 1960.

Introduction, *Under Western Eyes*, by Joseph Conrad, Garden City: Anchor-Doubleday, 1963.

E. M. FORSTER, JOHN GALSWORTHY, AND HENRY JAMES

Catalogue of Books from E. M. Forster's Library, Cambridge: Heffer, 1971.

Dupré, Catherine, *John Galsworthy: A Biography*, New York: Coward, McGann and Geoghegan, 1976.

Edel, Leon, *Henry James*, 5 vols., Philadelphia: Lippincott, 1953–72.

Ford, Ford Madox, "John Galsworthy," *Mightier Than the Sword*, London: George Allen and Unwin, 1938.

Forster, E. M., *Abinger Harvest*, New York: Harvest-Harcourt Brace Jovanovich, 1936.

Aspects of the Novel, New York: Harcourt, Brace, and World, 1927.

The Celestial Omnibus and Other Stories, London: Sidgwick and Jackson, 1911.

The Development of English Prose Between 1918 and 1939, Glasgow: Jackson, 1945.

"The end of the samovar," rev. of *An Honest Thief and Other Stories*, by Feodor Dostoevsky, trans. Constance Garnett, *Daily News* (London), 11 November 1919.

The Eternal Moment and Other Stories, New York: Harcourt, Brace, 1928.

Howards End, London: Arnold, 1910.

The Longest Journey, Edinburgh: Blackwood, 1907.

Maurice: A Novel, London: Arnold, 1971.

A Passage to India, New York: Harcourt, Brace, 1924.

A Room with a View, London: Arnold, 1908.

Selected Letters of E. M. Forster, ed. Mary Lago and P. N. Furbank, 2 vols., London: Collins, 1983.

Two Cheers for Democracy, New York: Harvest-Harcourt Brace Jovanovich, 1951.

Where Angels Fear to Tread, Edinburgh: Blackwood, 1905.

"The woman and the onion," *Listener* 26.672 (27 November 1941), 720.

Furbank, P. N., *E. M. Forster: A Life*, 2 vols., New York: Harcourt Brace Jovanovich, 1978.

Galsworthy, John, *Another Sheaf*, London: William Heinemann, 1919.

The Forsyte Saga, London: Heinemann, 1922.

The Man of Property, London: Heinemann, 1906.

Gardner, Philip (ed.), *E. M. Forster: The Critical Heritage*, London: Routledge and Kegan Paul, n.d.

Garnett, Edward (ed.), *Letters from John Galsworthy*, London: Jonathan Cape, 1934.

Henry James: Representative Selections, ed. Lyon N. Richardson, New York: American Book, 1941.

James, Henry, *The Ambassadors*, London: Methuen, 1903.

The Bostonians, London: Macmillan, 1886.

Letters, ed. Leon Edel, 4 vols., Cambridge: Belknap-Harvard University Press, 1984.

Literary Criticism, ed. Leon Edel, 2 vols., New York: Library of America, 1984.

The Portrait of a Lady, Boston: Houghton Mifflin, 1882.

The Princess Casamassima, London: Macmillan, 1886.

Stories of Writers and Artists, ed. F. O. Matthiesson, New York: New Directions, 1944.

The Turn of the Screw, New York: Boni, 1924.

Kirkpatrick, B. J., *A Bibliography of E. M. Forster*, London: Hart-Davis, 1965.

Marrot, H. V., *The Life and Letters of John Galsworthy*, London: William Heinemann, 1935.

Stone, Wilfred, *The Cave and the Mountain: A Study of E. M. Forster*, Stanford University Press, 1966.

Index

Printed in the United States
85043LV00004B/312/A